THE RECORD
OF A
HOME GUARD BATTALION

To the
" Ever Faithful "

BEING THE HISTORY OF

THE 1st ('LOYAL CITY OF EXETER') BATTALION
DEVON HOME GUARD

1940 - 1945

BY

LT. COL. H. J. WILTSHER, O.B.E.

The Naval & Military Press Ltd

Published by

The Naval & Military Press Ltd

Unit 10 Ridgewood Industrial Park,
Uckfield, East Sussex,
TN22 5QE England

Tel: +44 (0) 1825 749494
Fax: +44 (0) 1825 765701

www.naval–military–press.com
www.nmarchive.com

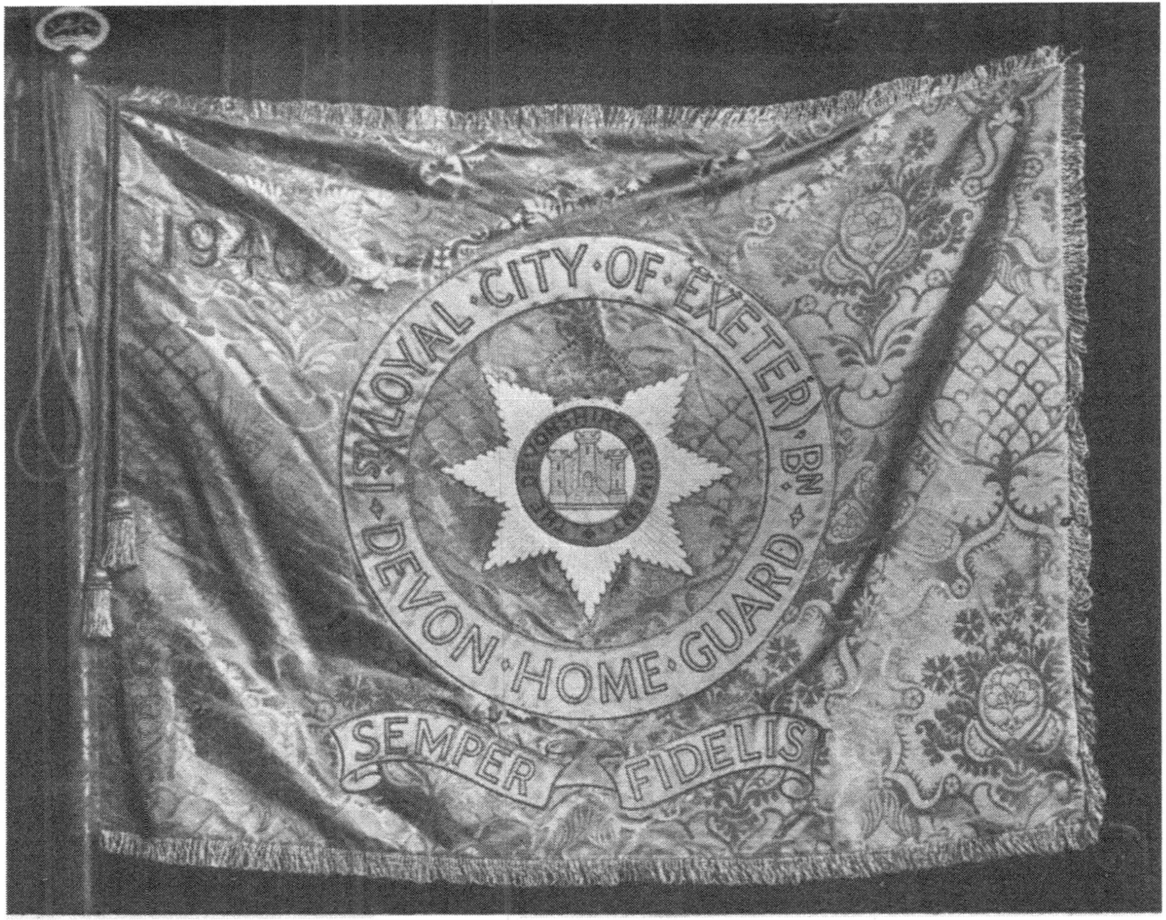
1940
1st LOYAL CITY OF EXETER BN
DEVON HOME GUARD
THE DEVONSHIRE REGIMENT
SEMPER FIDELIS

The Flag

FOREWORD

Lt.- Gen. W. D. MORGAN, C.B., D.S.O., M.C.

Chief of Staff
Allied Force Headquarters,
Mediterranean.

Formally G.O.C. Southern Command

The Home Guard in the United Kingdom has now passed into the pages of history. There it will find a place—and a high one—amongst those other Defence Forces which arose when the safety of the home-land was threatened.

The Home Guard expressed in the highest degree the unshakable determination of Englishmen to fight and die for their freedom.

Amongst Home Guard Battalions the 1st Battalion (Loyal City of Exeter) Devon Home Guard, under command of Lieutenant-Colonel H. J. Wiltsher, O.B.E. was noteworthy for its keenness, efficiency and its sense of duty and comradeship.

The City of Exeter has good reason to be proud of it.

The Flag Party

FOREWORD

Lt.-Gen. E. A. OSBORNE, C.B., D.S.O.

Lt.-Col. H. J. Wiltsher, O.B.E. has done much for the battalion which he has served in and eventually commanded. By no means the least of these services is the time and labour he has given to writing this Record.

By doing so, with no delay, he is making available for any member of the battalion, an outline history of its activities in a form that conveys a personal touch.

It gives me the impression of accuracy and completeness. Even if there are mistakes and omissions it is far better to have a Record like this than a more lengthy history produced in the distant future by an author who cannot have the same feeling for the Battalion as its Commanding Officer.

I hope that the great majority of those who served in the 1st (Loyal City of Exeter) Battalion Devon Home Guard will get a copy and that the possession of it will from time to time remind them of what an efficient Battalion it was, what good comrades they found while serving in it, and, with justification, that by being good Home Guardsmen they helped in the making of a fine Battalion and thereby "did their bit."

Such reflections may urge the individual to be a more active "Old Comrade" and so keep up the associations of the years 1940-1945.

The Record shews how that I, as Sector Commander on many occasions took the opportunity of complimenting all ranks of the Battalion.

I meant what I said and repeat that the 1st (Loyal City of Exeter) Battalion Devon Home Guard was a grand Unit and would have been ready to meet the enemy at any time anywhere.

INTRODUCTION

In all humbleness I set about recording the history of this the 1st (Loyal City of Exeter) Battalion Devon Home Guard, in which I have served from the first day, first as a Company Commander, then Second-in-Command of the Battalion, and finally as Commanding Officer. I have been greatly honoured, not only in having been associated with such a grand crowd of fellows, but in having been chosen to command them; their loyalty and realisation of their duty and the reasons for having joined, made my task pleasant. The Battalion is recognised as being an efficient one; the credit is shared by all ranks. This record is dedicated to all those who have been members of this Battalion, have given so freely of their time, and have sacrificed so much to ensure, through the busy 4½ years of service, that if the Hun did come, he would be dealt with in the only possible way, and that would be to wipe him out. I apologise to those who should be mentioned, but have not been. It will be remembered by all readers that the early Battalion records were destroyed in the blitz in May, 1942, and consequently this has involved much more work in compiling the early records, and even then they cannot be complete.

I am honoured that Lieut.-General W. D. Morgan, C.B., D.S.O., M.C., should have agreed to write a foreword. He has always taken a very keen interest in the Battalion, and has, on many occasions, said so many nice things about us, some of which are recorded in this record.

This introduction would not be complete without my grateful thanks to Lieut.-General E. A. Osborne, C.B., D.S.O., for also writing a foreword, and for his great help to the Battalion, and myself personally, since he has been our Sector Commander.

I have a debt of gratitude to Major E. P. Manson, M.C. and all his staff at the Devon Territorial Association for their great help to me and my staff, not only whilst I have been Commanding the Battalion but also during the time I have been compiling the records included in the back of this Book.

I, with much pleasure, place on record another example of the esteem in which this Battalion is held, and I offer my grateful thanks to Sir Arthur Reed, M.P. for his generous gift of the paper on which this book is printed. Mr. Reed was one of the original members of Battalion, having joined in May, 1940, and although his Parliamentary duties combined with his other many commitments have prevented him from carrying out regular duties he has always been ready to turn out in the event of trouble.

My introduction would not be complete without a very sincere "Thank you" from myself and the Battalion to Major W. L. Sparkes, Devonshire Regiment. As members of the Devonshire Regiment we were fortunate in having as the O.C. Devonshire Regiment depot an Officer such as Major W. L. Sparkes, he was always full of understanding and ready at all times to help the Battalion, and was certainly the ideal link between the Regular Battalions and the Home Guard Battalion.

I will, I know, be forgiven if I record here my sincere appreciation of the hard work carried out for the Battalion, and the personal help and loyalty given to me by the Second-in-Command, Major Bill Hoyt, he has been a tower of strength and all members of the Battalion will have at some time or other benefited by his efforts. These remarks also include the Company Commanders: Majors Tom Greenslade, D.C.M., Lionel Coles, E. N. Clulee, Claude Panes, Alex Young, M.C., Arthur Fry and Captain C. R. M. Frost. A grand team full of loyalty and efficiency.

I record my thanks to all those who have, in large or small degree, helped me by delving through records to obtain information or other necessary data to complete the picture, and especially I would mention Lieut. L. Rey for his untiring efforts in checking up many items to ensure correctness of detail as far as possible.

I am grateful to Lieut. M. C. B. Hoare, for his help in checking the original manuscript.

Mistakes in this record there may be, but I hope that it will bring forth many pleasant memories to members of the Battalion, and a feeling of pride in a job well and truly carried out in the service of the old country.

H. J. W.

CONTENTS.

ILLUSTRATIONS.

Chapter I

LOCAL DEFENCE VOLUNTEERS

Mr. Eden's Call

Mr. Anthony Eden broadcast a call for volunteers to defend the old Country against anything which the enemy might attempt to do.

MAY, 1940

All through the day of May 14th, 1940, the air seemed to be tense. Things were going from bad to worse for us. Everyone was expecting something to happen and felt helpless. It was known that an important broadcast was to be made that night, but no-one actually knew of the form the broadcast was to take. They seemed to be hoping that it was something that would enable them to fall into the picture of things and to do their bit if the worst came to the worst. As it was, the text of the speech was the answer and relieved the tension. There was a tremendous determination in the hearts of most men to give whatever help was possible; they only wanted the opportunity.

Before many hours had passed after the broadcast, over a thousand men were on the roll of Exeter, waiting for orders. During the next two weeks the volunteers heard nothing and to a certain extent this became a damper on their spirits. Every man was anxious to be doing something and to do it quickly.

It might be recorded that at that time all the volunteers were enrolled at the Police Station. This meant a considerable amount of extra work for the police because, although after the first few weeks the Local Defence Volunteers (as the movement was called) began to enrol men direct, Mr. A. E. Rowsell, the Chief Constable, was responsible for quite a long time for scrutinising and passing each enrolment, no doubt a very necessary precaution in those days.

On May 30th, 1940, Major A. Anstey, called a meeting at his home in Exeter. Major Anstey had been appointed Detachment Commander only the day before and he had lost no time in getting the early arrangements on the move. Those present at the meeting were himself, T. J. W. Templeman, J. Whiteside, Captain R. J. Paul, C. R. M. Frost, H. J. Wiltsher, E. N. Clulee, Captain F. J. C. Hunter and H. Enefer.

Major Anstey began the meeting by giving a short talk on the seriousness of the situation, and he then made the following appointments: —

T. J. W. Templeman to be Detachment Second-in-Command.
J. Whiteside—Adjutant.
H. J. Wiltsher—No. 1 (West) Company Commander.
Captain R. J. Paul—No. 2 (East) Company Commander.
C. R. M. Frost—No. 3 (St. Thomas) Company Commander.
Captain F. J. C. Hunter—Transport Officer.
H. Enefer—Assistant Transport Officer.
E. N. Clulee—Officer i/c Armaments.

Each of the three Company Commanders was then given a map and also their orders regarding the vulnerable points which had to be guarded and the patrol and observation posts which had to be manned. The whole position was fully discussed.

They were handed a roll book, each containing approximately 480 names. These were the men who were to form the company and they had been allocated to the companies by virtue of their place of residence.

The maps handed out were coloured in three sections giving the Company Commanders their area of responsibility, the sections being approximately equal: —

No. 1 (West) Company, from Cowley Bridge to Pinhoe Road.
No. 2 (East) Company, from Pinhoe Road to the River Exe.
No. 3 (St. Thomas) Company, from the River to Cowley Bridge.

Although there is no actual record of the strength of the detachment at that time, it was between 1,500 and 2,000.

There is no doubt that the task facing the Detachment and Company Commanders was a difficult one, owing to the fact that there was no organisation of any description. This had to be built up.

The Company Commanders went away from this meeting in the early hours of the morning on May 31st, with urgent work to get on with, the tasks facing them were many and varied, the Companies had to be organised into Platoons and Sections, according to the districts in which the men lived, and Platoon and Section Commanders had to be appointed. The latter was naturally a job of some urgency because it was impossible for a Company Commander to arrange his guards, patrols and observation posts, and organise the men, entirely on his own.

At this stage, owing to a misunderstanding at Detachment Headquarters, No. 1 Company, commanded by H. J. Wiltsher, became No. 2 Company, and No. 2 Company, commanded by Captain R. J. Paul, became No. 1 Company.

There is no doubt that a tremendous amount of work was done, and a lot of sleep lost by all Commanders both from Section to Detachment during those early days, and under most trying and difficult circumstances, and it is only right that a record should be made at this stage of the original Platoon Officers in each Company, the Detachment and Company Commanders having already been mentioned.

No. 1 Coy.   L. G. Coles, later to become Company Commander.
Captain R. W. Bell, later to become Company Second-in-Command.
Captain S. Wakeford, M.C., who resigned from the

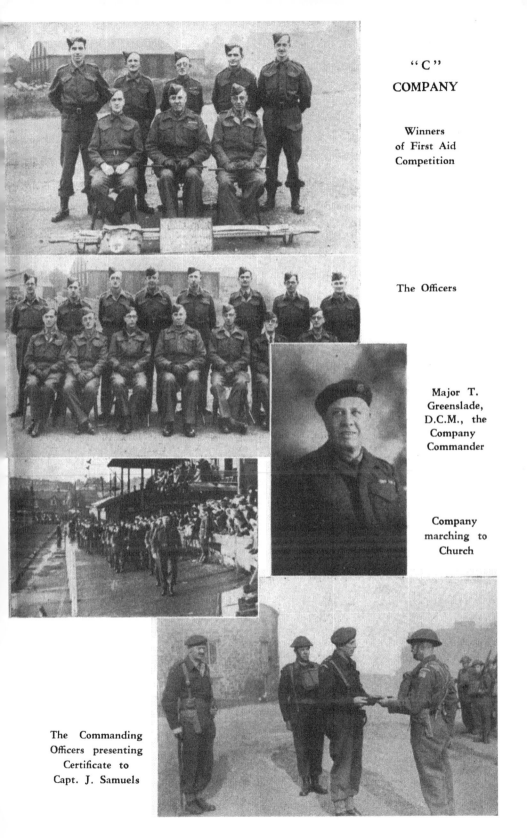

"C"
COMPANY

Winners
of First Aid
Competition

The Officers

Major T.
Greenslade,
D.C.M., the
Company
Commander

Company
marching to
Church

The Commanding
Officers presenting
Certificate to
Capt. J. Samuels

Battalion, on moving from the district.

D. W. Pullen, who eventually joined His Majesty's Forces and was killed.

No. 2 Coy. W. H. Hoyt, who became in succession, 2 i/c Company, Company Commander, and 2 i/c Battalion.

C. B. Trafford, who eventually resigned.

Major R. Row, M.C., who resigned on rejoining the R.E.'s.

K. Upright, who also resigned on joining the R.A.F.

No. 3 Coy. T. Greenslade, D.C.M., who became in succession 2 i/c Company, and then Company Commander.

J. D. Beedon ⎫
W. Dummett ⎬ all of whom resigned on leaving the district.
E. King ⎭

Brief details of the duties carried out by these three original companies in the very early days would not be out of place at this stage.

No. 1 Company's patrols and observation posts were at—Hill Barton Road—Digby's Halt—Swing Bridge, Countess Weir—Northbrook Park—Exeter School—Canal Banks.

Guards—Trews Weir Suspension Bridge—Electric Light Works—Oil Stores.

No. 2 Company's patrols and observation posts were at—Monks Road—Stoke Hill Farm—Cowley Bridge.

Guards—Admiralty Buildings, Paul Street—Centre Control, St. David's Station—Pynes Water Works—Staffords Bridge and North Bridge.

No. 3 Company's Patrols and observation posts were at—Barley Lane Reservoir—Exwick Three Gates—Constitutional Hill—Alpington Cross.

Guards—Pynes Water Works.

Captain F. J. C. Hunter, assisted by H. Enefer, worked very hard organising the many private cars, the owners of which had enrolled into a Transport Company.

JUNE, 1940

It was very soon realised that some form of Company Headquarters was necessary if the Company Commanders were to work efficiently, but it was to be some months before even the first Company Headquarters was established.

No authority could be obtained for such a move at this time and as a consequence Company and Platoon Commanders were working from their own homes, and when one realises that paper instructions were beginning to come in and that odd bits of equipment were being issued, and that all this had to be kept in the Company and Platoon Commanders' homes, it was to say the least, a severe strain.

Interposed with all the organising, there were Company Commanders' Meetings with the Detachment Commander in a small room at Pancras Lane, which now served as Detachment Headquarters. At these Meetings questions of policy were discussed and instructions issued by Higher Command, dealt with.

It was impossible in some cases to carry out the instructions issued to the letter, because of lack of facilities, but by sound common sense on the part of all Commanders difficulties were overcome.

One of the things which was early decided was that it was necessary for the Company Commanders to get to know the volunteers in their Company as far as possible, and to this end an instruction was issued to all the volunteers to parade at Pancras Lane: No. 1 Company on Monday evenings, No. 2 Company on Tuesday evenings and No. 3 Company on Wednesday evenings. A large number of the volunteers attended. On successive nights the respective Company Commanders attended with their Platoon Commanders and many good contacts were made with the volunteers.

Two volunteers, H. Coverdale and J. Culley, joined the detachment round about this time and offered themselves for full time unpaid work. Coverdale was immediately appointed Assistant Adjutant and Culley, acting Quartermaster. Both these volunteers put in a tremendous amount of work under very trying and difficult conditions. They both left the Detachment when paid Adjutants and Quartermasters were appointed by the War Office.

The training in the early stages was carried out by Platoons on a rough piece of ground in Pancras Lane, but it was not long before the small School House in Paul Street was obtained for Detachment Headquarters, and permission was given by the Civic authorities for the training to be carried out on the Paul Street Parking Ground, and in The Market, Queen Street.

It was now possible to organise, on a more reasonable basis, the training of the Detachment, and Major Anstey, the Detachment Commander, was able to offer certain training facilities to the Company Commanders.

He appointed E. N. Clulee to be in charge of what was called the Recruits' Training with the title of Officer i/c Training and he was ably assisted by C. Songhurst, M.M. Recruit training was carried out on almost every night in the week. These arrangements were made to fit in with the convenience of the Volunteers, some nights being better than others and the Companies sent their volunteers on the various nights to Paul Street for their elementary training.

A large percentage of the volunteers were old soldiers, but many of them had never handled a firearm before and even the old soldiers required a certain amount of brushing up. It should be realised that in addition to this training, the volunteers were still carrying out guards, patrols and observation duties.

The Detachment Commander at this time decided to appoint a Detachment Sergeant-Major and the obvious man for this appointment in those days was J. Martin, a good old soldier if ever there was one. Martin claims to be the first to join the Local Defence Volunteers on the evening of Mr. Anthony Eden's broadcast, and although this is disputed by many people, there is no doubt that if he was not the first, he was very near it.

Martin was Chief Instructor and his appointment as Detachment Sergeant-Major was thoroughly deserved, and met with the approval

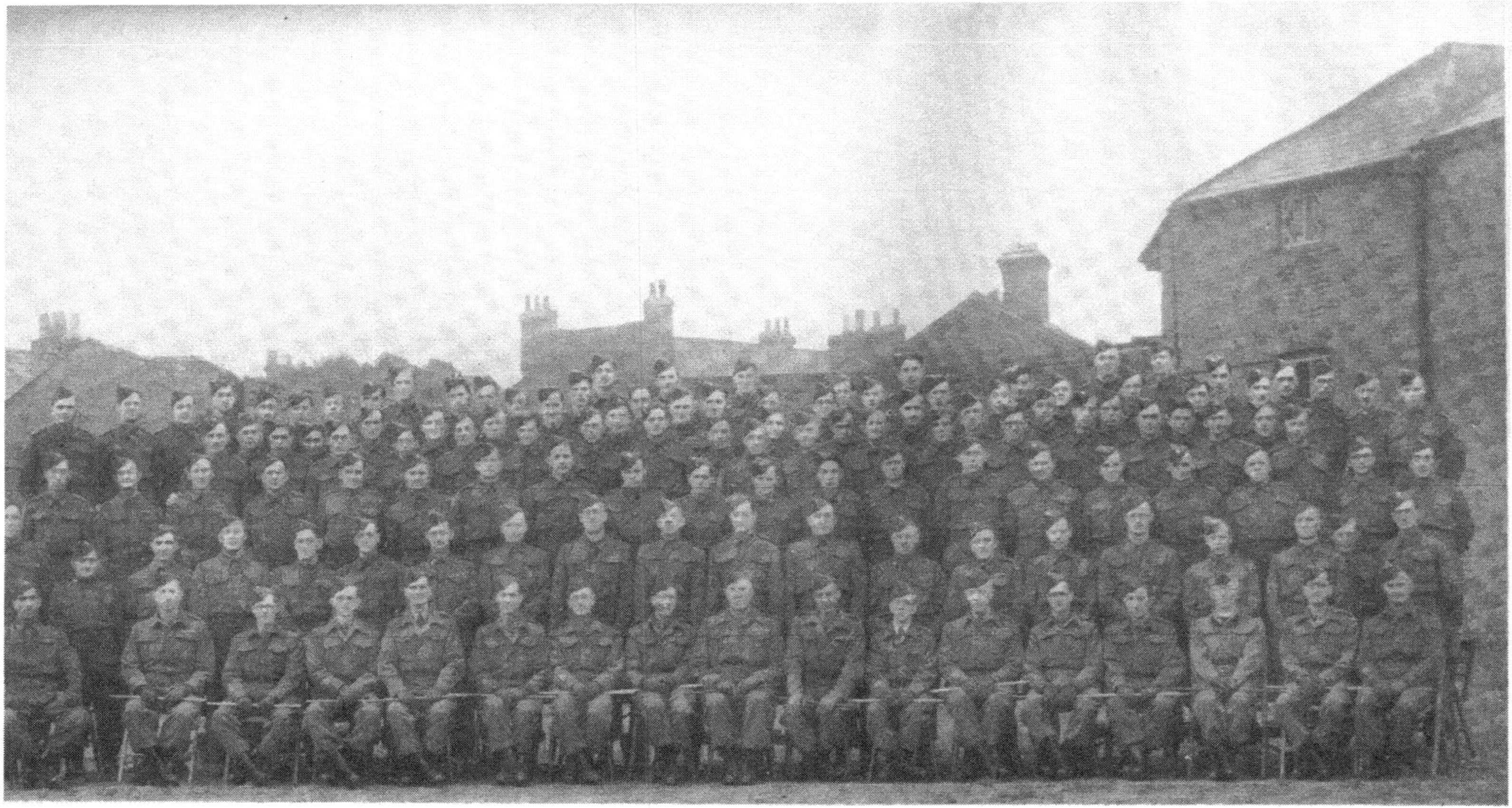

“C” Company

of everyone. He certainly knew his job and carried it out in a conscientious and efficient manner.

A. E. Crouch, acting Company Sergeant-Major in No. 2 Company, was transferred to Detachment Headquarters and appointed Deputy, D.S.M.

Every appointment in the early days of the L.D.V. had to carry a deputy.

W. Y. Patterson was appointed C.S.M. in No. 2 Company.

We were still very sadly lacking in firearms. Sixty borrowed rifles from the Exeter School O.T.C., and a few odd weapons of no use in training were all the facilities at hand for the Officer i/c Training. As a consequence the rifles had to be used for training during the evening and were then taken out by car to the various guards in and around the City. There was also the collection at 06.00 hours the next day when they were returned to Detachment Headquarters ready for training in the evening.

This went on for quite a long time and needed a certain amount of careful organising and time, and it is not to be wondered that occasionally there were groans from the guards asking, very indignantly, how they could be expected to guard a vulnerable point, or march up and down outside a building as a sentry, with nothing except their bare hands.

The volunteers on patrols and observation posts were still in civilian clothes and carrying anything they could get hold of. Shotguns, many and weird varieties of revolvers, usually without ammunition, and last but not least, a good hefty stick.

It is difficult to appreciate now the adverse conditions which existed in those days. The volunteers were called upon to do one whole night in six from dusk until dawn, plus of course, their training. During the winter months a man would perhaps not leave work until after dusk but he was expected to be at his post by at least 19.00 hours, be on duty until about 05.00 hours the following morning, and then go home and prepare for a day's hard work—and that was not all. There were no facilities for sleeping except sometimes an old cow shed or some such shelter as could be borrowed from local farmers.

Eventually some huts were obtained and erected in close proximity to the observation posts and the volunteers soon got to work to make these huts as comfortable as possible.

The observation and patrol duties entailed patrolling country lanes and across fields all through the night and in all weathers. No words can express the determination of the L.D.V. of those days. Every man had volunteered for a purpose and was determined to see that that purpose was fulfilled. They grumbled, as is the right of every Britisher to do, but they also realised the difficulties under which the Higher Authorities were working and were in the main, satisfied that the best was being done under the existing circumstances.

Looking back on those days there can be no doubt that the responsible authorities worked wonders in equipping the Home Guard as quickly as they did.

Alterations were now beginning to be made in some of the original instructions . This was only to be expected, the original instructions issued were issued on the spur of the moment, and under extreme emergency, and it was only natural that as things began to take shape and settle down more concise and lasting orders could be made.

Round about this time came a sudden call to "Stand To." This caused excitement and shall one say, expectation. The whole Detachment was not called out, but the Company Commanders were ordered to parade at Detachment Headquarters in Paul Street to await orders and all guards and patrols were warned to be on the alert. This emergency call lasted from approximately 20.00 hours until 05.00 hours the following morning when the "All Clear" was given.

The incident was not, however, without its excitement because, during this short peroid of "Stand To," one of the patrols reported that they had seen paratroops dropping in Hill Barton Road. This report eventually went through to Higher Authorities and whilst I cannot vouch for the accuracy of this statement, it is said that the Home Secretary himself was called out of bed. On investigation, the report was found to be without foundation but it all went to prove the alertness and keenness of the patrols.

The Detachment now began to receive denim suits. They were very slow in coming through at first but it was not long before most of the Detachment were fitted out with them. These suits were most useful for the work on hand but they were not too favourably received by the old soldiers, because of the bad fit. It was most unlikely that a volunteer soldier could be fitted out with a denim suit to his size and it was necessary in many cases to take in inches around the waist and turn many inches up on the bottom of the trousers.

Before this, the L.D.V. were always in doubt as to whether they were to be clothed at all, and the receipt of the denim suits raised their hopes that better things were to come.

With the denim suits appeared badges of rank. The Detachment Commander wore three blue bars on each epaulet, the Company Commanders and their deputies two, and the Platoon Commanders and their Deputies, one. Section and Squad leaders were authorised to wear the normal N.C.O.'s badge of rank on one arm only. On the other arm was worn the L.D.V. armlet which had now been issued.

JULY, 1940

July arrived with the Detachment still working very hard and spending long hours in training, patrols and duties. Too high praise cannot be given particularly to the Platoon and Section Commanders of those days, for the fact that duties were carried out in the way they were. Night after night they were found roaming about the City, checking the guards, calling up those who were late or absent, finding fresh men to take the place of those who, for various reasons, were unable to turn up.

No Headquarters existed except their own homes. and still odd bits of equipment were arriving in "dribs and drabs," and being issued out to them; but, in spite of all this, there was no slackening off; the good work still went on.

The Detachment Commander and His Staff were kept busy dealing with the many instructions which were being received. Company Commanders were busy on the general organisation of their Companies, attending meetings with the Detachment Commander, receiving orders and such like, and in addition, they were out many nights in the week visiting their picquets and guards.

All through this early period, the L.D.V., stood ready for anything, and held the fort during the tragic days of Dunkirk. Lads who were lucky enough to get away from Dunkirk and other places in France came home to find this body of men ready to fulfil whatever might come along and so give them time to recover from their terrible experience.

Another source of worry during those early days was petrol. Transport was most essential for the Officers of the Detachment to get their jobs done. Most of them had cars and, in addition, there was the Transport Platoon, all of whom had their own cars. The petrol which they were supplied with was supplied for their business purposes only and was not allowed to be used for any other purpose. A chance, however, had to be taken—and was! Eventually petrol coupons were issued but here again the amount was inadequate for the task in hand and another cause of trouble was that they were issued at the end of the month instead of the beginning. These difficulties were eventually overcome but they did cause a considerable amount of extra work and worry, particularly for the Transport Officer and the Company Commanders who were personally responsible not only for the issue of coupons to those who had cars, but also to see that a strict register was kept as to whom they were issued, and what they were used for. The matter was eventually settled quite satisfactorily.

Travelling allowances were also commenced during this time and a man using his car for Home Guard duties was allowed to claim on a mileage basis.

At this time the first consignment of U.S.A. Pattern P.17 .300 Rifles was received. These arrived in boxes packed in grease and many hours were spent by the volunteers in removing the grease and cleaning them ready for use. Classes were then arranged to instruct the volunteers in the new rifle and it was not very long before many of them were ready to fire on the open range, but they were unable to do so through lack of the necessary facilities. It should be recorded here that Major W. L. Sparkes, of the Devonshire Regiment, had been one of the Army Officers to volunteer to help the Detachment, and he was not long in coming forward and offering to give lectures; his help was gratefully received and appreciated.

No. 3 Platoon of No. 2 Company were fortunate in having Major R. Row, M.C., as their Commander, who realised the necessity for open range firing and hired, at his own expense, the Starcross Range, for three Sundays, paid for the ammunition out of his own pocket and was able to arrange for every man in his Platoon to fire.

Instructors Courses in the Browning Machine Gun were now being held in the Civic Hall, and these men, when they passed out, went back to their Companies and trained the Browning Machine Gun Teams.

During this month of July an advance issue of battle dress was made, but it was a very small quantity and the full issue was not to come for some time later. An issue of boots, however, had begun and this was very much appreciated by the volunteers.

This month cannot be passed over without reference to the wonderful work carried out by the Instructors at Detachment Headquarters, from the very early days. Many of the Instructors have now passed on to higher rank, but the leading light in those days was undoubtedly Detachment Sergeant-Major Martin, who later on, through business reasons had to relinquish his post. A great deal of the credit goes to him for the early spade work, the results of which were to last throughout the time the Detachment was in existence.

The other Instructors were, J. C. Samuels who eventually became Second-in-Command, No. 3 Company, R. G. Burvill, who eventually obtained the rank of Lieutenant and was appointed Battalion Gas Officer, having passed the necessary Courses, F. Howe, who succeeded Martin as Detachment Sergeant-Major, A. E. Crouch who was promoted to Lieutenant in command of a Platoon in No. 4 Company, H. S. Knight who became a Platoon Commander, and Sergeant Manley who remained on the Detachment Headquarters Staff throughout the life of the Detachment.

The Detachment Commander was now holding his meetings at the Police Court, Waterbeer Street, and at what was probably his last meeting he informed the Company Commanders that authority had been received from Higher Authorities for Companies to have Headquarters. This was a great blessing to companies, but a serious trouble now arose in the fact that it was impossible to get suitable accommodation, and company meetings had still to be held at the Company or Platoon Commanders' homes.

No. 2 Company were fortunate because there happened to be in their area the Old St. James School which was only used for meeting rooms for Girl Guides and Boy Scouts. The Vicar, the F. Lowman, M.A., agreed first of all to relinquish one large room and possession of this was taken in early September, 1940, but shortly afterwards the whole School was taken over by the Company and remained their Headquarters until the disbandment.

No. 3 Company, obtained the use of a room at John Stocker School for evenings only. Perhaps one might say it was better than nothing but it was really most unsatisfactory because the room was used by the scholars in the daytime and nothing could be locked up. Eventually they obtained possession of Drakes garage, Haven Road, and this remained their Headquarters to the end.

No. 1 Company Headquarters suffered through lack of Headquarters. The first real Headquarters was one office at Bedford Circus Drill Hall which also had to be used as a store. After this building was made untenable by enemy action, this Company spent nine days at No. 2 Bedford Circus where all their records were destroyed in the Blitz. The next move was to share Fonthill, Matford Lane, with the M.T. Company.

Finally, in 1943, Holloway Street Drill Hall was handed over to this Company and to be shared by H.Q. Company.

The three Field companies and Transport Company were now beginning to train under company arrangements, but facilities were still sadly lacking. It was a case of borrowing here and begging there. Somehow or other, through the hard work and ingenuity of the Officers and N.C.O.s, good results were being obtained. It was soon found that the best way to get anything to help in the training was to make it, and this was done. Very soon a number of dummy Mills 36 grenades appeared. Some of these were sectioned by Sgt. Prout of No. 2 Company, an old soldier of the last war who was also an instructor in this weapon. Home-made rifle-rests and aiming discs were very soon forthcoming and all the companies seemed to find some member who was willing and able to make most of the things they required.

It was not long before weird and wonderful home-made bombs were produced and whilst these might have been to a certain extent a little bit dangerous to the users, they would certainly have been very dangerous to the Hun if he should have appeared.

From early July, No. 1 Company were fortunate in being able to use the facilities of Exeter School, O.T.C. and the Battalions' thanks are again due to the Headmaster, Mr. J. L. Andrews, and Captain R. W. Bell, O.C. the O.T.C. for their great help.

No. 2 Company were similarly fortunately placed with being able to use all the facilities of the O.T.C. Dover College, which had been evacuated to Poltimore Park. The Headmaster of Dover College gave every facility to this Company for training, and there was a regular Company Parade at this place every Sunday morning.

.303 Rifles, miniature Range and ammunition were generously loaned by the O.T.C. and the Company owes a debt of gratitude both to the Headmaster and to Mr. Dale who was himself a Company Commander in one of the Home Guard Battalions.

H. J. Callender was now appointed C.S.M. No. 1 Company.

AUGUST 15th, 1940

August 15th, 1940, was a milestone in the Local Defence Volunteers. At the suggestion of Mr. Winston Churchill, it was decided that the name should be changed to Home Guard. This change created a very favourable impression throughout all ranks. All the L.D.V. armlets were withdrawn and Home Guard armlets substituted.

Another change of importance also took place at this time when all ranks were authorised to wear the Badge of their County Regiment, which bears the motto Semper Fidelis (Ever Faithful).

It was now decided that the Home Guard should be organised and administered by the War Office through the County Territorial Associations. The Commander-in-Chief Home Forces exercised operational control and was responsible for training. Each Sub-area was organised and commanded by the Military Area Commander. It is quite certain that these changes constituted a big step forward for this voluntary body of men, most of whom were anxious to be fighting soldiers and had, up to this time, been in some doubt as to their ultimate role. These alterations made a great stride towards settling their doubts and undoubtedly was the beginning of the ultimate smartness, keenness and tradition which continued to grow and which existed to such a large degree when the Home Guard was "Stood Down."

There was a scheme put forward for issuing emergency rations which according to instructions, were to be stored at the Police Station, but it was always hoped in those days that a Home Guardsman, if called out suddenly for duty, would be able to bring sufficient rations with him to last at least 24 hours.

AUGUST 21st, 1940.

The 21st August, 1940, was a very sad day for the Detachment. Major Anstey who had been in command since the first day, died after a very short illness. Everyone in the Detachment had not, in the short time available, had an opportunity of getting to know him, but those who did, and especially the Company Commanders and the Staff Officers at Detachment Headquarters realised that it was a tremendous blow to the Detachment, particularly at such an early stage. He had guided the Detachment through what I suppose was the most difficult times. He had had many worries and troubles but had always been able to settle them in the best interests of the Detachment and the majority, and, with things beginning to settle down when he would have been able to have taken more interest in the progress, he was called away.

He was an experienced soldier and ideally suited for the task in hand. He was always patient with those to whom patience was due, and he realised his Company Commanders' difficulties. It is a great credit that a man of Major Anstey's age should have taken on such a job, particularly in view of his very busy life in his civilian capacity as a well-known solicitor and an Alderman of the City. It does make one wonder whether the additional work of organising the detachment and the efforts which he put into it, might not have had some effect in hastening his end.

A short time previous to this Capt. F. J. C. Hunter had been made Staff Officer in order to assist Major Anstey and H. Enefer had succeeded him as Transport Officer.

AUGUST 24th, 1940

The 24th August, 1940 was the date of Major Anstey's funeral, and those of the Detachment, and there was a large number, who were able to get away from their work, paraded in Paul Street under Capt. F. J. C. Hunter, and marched to the Cathedral where a service was held.

Major Anstey's loss was undoubtedly greatly felt throughout the Detachment.

A few days after Major Anstey's funeral, Capt. F .J. C. Hunter was appointed Detachment Commander and T. J. W. Templeman who had been unable to take on the command, owing to his civil commitments, agreed to carry on as Second-in-Command.

AUGUST 30th, 1940

August 30th saw the first issue of steel helmets. These however

" A " COMPANY

" A " Company marching past saluting base.

" A " Company Officers

Company Commander Major G. Coles

" A " Company at Stand-Down Parade

"A" Company marching past Battalion Flag

only came through in small numbers and it was, therefore, generally decided that they should not be issued until there was sufficient for every man. Arrangements were made that helmets should be issued to the men going on duty and returned by them in the morning. This, of course, necessitated further work in cleaning and disinfecting.

SEPTEMBER 6th, 1940

The 6th September, 1940, was another turning point in the progress of the Detachment. The first Orders were issued and one paragraph was of particular interest because it announced the formation of a new Company to be called No. 4 (Mobile) Company. This was a most unusual formation in those days. P. A. B. Cherry who had been in charge of the H.Q. Machine Gun Section was chosen to take command of the Company and J. B. Fayerman was made Deputy Company Commander.

Each man joining this Company had to sign a declaration to the effect that they would go wherever they were required in the County of Devon and Cornwall in the case of an emergency. This condition was later cancelled.

Tremendous enthusiasm was shown by the fact that all Officers, N.C.O.s and men used to return their subsistence allowance to put into a Company Fund from which they purchased, over the course of two years, a motor van, four motor cycle combinations, eight motor cycles, a field cooker and other equipment, most necessary to make the company efficient, but which were not an issue.

F. W. Frost was detailed to take command of Headquarter Machine Gun Section, with the rank of Platoon Commander.

T. H. Vaughan was appointed C.S.M., D Company.

SEPTEMBER 7th, 1940

A Special Day of Prayer was ordered for Sunday, 9th September, 1940, and all Companies were to parade independently and attend a Church Service in their own area, but on Friday, 7th September, 1940, a state of emergency was declared and all the Companies were ordered to "Stand to." As a consequence the Church Parade was cancelled.

The "Stand To" lasted for ten days and it is quite certain that those volunteers who were members of the Detachment at that time will never forget their experiences. The weather was not too bad but the duties entailed were many and necessitated a man doing a full night's duty once every three nights and on occasions, every other night.

Observation posts were manned throughout the hours of darkness. Road Blocks were guarded with a full picquet of one squad, sentries being posted in the usual way. The method was, for the Regular Army to man the Road Blocks during the day time and for the Home Guard to take over from them in the evening, and then being relieved by the Regular Army at 06.00 hours the following morning.

Accommodation was bad. In isolated cases there might be a shed and in one case there was a tent, but generally protection from the weather was sadly lacking. Many men slept under the stars and in the morning hurried to prepare for a hard day's work. This was the

time when the invasion was expected and, in fact, from later information it would seem that an invasion had been attempted.

Every man realised the seriousness of his task and was fully prepared to do his best should the Hun make any attempt to put his foot on the sacred soil of Britain.

As usual in these times there were varied incidents and many a story could be told by volunteers in respect of some of the people they challenged and checked. The civilian population had at this time not quite got used to the Home Guard. There was, as a consequence, a few incidents where the volunteers had to eexrt their authority, and where authority was resented. This only took place where civilians were unreasonable and in any case such incidents were extremely rare.

Home Guardsmen, however, were determined to take no chances and where obstruction was met it was dealt with very strongly. It says a great deal for the Home Guardsmen of this Detachment that there were no serious incidents.

It was an order in those days that all petrol pumps in the City had to be immobilised each night and it was the duty of the Home Guardsmen to see that this was done during this time of emergency. Men were specially detailed for this job.

No rations were supplied and a volunteer was expected to bring haversack rations out of his civilian rations. This created hardship in some cases, but somehow or other it was managed, often, no doubt, by a considerable amount of sacrifice on the part of the wife.

To come on to a lighter strain, it was a standing joke during this "Stand To" and amongst the Home Guard that the volunteers worked all day and relieved the Regular Army in the evening so that they could go to the pictures or take their girls out. This was not quite true because the regulars were mainly confined to barracks on emergency duties.

SEPTEMBER 17th, 1940

It is quite certain that the end of the state of emergency which was on September 17th came as a relief to all the members of the Detachment. Everyone was certainly satisfied that they had carried out a good job of work and had at least done something to justify their formation, but the inconveniences and strain of the continued night duty and the knowledge that the organisation and equipment necessary to deal with any organised attack was incomplete and also that more training was necessary, was the main cause for their feeling of relief.

I would especially dedicate this paragraph to all those men who joined the L.D.V., during the early period and served continually through to the end of the "Stand To" period, May, 1940 to September 17th, 1940.

During the first two weeks the danger was great. Every man was facing the unknown and accepted the fact. They joined for a specific purpose of guarding their homes, their families and the Old Country against the Hun. They had joined knowing that they were unclothed,

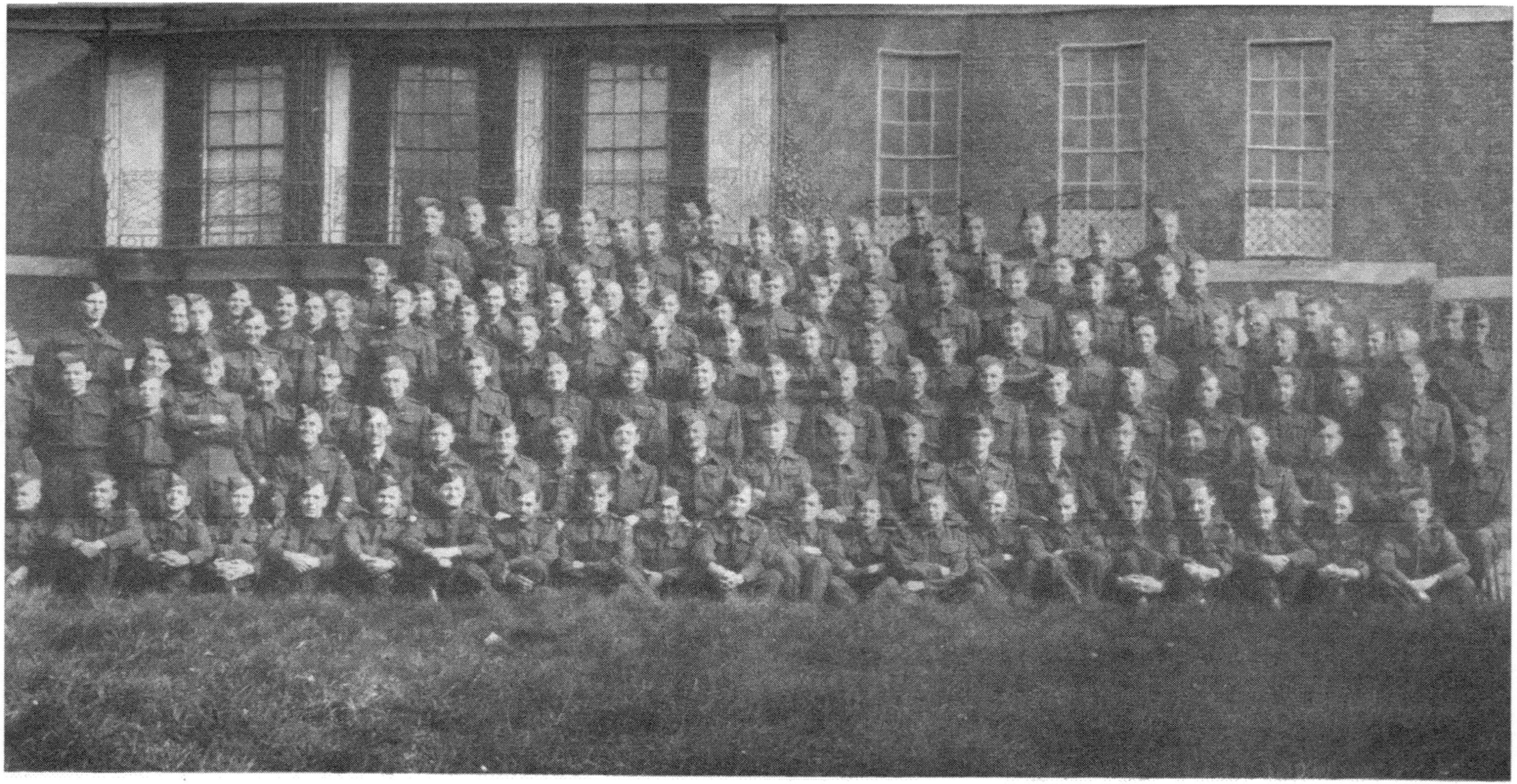

"A" Company

unarmed and untrained, but without a thought for themselves they were ready to answer the call made by Mr. Anthony Eden. There is no shadow of doubt that they would have given a good account of themselves if the Hun had landed in this country.

One can see a similarity between this L.D.V., or as they were called by this time, Home Guardsmen of May 14th, 1940, and the 1914 veterans—with all due respect to those 1914 veterans many of whom were again called to arms in the Home Guard, against their old enemy, the Hun.

F. E. Coram was appointed C.S.M. No. 3 Company.

J. Howe was appointed C.S.M. H.Q. Company.

CHAPTER II

GROWTH AND PROGRESS

SEPTEMBER 13th, 1940.

In Detachment Orders No. 2 dated September 13th, 1940, was copied a letter of congratulations from the Secretary of State for War, and this is set out in full as it is worthy of a part in the record of the Home Guard.

H.M. Secretary of State for War.   Congratulations to the Home Guard

"On the anniversary of the outbreak of War, I wish to offer my warmest congratulations to all members of the Home Guard upon the rapid growth and progress of the Force.   The duties of the Home Guard are many and diverse.   However exacting their duties have been and wherever they have been performed, the same spirit of devotion and loyalty has been everywhere manifest.

Already during the intensive operations of the past weeks upon the Home Front, the Home Guard has had opportunities to prove its capacity for service.

The Country has good reason to be grateful to men who are devoting all the time that they can give to such an essential and patriotic service."

We were now getting many and varied instructions of all types which had to be carefully read and in some cases acted upon, but in others filed for reference.

Somehow or other the various Commanders managed, in spite of their own private work, to keep track of, in any event, the most important.

The second change in the original senior Commanders, that was those who were present at Major Anstey's original meeting on May 30th, now took place. C. R. M. Frost who had been appointed to command No. 3 Company found it necessary to resign owing to pressure of other work.

J. C. B. Dart who had been Second-in-Command of the Company assumed command, but was only able to hold it for a very short time, he being another who found that owing to the amount of work thrust upon a Company Commander he was unable to undertake the task, and he therefore, resigned.

T. Greenslade, D.C.M., who was originally a Platoon Commander and who became Second-in-Command of the Company when C. R. M. Frost resigned, was now appointed Company Commander to date from the 27th September, 1940 and held that appointment until the disbandment.

Another move of interest was made at this time. The Deputy Detachment Sergeant-Major, A. E. Crouch and Sergeant F. Howe were transferred to No. 4 (Mobile) Company to assist in the intensive training necessary to make the personnel of this Company fit for their new role of mobility as quickly as possible.

During this month of September a warning was received that German paratroops might be expected to be landed in this country dressed in British battle dress. This, it will readily be appreciated, made an additional and serious complication for the Home Guard.

During this month the detachment received a total of 797 rifles and 26,000 rounds of .300 ammunition.

SEPTEMBER 20th, 1940

In Detachment orders No. 3 dated September 20th, 1940, it was announced that the Detachment had been allocated the miniature range at Higher Barracks and Topsham Barracks, and also the 30 yards open range at Prince of Wales Road. This was a big step forward and one which did a great deal to relieve the monotony of continued training and improve the efficiency of all members of the Detachment. It was a step also which enabled the instructors to ascertain to what extent the hard work which they had put into the musketry instruction had taken effect, and enabled those men who could prove their skill in this form of training, to carry on with more advanced training.

Serge battle dress was now beginning to be issued to all and it was not very long before the whole Detachment was completely equipped. It certainly does great credit to the Ordnance that, in spite of the fact that we had been through Dunkirk, they were able to fit out something like a million and a half men with battle dress.

Ninepence a garment was allowed for alterations which, in quite a number of cases, were necessary. It was doubtful whether the alterations could be carried out for that sum but carried out they were, at any cost, to the credit of the Home Guardsmen who believed that smartness was the essence of efficiency.

In the early stages of the L.D.V., Brigadier W. H. Brooke, C.B.E., M.C., D.L., had been organiser of the L.D.V. for the whole of Devon, Cornwall and Somerset, obviously a tremendous task for one man. Gradually part of the responsibility was taken away from him and he finally settled down as a Group Commander for the East Devon Group to which the Exeter Battalion belonged. The Detachment owes him a debt of gratitude for his sympathy and help which he was always ready and willing to give. His enthusiasm was a great inspiration to the members of this Battalion.

SEPTEMBER 27th, 1940

Detachment Orders No. 4, dated 17th September, 1940, announced the appointment of L. G. Coles to be Commanding Officer No. 1 Company, vice Captain R. J. Paul who had resigned on joining the R.A.F. This was another break in the original command of the Detachment. L. G. Coles had been Paul's deputy since the early days.

N. Thacker was transferred from No. 2 Company where he had been Section Sergeant to assume the appointment of Deputy to L. G. Coles.

OCTOBER 9th, 1940

On October 9th, 1940 authority came through for Subsistence Allowance, which was to be paid to the volunteers at the rate of 1/6 for five hours and 3/- for eight hours. It was decided that this should be retrospective to the 1st August, 1940. Obviously this was very well received but the fact that it was made retrospective placed another burden on the shoulders of the Company Commanders and their Staff in forcing them to go through their past records; however, nothing was too much trouble for them so long as it was for the good of the volunteers.

Volunteer W. H. Hewett was appointed Detachment Quarter Master Sergeant and held that position until the disbandment of the Home Guard.

OCTOBER 15th, 1940

On the 15th October, 1940 the Detachment Commander, Capt. F. J. C. Hunter held a meeting in the Magistrates Court, for all Company and Platoon Commanders. This was the first time all of the Officers of the Detachment had been called together and it proved to be a very useful meeting and showed that the organisation was beginning to settle down to uniformity and orderliness.

On the 20th October No. 2 Company held a Church Parade at St. David's Church, under the command of H. J. Wiltsher, and all ranks were delighted that one of their own volunteers, the Rev. C. E. Burkitt, who was the Vicar of St. David's, took the service.

The Detachment Commander, Capt. F. J. C. Hunter, supported by the Company Commander, took the Salute after the service.

Major R. Row, M.C., who from the beginning and up to this time had been No. 3 Platoon Commander in No. 2 Company, was appointed Deputy Company Commander in that company, vice V. H. L. Searle who resigned the appointment, this change taking effect from October 12th.

More organisation was published in Detachment Orders No. 8 dated October 22nd. The official recognised appointments were now to be Battalion Commander, Company Commander, Platoon Commander, Section Commander, and Squad Commander. It will be noted by these appointments that the organisation was becoming more on military lines. Before this date the Commanding Officer had been known as the Detachment Commander and there were no Squad Commanders.

On October 23rd, No. 1 Company held a Church parade at St. Mark's Church, under the command of L. G. Coles.

NOVEMBER, 1940

Early in November it was decided that the G.W.R. Home Guard who first of all were part of No. 2 Company and then attached to H.Q. details, should become an independent Company to be called No. 6 (G.W.R.) Company. The formation of the Company to date back to the 13th August, 1940. C. R. Panes who had been in charge of this Unit since its inception was appointed Company Commander. L. F. Nickels was appointed Deputy Company Commander, the appointment to take effect as from November, 1940.

The strength of the Company at this time was 187. All the personnel of this Company were recruited from the G.W.R. and their first and only Company Headquarters were at St. David's Station. In the early days even before their personnel were made into a Company, they provided patrols at vital points such as the City Basin, St. David's Station, Staffords Bridge and North Bridge, but later owing to difficulties in getting sufficient men because of intensive railway duties, No. 1 Company took over the responsibility of the City Basin, and No. 2 Company, Staffords Bridge and North Bridge.

During the blitz on Exeter in May, 1942, this Company suffered one casualty. A seventeen-year-old volunteer was killed whilst taking shelter on his way home from his first guard duty.

In 1944 part of this Company was formed into a light A.A. Troop, but more of this at the appropriate time.

Battalion Orders No. 10 dated November 15th set out the official designation of the Battalion as decided by the War Office. It was to be the 8th Battalion (Exeter) Devon Home Guard. The Battalion Commander, Capt. F. J. C. Hunter took exception to this title and went some length to draw the authorities' attention to the fact that the City of Exeter had formed the 1st Loyal Volunteers in 1798 and that, in his opinion, the Battalion should be the 1st (Loyal City of Exeter) Battalion Devon Home Guard.

On Sunday, November 10th, 1940, the Battalion held its first route march. The Companies marched independently to the Parade Ground at St. Luke's College Football Ground, where they were paraded as a Battalion under the Battalion Commander and moved off at 10.30 hours. Major T. J. W. Templeman, Battalion 2/i.c. was in command on the march.

The route taken was College Avenue, College Road, Heavitree Road, Sidwell Street, Blackboy Road, Pinhoe Road, Hamlins Lane, where the Battalion broke off for 10 minutes. After reforming the route march continued along Hamlins Lane, South Lawn Terrace, North Street Heavitree, Magdalen Street, South Street, High Street and past the Guildhall at 12.00 hours where the Right Worshipful the Mayor of Exeter, R. Glave Saunders, took the Salute.

The Battalion then proceeded to London Inn Square where the Companies marched off independently under the command of the Deputy Company Commanders, the Company Commanders breaking off in order to join the Battalion Commander in the Mayor's Parlour at the invitation of His Worship the Mayor.

The Battalion was accompanied on the Route March by the Band of the I.T.C. by the courtesy of Lt.-Col. G. Coates, who was in command of the I.T.C. at that time.

The dress worn by the volunteers will no doubt be of interest because it will show to those who will have forgotten, or to those who never knew, the equipment which had been issued up to that time.

Battle Dress, forage cap, leather belts with bayonet, scabbard, frog, rifles with slings, gas masks and black boots.

Provision had to be made because of the weather being unkind, but at this stage there were insufficient greatcoats for every man in the Battalion and they were advised to wear warm under-clothing.

Gaiters could not be worn because here again there were insufficient for the whole Battalion.

The total on parade for this Route March was 945 and a film of the march past was taken by the Gaumont British News Corporation and shown at the Gaumont Cinema, Exeter, every day from Thursday, November 14th, until Wednesday, November 20th.

In Battalion Orders No. 11 dated 12th November, 1940, the Battalion Commander, Capt. F. J. C. Hunter, congratulated the whole Battalion on their turn out for the route march especially mentioning the fact that hard training had been carried out, and which had contributed so much to the efficiency of the march discipline.

At this time the following factory units were serving with the Battalion. The Admiralty Platoon, The Civil Defence Platoon, The Fire Brigade Platoon, Devon County Council Platoon, Express & Echo Platoon, H.M. Prison Platoon, Research Department Platoon, and the Records Department Platoon. All these were small Units, formed to keep the personnel of the different factories or organisations together in one body, but they were all eventually disbanded and the personnel either left the Home Guard or were merged into the field companies with the exception of the Gas Company Platoon which remained a Unit and part of "C" Company, until disbandment.

NOVEMBER 12th, 1940

In the following Battalion Orders dated 12th November, a Headquarter Company was formed under the command of E. N. Clulee and the Unit at that time comprised the Transport, Machine Gun Detachment, Admiralty Platoon, Gas Company Platoon, plus certain Headquarter details who formed the permanent Battalion Headquarter Guard. E. N. Clulee already held the rank of Company Commander, and remained H.Q. Company Commander until disbandment.

This Company's original Headquarters were at Paul Street, but they were to see many changes. The first change was to Bedford Circus Drill Hall. After the first blitz they moved with the Battalion to No. 2 Bedford Circus, and then after the second blitz they were at Penleonard Close (St. Leonard's Road), Fonthill, Priory Drill Hall, until finally taking up their quarters in Holloway Street Drill Hall, where they remained until "Stand Down." There were various changes in the Second-in-Command of this Company, which will be noted throughout this record.

F. Howe was the original Company Sergeant-Major, later to become Regimental Sergeant-Major. He was followed by G. H. Finn, later to become Artillery Staff Officer and W. L. Lovell, who was Company Sergeant-Major until "Stand Down."

It is a boast of H.Q. Company Commander that H.Q. Company was the most consistent Company in the Battalion and held the record for the number of second places in all kinds of competitions. If this is true then, as a specialist company, they have a record to be proud of.

Many volunteers who had been through this Company have received appointments of responsibility in the Battalion.

The Recruits were still being trained in the Civic Hall under Headquarter Instructors, but Companies were now carrying out their own training programmes. Owing to the issue of P.17 .300 Rifles, all shotguns and .303 Rifles were withdrawn from the volunteers. Platoon Commander, G. H. Vooght who had acted as Establishment Officer since the very early days was appointed to the rank of Deputy Company Commander. This volunteer had done a considerable amount of work under adverse conditions.

As it can be readily appreciated, weekly Battalion Orders showed many alterations, particularly in the way of promotions.

The early days up to now had undoubtedly proved a very severe test to many keen and enthusiastic volunteers, and it was only to be expected that some men, however willing in spirit, would, by means either of age or health, be unable to carry on.

Capt. F. J. C. Hunter, the Battalion Commander, very soon realised the necessity for encouragement in miniature and open range firing, not only to increase the efficiency of the volunteers but also to sustain their interest and to prevent normal training becoming dull. He, therefore, presented a handsome silver cup for a miniature range shooting competition between Companies of the Battalion. The trophy was to be shot for monthly and the teams were to be four men per company. One of the many good rules was, that no man was allowed to fire twice in his company team until every member of the Company had fired. This prevented the best shots in the Company from firing every month and gave every man an interest in the competition. The shoot for this cup became something which was keenly looked forward to and there were many very close finishes in some of the matches. The results of this competition can be seen at the back of this book.

Courses for N.C.O.s were now being started. There were also special courses for the training in the Machine Gun and the 36 Grenade. This latter weapon was now an issue to the Home Guard, much to the satisfaction of the old soldiers.

DECEMBER, 1940

On Sunday, December 8th, 1940, No. 3 Company held a parade at the John Stocker School and marched to Alphington Church where a service was held. The Company Commander Major T. Greenslade, D.C.M., was in command.

On December 7th, Col. Short, a Staff Officer from the War Office came to Exeter and lectured to the Battalion in the Civic Hall, the subject being, the training of the Home Guard. This was an important lecture and the lecturer undoubtedly made it very interesting. It was well attended and all ranks appreciated the position as it was put across by the lecturer.

The possibility of air raids was now exercising the minds of the authorities and whilst there was no compulsion the Army Commander directed that assistance should be given by the Military, including the Home Guard, to the civil authorities during and after air raids, and that such assistance should be a military duty to be carried out by the Home Guard as a military unit under the command of their own officers. This presented no hardships because it did not interfere in any way with the training of the Home Guardsmen and there is no doubt that, without this order, Home Guardsmen would have been one of the first to have turned out to give whatever assistance they could.

Arrangements were now being made for telephones to be installed at Company Headquarters. This would have been a great boon to the Company Commanders, if they had been able to secure Headquarters, but the telephones were installed very quickly after Headquarters were requisitioned.

DECEMBER 18th, 1940

On December 15th, 1940, H.Q. Company, under the command of E. N. Clulee, paraded at Paul Street Parking Ground, and marched to St. Mary Arches Church, where a service was held. The company then undertook a short route march.

Brig. W. H. Brooke, C.B.E., M.C., D.L., the Group Commander, was a frequent visitor to both Battalion and Company Headquarters and his visits were always encouraging and instructive. He, with the Battalion Commander, visited No. 2 Company during their training at Poltimore Park and was agreeably surprised at the facilities which were being given to this Company by the Dover College O.T.C.

I have previously referred to Battalion Orders No. 10 dated November 5th, 1940, which set out the fact that the official designation of the Battalion was the 8th Bn. (Exeter) Devon Home Guard, and that the Battalion Commander, Capt. F. J. C. Hunter, had objected to this title. The objections had borne fruit, because in Battalion Orders dated 18th December, it gave the new official designation, which is as it is now, the 1st (Loyal City of Exeter) Bn. Devon Home Guard, and I will repeat here a message from the Battalion Commander to all ranks:

"Members of the Battalion will share the Battalion Commander's pride that this title has been bestowed upon it. Exeter was the birthplace of the 1st Rifle Volunteers raised in 1852, and the movement resulted in the recruitment of Volunteer Regiments throughout the Kingdom. Volunteer Regiments were also raised in the City as far back as 1798 by the Exeter Loyal Association to guard against the menace of an invasion which at that time threatened the Old Country. The Colours of this Association are preserved in the Exeter Cathedral. It therefore seems fitting that this Battalion should bear the title which has been given to it."

It would be superficial for me to say more except, that the title has been jealously guarded by the members of the 1st Battalion right to the end.

There was another important alteration at this time and one which was to effect the Battalion directly, for at least eighteen months and indirectly, perhaps, until the end, as from 1200 hours on Monday, December 16th, 1940, the Headquarters of the Battalion were to move to the Bedford Circus Drill Hall, Bedford Circus, Exeter. This was the Headquarters of the 4th Battalion Devon Territorials. When one considers the cramped Headquarters at Paul Street and the difficulties under which the staff had to operate, it will be easily seen what a big difference the move from one big room to a properly constructed Headquarters was to make for the efficiency of the Battalion.

With our own Battalion Headquarters, in an adequate building the volunteers were able to take a greater pride in their unit, and the Battalion Commander with his Staff was able to exercise greater control and provide more facilities for training.

On Sunday, December 22nd, 1940, No. 1 Company held a route march commencing from Victoria Park Road. The Parade was under the command of L. G. Coles, the Company Commander.

On the same day, No. 2 Company attended a Church Parade at the Congregational Church, Southernhay, the company having first of all paraded at their Company Headquarters in St. James Road, under the command of the Company Commander, H. J. Wiltsher.

More information was now coming through regarding the possibilities of an attack on this country by the Germans. At this time we were being warned that the Germans were expected to drop incendiary bombs on this country. This was a new weapon but before the Home Guard were to finish, they were to learn a lot about the incendiary bomb from actual experience.

Suggestions were now beginning to be made about the possibility of the reconstruction of the Home Guard. No one seemed to have any idea what that meant but there was, in fact, an order given at this time that all the appointments and promotions in the Battalion should be on an acting basis.

No. 3 Company who, up to this time, had been using a room in the John Stocker School, were able to requisition Drakes Garage, Haven Road, for their Headquarters. This was not altogether satisfactory, but it was the best obtainable at the time, and certainly very much better than what they had had previously. In spite of many efforts they were destined to remain in these Headquarters until the end of the Home Guard.

We had now arrived at Christmas time and no Battalion Orders were issued for the Christmas Week, the Battalion having been given a well deserved holiday.

It was decided to form a Signals Platoon. J. S. Forsyth was given the task of forming this Platoon and he was ably assisted by W. V.' Bristow. Forsyth decided on a novel method to secure recruits. He borrowed a public address travelling van and toured the streets of Exeter for two weeks explaining the needs of the Signal Platoon, and within a month a band of technicians had joined and the strength of the Platoon was completed.

The next move was to appoint a pigeon officer. He invited the pigeon fanciers in the town to a meeting and the position was explained to them. Before the meeting broke up the officer had signed on 12 pigeon fanciers, with their lofts and their carrier pigeons. The 1st Battalion now had the first carrier pigeon service of any Battalion in the country. This pigeon section formed their own transport and it was not long before the birds were being flown in conjunction with the Regular Army trunk lines.

The early training of the Signals Platoon was assisted greatly by the Regular Army. There is one incident of note in connection with the training of this Platoon which happened when they were on the bombing range, throwing live 36 grenades. H. S. Knight was in charge of the instruction when a man dropped a live grenade after having pulled out the pin. H. S. Knight pushed the man out of the way, picked up the grenade and threw it over the parapet. The fact that the grenade burst in the air shows how close it was to causing serious injury. The prompt action of this instructor is deserving of mention.

We were now receiving a warning that there was a possibility of improper use of telephones by enemy agents. If the possibility was a live one then the warning was undoubtedly necessary. Every precaution was being taken in the Battalion to prevent any misunderstanding in the event of such messages being transmitted.

Further instructions were received drawing attention to the fact that under the Defence (Gen. Regulations) 1939, Home Guardsmen, as members of H.M. Forces, had equal powers to those of police Constables in enforcing light regulations. The instructions which followed, however, made it difficult for Home Guardsmen to carry out this order very effectively. but if it did nothing else it at least gave them the confidence to draw the attention of the guilty party to any infringement of the regulations. There were many occasions where Home Guardsmen were not only the means of rectifying faulty lighting but also of saving the guilty party from a possible police persecution.

Again it was agreed that, as the Home Guard formed a part of the armed forces of the Crown, the members, when in uniform or wearing the authorised armlet, could use garrison and regimental institutes conducted by N.A.A.F.I., to the same extent as other members of H.M. Forces. This privilege was not very much used but it certainly was appreciated by Home Guardsmen. It was another sign that he was being acknowledged as a full member of the armed forces.

This brings us to the end of 1940, a year full of anxiety, hard

Arrival at Company Head Quarters
after Church Parade

Company arriving
at Cowley Church
for Divine Service

Some of the
Officers

Some of the
N.C.O.'s

" E " (G.W.R.) COMPANY

Major C. R. Panes Company Commander

work and perplexities, but it proved that, in a short space of time, there had been brought about a comradeship and *esprit de corps* second to none, and the year had undoubtedly sealed the framework of the efficient body it was to become at the end.

No one could visualise what lay ahead. Trouble was expected and, being expected, it was being prepared for. Every individual member of the Battalion was facing a future with great confidence in his ability to overcome anything which the Hun might decide to do.

JANUARY, 1941

1941 opened with the Battalion organised and settling down to hard work. Patrols and guards were still being carried out and observation posts manned, but January was to see the commencement of concentrated preparation for defence. It was to bring forth the digging of trenches, and setting up of barbed wire, and here again the old soldier of the last War came in very useful. In spite of the hard work the men were undoubtedly very pleased that they were being given the opportunity of preparing at least some form of defence which would enable them to carry out the job that they had in hand with better prospects of damage to the Hun and protection to themselves.

The training being carried out was one evening parade per week and in addition to this every man, was doing at least a duty per week, and trench digging or wiring all day every Sunday. The first turf for the trenches was lifted about the middle of January, 1941. There were in the region of 40 or 50 individual posts in each Company, where a trench had to be dug. Many difficulties were experienced because the actual spot chosen by the military authorities as being the best from a defensive point of view, very often soon became waterlogged and the site either had to be altered or more digging had to be carried out to drain it. The hard work put into this task by the volunteers of the Battalion is difficult to believe in these days, but in many cases the evidence still remains.

There was one trench where the authorities would not give permission for it to be moved and as it was impossible to drain it, a hand pump had to be borrowed and every Sunday before the work could be continued, the water had to be pumped out of the trench.

One Sunday it snowed from the time the men paraded which was round about 09.30 hours until they finished at 16.00 hours, but a large percentage of the volunteers, realising the urgency of the work, carried on with the job and enjoyed it.

Haversack rations were taken by the men for the midday meal, but the Company Commanders generally managed to arrange for supplies of hot tea and hot soup.

Wiring was another tremendous task. The length of the Battalion's defended areas around Exeter was 14½ miles. This had to be wired in front of the trenches by triple dannert and in many cases a trip wire also. The Military carried out the wiring of roughly 3-4 miles out of the whole length, and the Battalion erected the remainder. It went across fields, over ditches, and the only spaces left were across arable fields, and in these cases dannert wire with the necessary pegs had to be stored close to the hedge and arrangements made for the wire to be put up immediately on recipt of 'Action Stations.'

The original siting of the wiring was in many cases a difficult task. The volunteers were obviously not concerned with this, but the Battalion and Company Commanders, in conjunction with the Military authorities, spent many hours tramping round the countryside before the final positions were decided.

When a trench was dug in any field where cattle was likely to be put, a cattle fence had to be built around the trench. The biggest grouse was that, whilst volunteers realised the urgency of the job and were prepared to carry it out, they were handicapped considerably by a shortage of tools, and many of the volunteers brought their own and somehow or other by the comradeship amongst all ranks, a realisation of the necessity of the work, and great loyalty, the job was completed in spite of the fact that generally there were only three pairs of wiring gloves available for each company, and the men in their anxiety to get the work done, risked nasty cuts and poison by handling the wire with their bare hands. Whatever can be said about the Home Guard, this is one thing that might be missed but cannot be forgotten.

A hard and unpleasant job of work well and truly carried out without thought of reward.

It is impossible to give a date for the completion of all the trench digging and wiring, because, although the main job was completed during the early summer, there was always something to be altered or renovated, and the completion time varied with each Company.

During January, 1941, a First Aid Section was formed and attached to Headquarters. W. Rackwood Cocks was appointed to take charge of this Section with the rank of Platoon Commander.

Attention was now being given to the fire watching at the various Headquarters, but in those days it was not recognised as a Home Guard duty but as a volunteer fire fighting party, recognised only by the local authorities. Fire picquets were supplied by each Company for its own Headquarters. Another duty entailing the use of the volunteers, and again reducing their free time.

On Sunday, 22nd January, No. 3 Company held a Church Parade at Exwick Church under the command of T. Greenslade, D.C.M., Company Commander.

Southern Command were running a Weapon Training School at Woolacombe, and a vacancy was allocated to this Battalion. This was a fortnightly course and it was therefore very difficult to get a volunteer who was able to spare two weeks away from his normal work.

.300 ammunition was still very scarce and strict economy had to be exercised in its use for training purposes, the Battalion Commander naturally being much concerned with his operational stock, which was very low. Undoubtedly the lack of practice ammunition was a great drawback to the training of the Home Guardsmen in

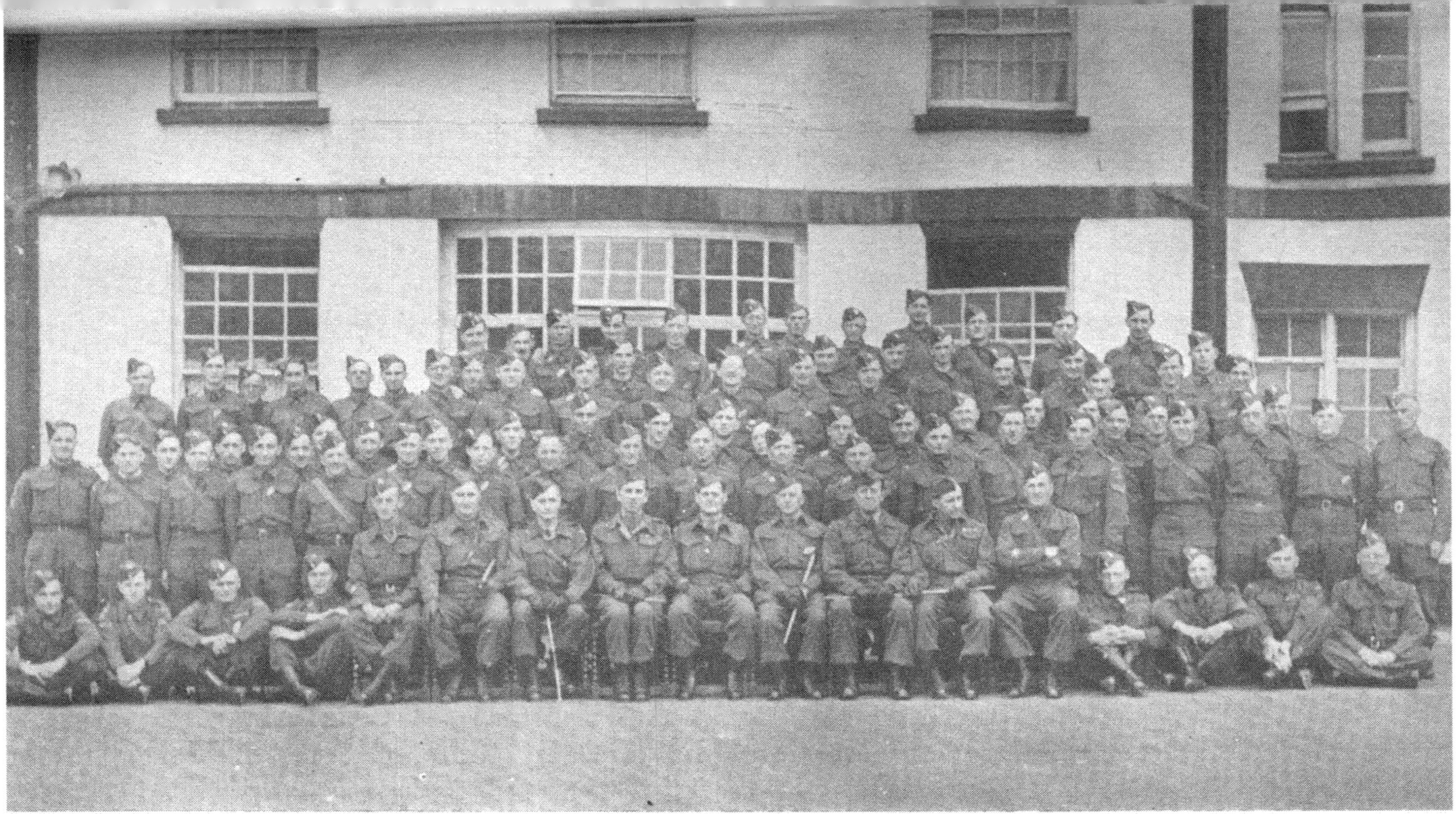

" E " Company

musketry as it was quite rightly felt by every man who had a rifle that he would be very much more efficient if he had had an opportunity of firing it even if he only had five rounds.

The Home Guard were still wearing armlets which were khaki bands with 'Home Guard' in black, and a reminder had to be issued that these had to be worn at all parades, lectures or demonstrations, whether in uniform or otherwise.

Instructions were issued during this month that Devon and Cornwall were to be two zones in the South-West area, and that the then existing zones were to be known as Groups. This was one of the many alterations which were to follow.

We had now received a few Lewis Guns and an Instructors Course was started.

The Battalion was by this time formed in the way in which it was to remain for quite a long time and in Battalion Orders, dated 5th

FEBRUARY, 1941

February, 1941, the actual numbering of the Companies was set out.

No. 1 Company commanded by L. G. Coles.

No. 2 Company commanded by H. J. Wiltsher.

No. 3 Company commanded T. Greenslade, D.C.M.

No. 4 (Mobile) Company commanded by P. A. B. Cherry.

No. 5 (Transport) Company commanded by H. Enefer.

No. 6 (G.W.R.) Company commanded by C. R. Panes.

H.Q. Company commanded by E. N. Clulee.

H.Q. Company through no fault of their own, seemed to be for a long time in a continual state of alteration and it will be interesting to set out here the various units which this company now consisted of:

Fire Brigade Platoon, Admiralty Platoon, H.M. Prison Platoon, Research Department Section, Civil Defence Platoon, Records Department Section, Machine Gun Section, First Aid Section, H.Q. Instructors, H.Q. Guard.

It will be noted that No. 5 (Transport) Company had now been taken away from H.Q. Company and made a company on their own.

Most of those in H.Q. Company units were eventually disbanded.

On Sunday, February 12th, 1941, No. 6 (G.W.R.) Company attended a Church Parade at Cowley Church followed by a route march under the command of C. R. Panes, Company Commander.

C. A. Songhurst was appointed to the rank of Deputy Company Commander and to remain on the training staff.

W. F. H. Payne, who was a Section Commander in No. 2 Company, an old soldier of the South African War and others which followed, and destined later to become C.Q.M.S. No. 2 Company, and to be awarded the British Empire Medal for his work in the Home Guard, was our first serious casualty.

Whilst out on patrol with a part of his section near St. David's Station on a very dark night, he was knocked down by a motor vehicle and sustained two fractures of the right leg. Payne was in hospital for a long time but he eventually recovered in spite of his age and returned to do a lot more good work for the Company in general and the Battalion as a whole, and he was still a member of the Battalion when the Home Guard was disbanded.

It was now being realised that camouflage was a very important subject for the Home Guardsmen and a lecture on this subject was given by Mr. Penrose.

Battalion Orders No. 24, dated 19th February, Part II, announced the appointment of Major J. W. Western, O.B.E., T.D., as Second-in-Command of the Battalion as from the 12th February, 1941, vice, T. J. W. Templeman, who relinquished his appointment for business reasons.

None of the Company Commanders at that time were able to take on the appointment as Second-in-Command of the Battalion owing to their own business commitments. T. J. W. Templeman was immediately appointed Liaison Officer between the Home Guard and the Civil Defence and a most admirable appointment, Templeman being not only a past Mayor of the City but also well acquainted with all the Civic authorities.

T. J. W. Templeman had been the original Second-in-Command of the Battalion, he having been appointed to that position by Major Anstey at the original meeting on May 30th, 1940. He had done a lot of work for the Battalion especially behind the scenes and the Battalion owe him a debt of gratitude for that. Templeman carried on and right to the end was still Liaison Officer, in addition to which he was always helpful as being the legal adviser to the successive Commanding Officers, and also to any man in the Battalion who found himself in trouble or in need of advice.

Major Western joined the Battalion on the 27th September, 1940, and shortly after took on the job as Assistant Adjutant to Coverdale.

Battalion Orders dated 24th February, 1941, the War Office confirmed the following appointments:

Zone Commander, Col. H. D. Goldsmith, D.S.O., D.L.

Group Commander, East Devon Group, Brig. W. H. Brooke, C.B.E., M.C., D.L.

Both of these Officers have at all times been of great assistance to the Battalion.

The War Weapons Week saw a parade through the City to which the Battalion sent a Detachment and the O.C. Troops, Exeter, congratulated The Commanding Officer in the following letter.

"On behalf of the Mayor, the Display Sub-Committee and the townspeople of Exeter, I should like to thank you for your very great assistance in providing a representative detachment, and to express their admiration of the Officers and Men who gave up their Saturday afternoon. It was obvious that much time and trouble had been expended on the general turn-out, and I have heard many comments expressed by some of the very large crowd of spectators, who lined the route, indicating their interest and pride. I am told there is no doubt that this parade on the opening day of War Weapons Week, provided a great incentive to subscribe to the National Savings Campaign."

During this week a message was received from the East Devon Group Commander, Brig. W. H. Brooke, and this also is worthy of repetition.

"We are entering on a critical period. The success or failure of the enemy's invasion will depend largely on whether our defensive preparations, especially barbed wire fencings, are complete. All training must now be sacrificed to the completion of our defences. I appeal to every Home Guardsman, who can, to give every moment he can spare to the completion of the task. The safety of the Country depends on it."

In Battalion Orders No. 25 dated 26th February, 1941, Part II, was announced the appointment of F. J. C. Hunter as Commanding Officer of the 1st (Loyal City of Exeter) Bn. Devons Home Guard, with the rank of Lieut.-Colonel, as from the 1st February, 1941.

This was a very big step forward for the Home Guard as it had now been decided that all Home Guard Officers should carry the rank equivalent to their appointment.

In March, 1941, permission was given by the War Office for all Officers to wear their appropriate badge of rank: Company Commanders to be Majors or Captains, Deputy Company Commanders to be Captains, Platoon Commanders—Lieutenants, Deputy Platoon Commanders—2nd Lieutenants, and in a following A.C.I. Warrant and Non-Commissioned rank was introduced and recognised.

The establishment was laid down for Battalion, Companies and Platoons on similar lines to the Regular Army. This was another step forward and one which was fully appreciated by all Home Guardsmen because it was bringing them in line with the Regular Army and it would not be going too far to say that the general feeling was that every Home Guardsman wanted to be acknowledged as part of the Armed Forces.

On the 12th March, Platoon Commander W. H. Hoyt was appointed Second-in-Command of No. 2 Company vice Major R. Row, M.C., who had resigned having been called up by the War Office under the Emergency Reserve of Officers.

Major Row had been with the Company since its formation. He was one of the original Platoon Commanders appointed by the Company Commander, H. J. Wiltsher, and his loss was a great one for the company. He himself quite frankly admitted that he was very reluctant to leave because although the Company had only been in existence for ten months he could appreciate the feeling of good will and comradeship and was loath to give this up. He took with him the good wishes of everyone in the Company.

W. H. Hoyt, also an original Platoon Commander in No. 2 Company, had commanded No. 1 Platoon since formation, and he was later destined to become Company Commander and then Second-in-Command of the Battalion.

On March 26th the Commanding Officer, Lt.-Col. F. J. C. Hunter decided to inaugurate a Battalion Orderly Officer. This Officer was to be either a Lieutenant or 2nd Lieutenant, and his duty was an all night one at Battalion Headquarters, including the inspection of outlying guards and picquets.

On Sunday, 30th March, 1941, H.Q. Company, under the command of E. N. Clulee, attended a Church Parade at St. Mary Arches Church.

G. T. Page was now appointed C.S.M. No. 6 Company.

A. Coates was appointed C.S.M. No. 3 Company.

APRIL 9th, 1941

In Battalion Orders No. 31 dated 9th April there appeared a copy of Southern Command Orders confirming the ranks of all the Officers in the Battalion to take effect from the 1st February, 1941.

The Commanding Officer had already been promoted to Lieut-Col. and it will be interesting to set out the Senior Officers who had been appointed to the rank of Major: —

J. W. Western, O.B.E., T.D., Second-in-Command of the Battalion.

T. J. W. Templeman, Liaison Officer.

L. G. Coles, No. 1 Company Commander.

H. J. Wiltsher, No. 2 Company Commander.

T. Greenslade, D.C.M., No. 3 Company Commander.

P. A. B. Cherry, No. 4 (Mobile) Company Commander.

H. Enefer No. 5 (Transport) Company Commander.

C. R. Panes, No. 6 (G.W.R.) Company Commander.

E. N. Clulee, H.Q. Company Commander.

Of the a./m., Lt.-Col. F. J. C. Hunter was killed in the Blitz on Exeter in 1942, Major J. W. Western, O.B.E., T.D., resigned on account of health reasons on May 30th, 1943, Major H. J. Wiltsher, after being Second-in-Command of the Battalion from May, 1942 to May, 1943, assumed command of the Battalion, Major P. A. B. Cherry moved out of Exeter and was transferred to another Battalion, H. Enefer left the Battalion on the reformation of No. 5 (Transport) Company under the command of the R.A.S.C. The remainder still held the same position on the disbandment of the Battalion.

Another step was taken in April, which was to increase the efficiency of the Home Guardsmen. In an A.C.I. it was decided to institute the award of a Proficiency Badge to members of the Home Guard and it was not long after all the details were received that a number of men were parading at Battalion Headquarters to go through the test and there were very few failures, showing the extreme keenness of the volunteers to make themselves as efficient as possible. The men were undoubtedly proud to be privileged to wear the Proficiency Badge, a red diamond worn on the lower part of the sleeve.

Round about this time a course was held for N.C.O.s in the Browning Automatic Rifle. This gives another indication of the increased variety of arms which were being issued to the Home Guardsmen and this variety undoubtedly put a great strain on the training facilities available.

One or two outside competitions were being carried out and it is interesting to note that H.Q. Company challenged the Pinhoe Platoon of the 3rd Battalion to a Miniature Range Shooting Match and that H.Q. Company won.

The Battalion Commander had now decided to appoint an Intelligence Officer and A. M. Hichisson was duly installed in this position, with the rank of Lieutenant. No one can say that this Officer has not done his full share of work for the Battalion and he remained in that position until the disbandment.

MAY 10th, 1941

On Saturday, May 10th, 1941, the Battalion went on a recruiting march. The Assembly was at the Exeter City Football Ground where the Battalion paraded under the command of Lt.-Col. F. J. C. Hunter, but marched off under the command of the Second-in-Command of the Battalion, Major J. W. Western, O.B.E., T.D.

This march which, from the Home Guard point of view, was quite an ambitious one, was very successful. Before the march off, Col. H. F. G. Hay, the Group Commander, South Devon Group, to which this Battalion at that time belonged, inspected the Battalion at 15.35 hours and then proceeded with the Battalion Commander to join the Right Worshipful the Mayor of Exeter (R. Glave Saunders) on the Saluting Base at the Guildhall, the Mayor taking the salute as the Battalion marched past.

The route taken by the Battalion will be interesting. Commencing at St. James Park, it followed along St. James Road, Sidwell Street, High Street, Fore Street, Exe Bridge, Cowick Street to Buddle Lane, where the Battalion halted and fell out for ten minutes. The route then continued along Okehampton Street, Exe Bridge, Edmund Street, West Street, Coombe Street, South Steet, Magdalen Road, Southernhay East, London Inn Square, Longbrook Street, Pennsylvania Road, Union Road, Old Tiverton Road to the Football Ground where the Battalion was dismissed.

It has already been pointed out that this was an ambitious route march and there is no doubt that it was, having regard to the fact that the members of the Battalion had no opportunity of training for route marches.

The march throughout was led by the Devonshire Regiment Band, by kind permission of the Commanding Officer, I.T.C., Devonshire Regiment.

It was never definitely ascertained whether this march was a successful one from a recruiting point of view. It had been arranged that all those joining should fall in at the rear of the Battalion, but it could be understood that there were not many who availed themselves of this opportunity, although there were at least a dozen who are to be admired for their keenness and enthusiasm and it is to be hoped that they will read these notes.

During the early part of this year certain alterations to the defence line had been made by Regular Army Officers in conjunction with the Battalion Commander, and it was, therefore, decided that on May 11th, 1941, there should be a "Manning" Exercise in the new defence positions. The whole Battalion was turned out as for "Action

Stations," and were in their defended position by 14.30 hours. An inspection was carried out by the Brigade Commander, and other Regular Army Officers and the questionnaire was a very exacting one.

General reports were very satisfactory, and there is no doubt that the Exercise was of great importance.

In the early days of May the Battalion Commander copied in Battalion Orders a direction issued by the G.O.C. Southern Command. It related to the question of saluting and pointed out the reasons why Officers should be saluted. It particularly drew attention to the fact that the Home Guard Battalions were entitled to wear the badge of their County Regiments and suggested that these County Regiments might think badly of their County Home Guard Battalions if they did not conform to the ordinary practice of the Regular Army. This Battalion did not require much reminding as it had always been keen to keep up a military standard and although no orders had ever been issued to the Battalion regarding saluting, the practice was invariably carried out.

This month saw the inauguration of a further competition for a cup presented by the Company Commanders. This was to be awarded to the Company with the highest aggregate score and was to date back to March. The first winners were No. 4 Company followed by No. 6 Company, H.Q. Company, No. 2 Company, No. 3 Company, No. 1 Company, and No. 5 Company.

2nd Class Warrant Officer, F. Howe who for some time had been H.Q. Company Sergeant-Major, was now appointed Regimental Sergeant-Major, and promoted to Warrant Officer Class 1, vice J. Martin with effect from May 5th, 1941. This promotion was thoroughly deserved. No man had been more keen or enthusiastic over the well-being of the Battalion since the very first day. No-one had done so much good work without thought of reward, and it would be difficult to estimate the amount of time Sergeant-Major Howe had given quite freely to the training of the recruits in the early days, and later on as C.S.M. in H.Q. Company.

R.S.M. Howe was to retain his position until the disbandment of the Home Guard and the writer of these notes is grateful, to him for the efficient manner in which he has carried out the many duties assigned to him, and for his interest in the training of the Battalion.

Jimmy Martin had found it necessary to relinquish his appointment as R.S.M. owing to a new civil job which he had taken on, but he was determined that he would not be kept out of things, and applied for the post of Battalion Armourer which was granted, with effect from the 5th May, 1941, and with the rank of Staff-Sergeant. Jim was one of the mainstays of the Battalion and it was a great relief to everyone to know that he was not leaving us.

G. H. Finn was now appointed C.S..M. of H.Q. Company.

Battalion Orders dated May 14th, 1941 set out a message by Lieut-Gen. The Hon. H. R. L. G. Alexander, C.B., C.S.I., D.S.O., M.C., G.O.C. Southern Command. This Special Order of the Day comprised a special message from His Majesty the King to the Home Guard, and was as follows: —

"I heartily congratulate the Home Guard on the progress made by all ranks since it was established a year ago to-day. On many occasions I have seen for myself the keenness with which they are fitting themselves for the discharge of vital duties in the defence of our homes. They have already earned the gratitude of their fellow citizens for the prompt and unstinted assistance which they are constantly giving to the Civil Defence services. The Home Guard stands in the direct line of the various bodies of militia, trained bands, fencibles and volunteers, the record of whose fine spirit and military aptitude adorn many a page of our history. I thank them for the service which they freely give at considerable sacrifice of leisure and convenience, and I am confident that co-operation with their comrades in arms of the Field Army, they will fit themselves to meet and overcome every emergency and so make their contribution to the victory, which will reward our united efforts."

GEORGE, R.

There was also included in these orders a message from the South Devon Group Commander, to which Group we were attached at this time. He expressed his pleasure at the turnout, bearing of the men, and the march discipline during the recruiting march.

It was decided by the War Office at this time that members of the Home Guard ranking as privates should in future be designated "volunteers." This was a very appropriate decision.

We were now being issued with, to put it in the army fashion, "Titles, Shoulder, Home Guard," and these are the actual flashes which were still being worn on disbandment. There was also issued at the same time the regimental flash which was the letters "DVN" denoting the County of Devon, with the number of the Battalion which in this case was "I."

More equipment was beginning to come through and one of the items issued at this time was first aid dressings.

On May 21st, 1941, Capt. J. Hillyard, Second-in-Command of the Transport Company was congratulated by the G.O.C. Southern Command, for his courage and soldierly conduct at Dunsford, when at great personal risk to himself he attempted to rescue a pilot from a burning enemy plane. These congratulations formed the heading of Battalion Orders for that week.

Capt. C. A. Songhurst, M.M., now took over full direction of the training of Recruits.

Among the enrolments which took place during the week commencing May 21st, 1941, was one which should be specially noted. The Rev. Preb. E. Reid, M.A., of St. Mary Arches, was appointed Honorary Chaplain to the Battalion. If ever a Battalion was lucky in its Padre, this Battalion was, and still is. Nothing was too much for him to do. To say that he was loved by all ranks is not an exaggeration, but expresses the feelings of the members of the Battalion. One was always certain of a full Battalion Parade when the Padre was to conduct the service and preach the Sermon.

Nothing of special interest took place to mark the first anniversary of the Home Guard except the King's message, but there is no doubt that the organisation and efficiency of the Battalion, after one year of service, was something which every member of the Battalion could be proud of. No one in the early days, would, I am sure, have dared to venture a suggestion that the Battalion would have reached the state of efficiency that it had reached, at the end of one year.

On the 25th May, 1941, an Exercise was run by Lt.-Col. M. G. Beck, O.C. Troops, Exeter. Col. Beck directed the Exercise assisted by Major A. W. Valentine, M.B.E. and Major R. A. Smith, all of the Devonshire Regiment. Lt.-Col. F. J. C. Hunter, commanded the 1st Battalion and in the disposition of troops Nos. 1 and 3 Companies were to act as attacking forces on orders issued by Major Valentine, and No. 2 Company were to occupy their own Sector of the Exeter perimeter defence under "Action Stations" conditions. No. 4 Company were in reserve.

The Exercise commenced at 10.00 hours and terminated at approximately 12 noon. The Exercise was most instructive and enjoyable but again was hampered by the fact that no blank ammunition was available. Strong attacks developed which enabled the defended Sector to be completely tested and many good lessons were learnt.

The work of the Officers of the Battalion was still increasing, but, with the support of all the personnel, the work was more of a pleasure than a duty.

Companies were now beginning to run Platoon Exercises of their own and soon found that this was the kind of training that the troops wanted, both from an interesting and efficiency point of view.

This brings us to the end of May, 1941, the first anniversary of the Home Guard and a suitable place to end a chapter.

Great strides had been made during this year and everyone could feel satisfied that they were infinitely more prepared to meet the Hun than at any time previously.

During the winter, No. 2 Company had run a football team and they were very successful in the various competitions in which they took part.

Chapter III

TRAINING BY COMPANIES

JUNE, 1941

The second year of the Home Guard started with spirits high and I am sure that in the hearts of many there were hopes that at some time they would be given the opportunity of having a crack at the old enemy, the Hun.

Recruits were still being trained under Battalion arrangements, but the Companies were now organising their own training. The general scheme was, for each Platoon to parade on one night each week and the complete Company every Sunday, which was still being mostly occupied in trench digging and wiring.

The Battalion had lost quite a number of its members for various reasons, but there were still enrolments which kept the strength of the Battalion, more or less, static.

In Battalion Orders, dated June, 1941 the Commanding Officer congratulated Sergeant R. B. Newman for his prompt and courageous action in the following incident.

On Whit-Monday, June 2nd, Sergeant R. B. Newman of No. 3 Company, was walking along the banks of the Exeter canal near Double Locks, when he heard a shout. He then noticed a small boy in the water. Sergeant Newman and a gunner both plunged in fully dressed, rescued the child and handed him over to his mother, little the worse for his immersion.

The Commanding Officer in Battalion orders dated June 11th, 1941, now laid down that the Commanding Officer's Cup and the "Aggregate Cup," both of which were awarded for miniature range shooting, were to be presented to the Right Worshipful the Mayor of Exeter at the end of the War to be retained in the Guildhall as a memento of this Battalion.

This month saw the first appointment of a Permanent Staff Instructor for the Battalion, and Home Guardsmen C.S.M. Callender, No. 1 Company, relinquished his Home Guard appointment after receiving the new appointment as P.S.I. C.S.M. Callender had done good work for No. 1 Company, and he took up his new appointment with the good wishes of the Battalion.

P. C. Jefferies was immediately promoted to 2nd Class Warrant Officer and appointed C.S.M. No .1 Company and retained that position until disbandment. F. E. Coram was now appointed C.S.M. No. Company.

The Home Guard had now received a new weapon which was called the Northover Projector and which could be used for firing Molotov and A.W. Bombs, both being fire bombs, the latter being self igniting. Later 36 Mills Grenades were fired from this projector.

The appearance of the weapon did not at first give one any great confidence but it was soon found to be simple in operation and accurate. Its main task was to set fire to tanks and if enemy A.F.Vs. had ever landed in this country they would undoubtedly have had a hot reception. The appearance of this new weapon necessitated more courses of instruction for Officers and N.C.O.s; another task cheerfully and willingly carried out by these men who were already overburdened with duties.

2nd Lieut. R. G. Burvill, who, before being commissioned was one of the original instructors, was at this time appointed Battalion P.A.D. Officer.

Another competition which was commenced during July was the Officers' Inter-Company Miniature Range Shooting, the team to consist of four Company Officers, and the Trophy was a silver cup presented by Lt.-Col. F. J. C. Hunter. The winners of the trophy were No. 2 Company.

JULY 9th, 1941

The announcement of the resignation of Mr. H. J. Coverdale was included in Battalion Orders dated July 9th, 1941, his resignation to take effect as from the 7th July. Coverdale had taken over the duties of Adjutant from J. Whiteside in the early days, and during the time that he held that appointment he had made it a full-time job, and the Battalion undoubtedly owe him a debt of gratitude for the tremendous amount of work which he carried out.

The main reason for the change was the War Office decision that each Home Guard Battalion should now have a regular Army Adjutant, and Captain F. H. Daykns was appointed Adjutant and Quartermaster, with effect from July 7th, 1941 .

Dr. J. N. Watson was promoted to Major and appointed Battalion Medical Officer. Dr. Watson was another who remained with the Battalion in his appointment until the disbandment.

More Courses were being held a the War Office School of Instruction at Denbies, Dorking, and the Camouflage School at Farnham, but the old difficulty still existed of Home Guardsmen not being able to get away from their business for a week at a time.

Gas training was now receiving attention as all volunteers had received respirators and the Gas Officer looked forward to a busy time putting all the Volunteers through the Gas Chamber after the necessary instruction had been completed.

W. J. Wright was appointed C.S.M. No. 2 Company.

On the 26th/27th July an Exercise was held in which all the Companies were ordered out on "Action Stations." The Field Companies were to be in defence and an attack was made by No. 4 (Mobile) Company. The attacking force was naturally too small to attack all round the perimeter of Exeter, but the uncertainty of where they were going to attack, this decision being left to the O.C. No. 4 Company, kept the defending companies on the alert. The attack was actually made in more than one area and was very well carried out. There was a frontal attack on No. 2 Company's area but the main attack was across the river for which boats were used and eventually the enemy got into the City and were able to attack Battalion Headquarters. The main defences where they were actually attacked, stood the test satisfactorily and many lessons were learned, particularly in regard to the actual positions of the various defence posts. One big lesson which was brought out but which was not acted upon for a long time afterwards was that the best form of defence under the circumstances was defence in depth and that a thin line once broken could not be restored without adequate reserves.

No. 4 Company had the assistance of S/Sergeant Hickman of the Marines. This was known throughout the Battalion and a good look was kept for this most efficient N.C.O. He was, in fact, finally captured by No. 2 Company and taken to Battalion Headquarters, where, like a good soldier, he refused to talk. This point is mentioned because it gives an opportunity of recording in this book the Battalion's deep appreciation of the great assistance given to No. 4 Company particularly, and the Battalion in general by S/Sergeant Hickman. Hickman was undoubtedly a most efficient N.C.O. and he was eventually commissioned in the Marines and is now a Captain in a responsible post in a Marine training depot. Right up to the end of his time in the Exeter area he continued to assist the Battalion and, when he left on his promotion, he carried with him the good wishes of those who had met him. It can be safely said that all Companies owed much to him.

At the end of the month a further task was given to the Home Guardsmen and that was to watch out carefully for fire among the crops. It was recognised in those days that one of the aims of the enemy would be to set fire to the standing crops in the fields. The Battalion held itself in readiness to turn out, but they were not troubled.

AUGUST, 1941

On the night of August 17th, 1941, No. 2 Company by an arrangement between Major H. J. Wiltsher, the Company Commander, and Col. Greening, 22nd (S.R.) Bn. Commander, attacked Exmouth Junction, which was defended by part of "B" Company, 22nd (S.R.) Bn. Home Guard, commanded by Major Turle, their Company Commander.

The two Company Commanders having arranged the Exercise, transformed themselves into Umpires and a most interesting Exercise took place. In all such exercises it is usual for the dead to remain alive and active and for those alive to claim many casualties with one bullet, but it all served to show the Defending Commander, any weaknesses which may exist in his defended area.

The inquest took place directly after the Exercise, and then tea was supplied by the Southern Railway.

Strange as it may seem the Battalion entered a Relay team in the Open Relay Race at the 1st Eng. Company, Royal Marines, Athletic Sports on Sunday, August 19th, 1941, and won the trophy. I say strange, because it was the general opinion that Home Guardsmen were all old men. This was not so. There were many young and keen members in this Battalion and, I suppose, in all Battalions.

On August 20th, 1941, Capt. C. A. Songhurst, M.M., relinquished his position as Second-in-Command, of H.Q. Company, which post he had held in conjunction with his responsibility for training, and was transferred to Battalion Headquarters as Assistant Adjutant.

Lieut. J. Samuels was appointed Second-in-Command of H.Q. Company and promoted to the rank of Captain.

On the 31st August a Service March Past took place. A detachment of all the services, including the 1st (Loyal City of Exeter) Bn. Devon Home Guard took part in the Parade. The route was, Blackboy Road, Sidwell Street, High Street, Exe Bridge, Haven Road and Haven Banks Fairground.

The Right Worshipful the Mayor of Exeter, accompanied by Brig. Gilmore, D.S.O., M.C., took the Salute at the Guildhall.

SEPTEMBER, 1941

His Majesty the King expressed a wish that Sunday, September 7th, should be observed as a day of National Prayer. A volunteer parade of the Battalion attended the Cathedral Service with the Regular Army.

In Battalion Orders dated September 10th, 1941, the Battalion Commander published a letter from the Zone Commander congratulating the Battalion on its turn out and bearing at the Services March Past, on Sunday, August 31st and it was specifically mentioned that the marching and dressing of the Battalion made a very good impression on the Brigade Commander.

OCTOBER, 1941

Companies were now preparing for the Military Tournament which was to be held at St. James Park on Saturday, October 4th, 1941. The day arrived with good weather and the proceedings were opened by the Battalion marching round the ground past the Grandstand where the Brigade Commander, accompanied by the Battalion Commanding Officer, took the Salute.

Major J. W. Western, O.B.E., T.D. was in command of the Battalion for the march past.

The whole proceedings were a great success. Seven silver cups had been presented to the Commanding Officer by various people, and it will no doubt be interesting to members of the Battalion at that time if the complete report is set out here: —

Route March
      Winners—No. 4 Company.
      2nd—H.Q. Company.
      3rd—H.Q. Company.

Machine Gun Competition
      Winners—No. 2 Company.
      2nd—No. 2 Company.
      3rd—No. 1 Company.

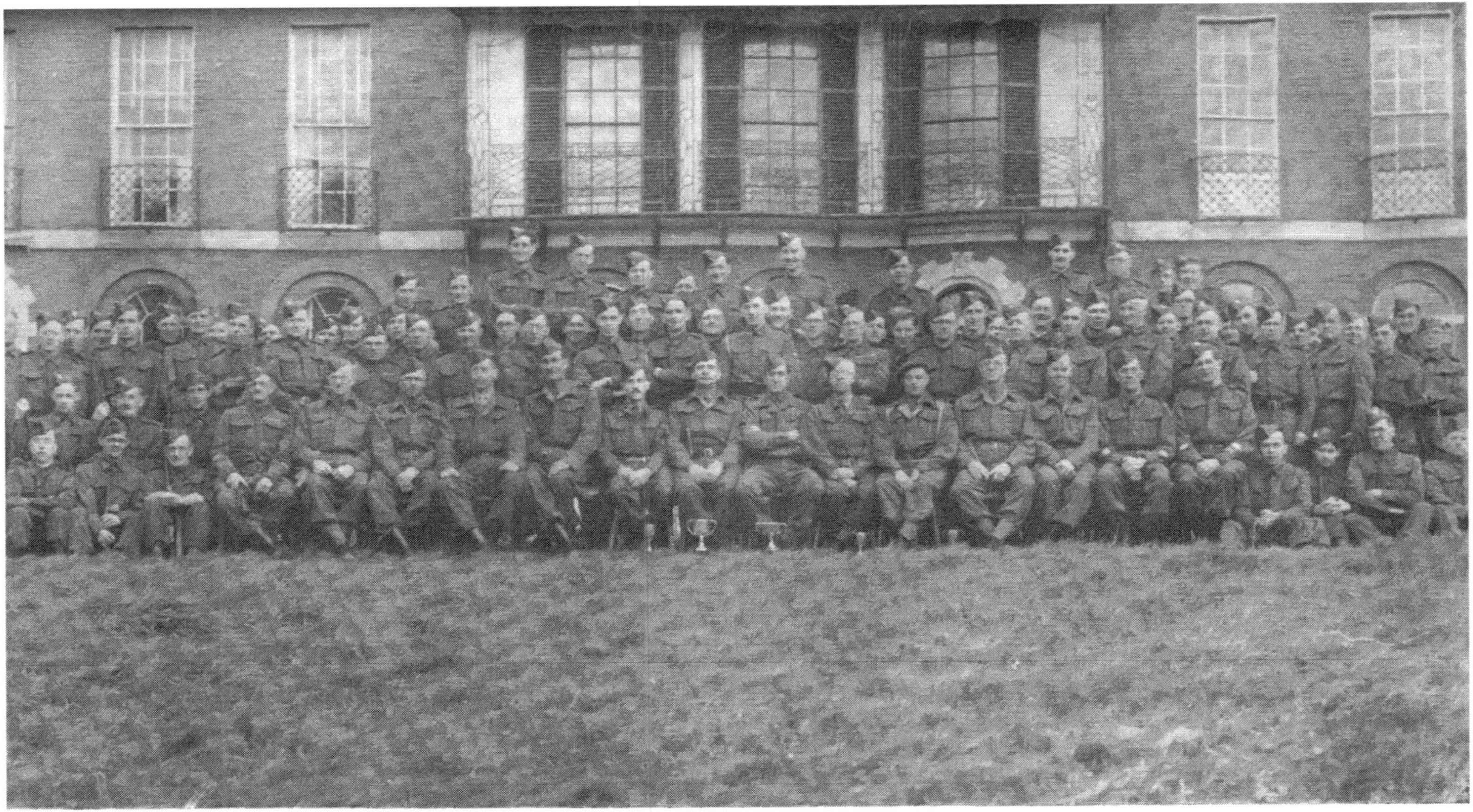

Head Quarters Company

Gas Race
    Winners—No. 1 Company.
Grenade Throwing Competition
    Winners—No. 2 Company.
    2nd—No. 1 Company.
    3rd—H.Q. and No. 4 Company tied.

Relay Race
    Winners—H.Q. Company.

Drill Competition
    Winners—No. 2 Company.
    2nd—No. 1 Company.
    3rd—H.Q. Company.

All companies gave a demonstration display and this was won by No. 4 Company to whom a silver trophy was awarded.

The meeting was enjoyed by the competitors and also a large crowd of spectators who filled the stand and the ground, and it was a great pity that, owing to so much training and duties, which had to be carried out, time could not be spared to repeat this splendid effort.

It was decided at this time that the Machine Gun Section which had been up to that time a Unit in Headquarters Company and who now possessed nine Browning Machine Guns should be formed into a Company. Lieut. F. W. Frost became the new Company Commander with the rank of Captain, this unit was a most keen and efficient one and in spite of the fact that on "Action Station" they would have been split up between the Field Companies their "Esprit de Corps" was always 100 per cent. When Captain Frost left the unit to take up duties as Battalion Machine Gun Staff Officer he was replaced by Lieut. G. T. Richards. It should be recorded that this unit has been most successful in the Miniature Range Competition both when they were attached to H.Q. Company and after they were formed into a Company.

On the night of October 11th/12th an Exercise was arranged in which No. 2 Company, under the command of Major H. J. Wiltsher were to attack Central Station, Exeter, which was to be defended by "B" Company, 22nd (S.R.) Bn. H.G. under the command of Major Trule. This was a most interesting Exercise.

No. 2 Company of the 1st (Exeter) Bn. were assumed to be enemy paratroops who had landed on the outskirts of Exeter and were endeavouring to capture the Central Railway Station in order to dislocate traffic. All ranks entered into this Exercise with complete enthusiasm. The attack was timed to start at 01.00 hours on the morning of October 12th, the defence having got into position during the previous night. "Cease Fire" was at 05.00 hours. The attack took place from three directions and again many lessons were learnt, and any weaknesses in the defensive positions were noted and rectified.

On the conclusion of the Exercise, the troops on both sides were issued with tea very kindly supplied by the Southern Railway.

We were now getting regular allocations for the Bombing and

Northover Ranges, both of which were situated on the top of Haldon. Both the sites were old quarries and many members of the Battalion gave up a lot of their time and carried out a lot of work in building the necessary throwing bays and organising the safety precautions. It can be readily understood how much these facilities were appreciated by the members of the Battalion, because it enabled them to handle the live ammunition without which a man cannot get confidence in the weapons which he may be called upon to use, and furthermore as transport was now available the actual journey out to these places made a change from the monotony of the continued training in Exeter.

During this month of October, the Battalion was issued with another new weapon, called the Blacker Bombard, later to be re-named the Spigot Mortar. The variety of weapons now being issued to the Home Guard was becoming somewhat perplexing and it became necessary to not only run further courses of instruction but also to make certain Officers and N.C.O.s in the Companies, responsible for the individual weapons.

There is no doubt that this Blacker Bombard (Spigot Mortar), was very effective, simple and accurate, but the unfortunate part was that, although they were dummy bombs which could be used for practice it was to be quite a long time before live ammunition was issued, and then there was the difficulty of finding a suitable site for firing.

C. B. Dare was appointed C.S.M. No. 4 Company.

On the night of the 25th October a very ambitious Exercise was arranged by the Battalion Commander, Lieut-Col. F. J. C. Hunter. He had decided he would test as much of the defences of Exeter as he was able with the troops available. He therefore ordered the whole Battalion with the exception of No. 2 Company to take up their positions on their defence line, with No. 4 Company acting as Mobile Reserves. Lieut-Col. F. J. C. Hunter not only directed the Exercise but also commanded the defence, which was to be called the Blue force. No. 2 Company with the assistance of "B" Company 22nd (S.R.) Bn. Home Guard, were to act as the enemy and were to be known as the Red Force, under the command of Major H. J. Wiltsher.

The defence was approximately 1,500 strong and the attacking force approximately 250 strong.

In the defence, No. 1 Company was under the command of Major L. G. Coles, No. 3 Company under the command of Major T. Greenslade, D.C.M., No. 6 (G.W.R.) Company under the command of Major C. R. Panes, No. 4 (Mobile) Company under the command of Major P. A. B. Cherry and H.G. Company under the command of Major E. N. Clulee.

Attached to the defence was also the Post Office Company, commanded by Major Williams, and the University College of the South West Home Guard commanded by Capt. Lloyd, both of these latter units being held in reserve.

Major Wiltsher split up his Red Force into three companies, A, B and C. In the centre sector, Major Turle of the 22nd (S.R.) Batta-

D. Cookhouse on
Exercise

D. MOBILE
COMPANY

Company
Commander
Major A. G. Fry

D. Company
Officers

D. Mobile in Action

lion commanded "A" Company, on the right flank Captain W. H. Hoyt, Second-in-Command of No. 2 Company, commanded "B" Company, on the left flank Lieut. A. P. Young commanded "C" Company.

The attacking Red Force represented Germans who were assumed to have landed at Dawlish Warren and had made their way towards Exeter with the intention of capturing the City. The locality of the attack was confined to a line drawn through the Exeter Golf Course, through Lower Weir, across the Rive Exe, St. David's Station, New North Road to St. Germans Road, All troops were in position at 21.30 hours on the night of the 25th October, 1941, zero hour was at 23.00 hours and the Exercise terminated at 03.00 hours on the morning of the 26th October, 1941.

The attacking force was given certain objectives in the City. Many fifth columnist tricks were practised by the attacking force, this being a very important form of training for the Battalion at that time as it was always expected that such methods would be used if the Germans ever made an attack on the City.

The result of the Exercise does not matter. The attackers certainly got into the City and in some cases claimed their objectives but there were counter claims from the defence that the attackers had been wiped out before they reached the defended area and had refused to die. Exercises depend to a great extent on umpiring and on this occasion the umpiring was undoubtedly good, but at night time it is very difficult to be able to see everyone and it is always impossible to be in two places at once.

Again certain weaknesses in the defence were brought to light, and the Battalion Commander expressed himself as being very satisfied with the results attained.

The weather was fortunately good and tremendous enthusiasm was shown by all ranks.

There were quite a number of particularly amusing incidents. In one case two of the attackers dressed themselves up as special constables, walked through the defence line and commiserated with the defenders on the fact that they, the defenders, were out until 03.00 hours, whereas they, the special constables, were coming off duty at 02.00 hours. The information which they gained through their tour of fictitious duty was passed on to the attackers.

One particular incident deserves mention as it proves the keenness of all concerned. Lieut. Rainbird, No. 2 Company, under the command of Captain Hoyt, was given orders to attack from Countess Weir and he was faced with the alternative of either crossing one or three waterways. These waterways were the River Exe, Exeter Canal and a leat joining the two. Believing that the hardest, the crossing of the three waterways would be the one from which the defence would least likely expect an attack, he decided to adopt that method. His men gallantly carried water craft across fields after dark and from one waterway to another and they got through the defences, not, however, without certain claims from the defences that they had been wiped out. They did not negotiate these obstacles without incidents and more than one man finished up with a wet shirt.

It goes to prove, however, the keenness of the Home Guardsmen in making themselves efficient in their job and learning as much as possible.

As is always the case in Exercises such as this the attackers have the much more interesting job, mainly because of their mobility. The defenders have the unenviable task of remaining in the one spot throughout the whole Exercise, not knowing what is going on.

There were many other incidents as must be expected, where one side claims total annihilation of the other side, but, where real bullets are not used, this is sure to happen. These incidents, however, did not detract from the actual lessons learned.

Fifth columnist activities have already been mentioned but there are others which are worthy of record and of interest to the members of the Battalion. One officer entered the City with three other members of the attacking force, all in civilian clothes and carrying billiard cue cases. They got through the outer defences but all of them, except one, were very cleverly intercepted and detained by members of "A" Company. One got through to the vicinity of Battalion Headquarters where he was arrested. He was taken into the defence Headquarters for interrogation by the Officer Commanding the defence, and whilst waiting in the guard room he threw the billiard cue case on the ground, claiming that it was full of explosive and that he had blown up the whole of the Headquarters. The Umpire's decision was that the particular guard room had been demolished and that the fifth columnist had killed himself.

The ultimate result of this Exercise was that the Company and Platoon Commanders found more work to do in strengthening the weak spots in their line.

The Inquest on the Exercise was held about a week later and was attended by all the Battalion Officers.

More courses were now being held in the new Sub-Artillery weapons at Higher Barracks but the main difficulty was that instructors had to be trained for all Companies before the information could be passed down to the Volunteers.

NOVEMBER, 1941

On the 23rd November, 1941, the Group Commander, Brig. W. H. Brooke, directed an Exercise in which No. 4 Company of the 1st (Exeter) Bn., under the command of Major P. A. B. Cherry, was detailed to attack the defences of Bampton, part of the 20th Bn. area of responsibility. This exercise was most interesting because the whole of the Civil Defence, Police, and the local inhabitants of that town played with the defending Home Guard and many useful and interesting lessons were learnt.

The 1st Battalion supplied, in addition to the attacking force, Officers who acted as Umpires. No. 4 Company were able to practise their role of mobility and their advance to the defences was carried

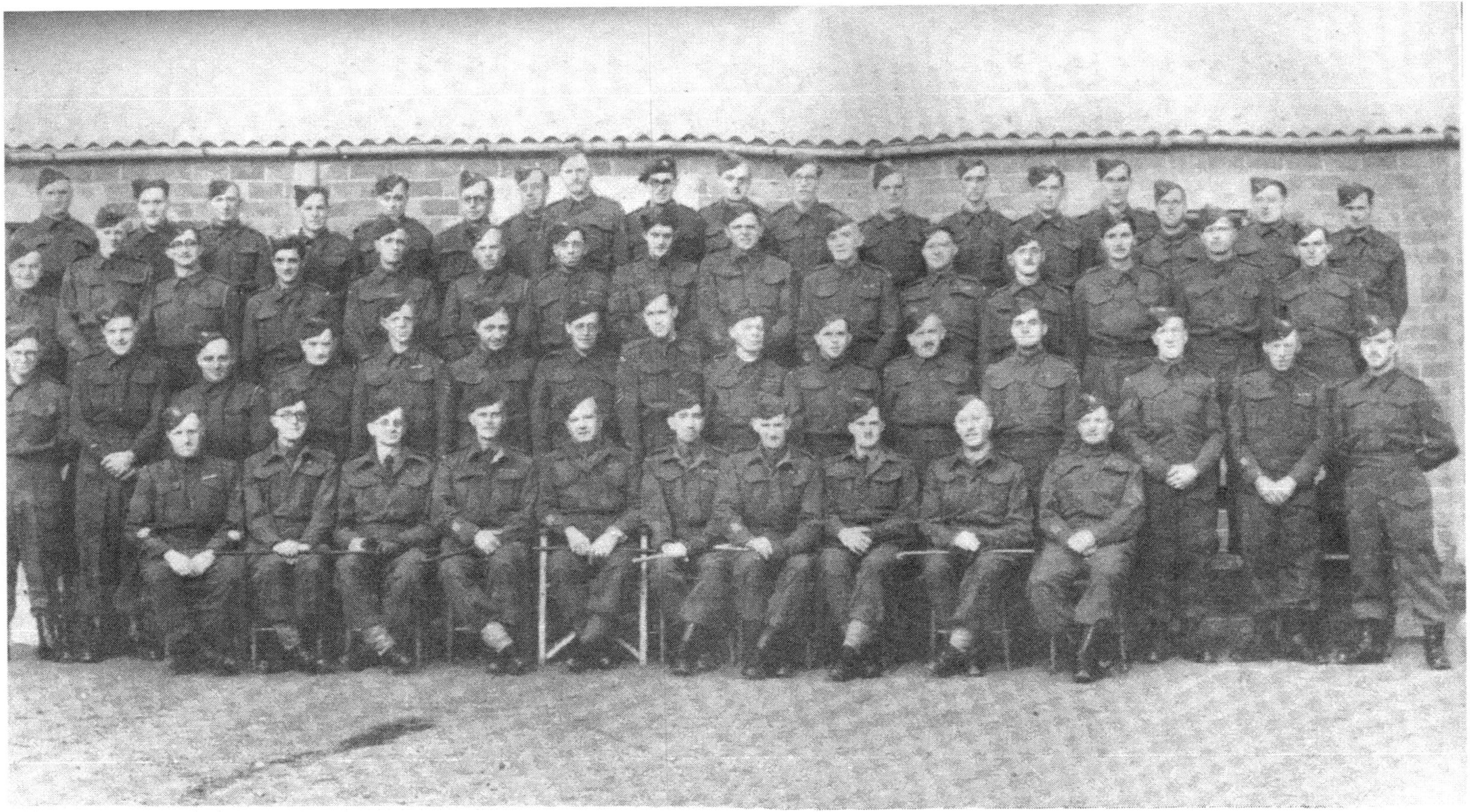

"D" Company

out in lorries. They then debussed and completed the assault on foot.

A Golf Match between the Battalion and the Royal Army Pay Corps was played on November 2nd, 1941, resulting in a win for the 1st Battalion by three matches to two.

During November, Major General Lord Bridgeman, Director-General of the Home Guard, visited Exeter and lectured to the senior Officers of the Devon Home Guard. This lecture was most interesting and instructive. During the lecture he gave certain information about many things which we were waiting to hear about. Perhaps the most interesting part, was the fact that he announced that Tommy Guns were expected to be issued to the Home Guard in the very near future. We did eventually receive some of these Tommy Guns, but soon afterwards they were withdrawn and Sten Guns were issued in their place.

Lord Bridgeman made a statement to the effect that the only reason the Government were able to release so many troops to be sent abroad was because of the existence of the Home Guard, and that the position in Libya at that time would not have been so satisfactory had it not been for the Home Guard.

DECEMBER, 1941

The Battalion were again given leave from all training from the 20th December, 1941 until the 4th January, 1942.

At the end of the year the Home Guard received a reminder that they were members of the Armed Forces of the Crown, whether in uniform or not and that all registration cards were to be properly embossed, signifying that the owners belonged to the Home Guard and that such registration cards were to be carried at all times.

Lieut. F. W. Frost was promoted to Captain at this time.

The year 1941 finished more quietly than had been anticipated at the beginning. Nothing of any outstanding nature had taken place. There had been plenty of hard work and hard training and there is no doubt that the Battalion had benefited considerably and was very much more efficient than at the beginning of the year. This was not only due to organising by the Senior Officers and the enthusiasm of the Instructors, but also to the keenness of the members of the Battalion and their loyalty.

Battalion Orders dated 31st December, 1941, carried a special Order of the Day, by Gen. Sir Alan F. Brooke, K.C.B., D.S.O., Commander-in-Chief Home Forces and Home Guard: —

"On relinquishing command of the Home Forces and of the Home Guard I wish to thank all ranks for their loyal support, and for their spirit of whole-hearted co-operation. The grave threat to which this country was exposed during the period of my command, necessitated my making the heaviest calls on all individuals, units and formations. This has resulted in long hours, tedious parades of night work and protracted exercises in inclement and wintry conditions. In every case you have met such calls with a cheerfulness which proved your determination to become worthy of the task entrusted to you. I leave my present command with heartfelt gratitude for all your help, with feelings of great honour of sharing with you, the sacred task of defending this Country against the threat of invasion. I am confident that my successor will receive the same loyal support that you accorded to me." 25th December, 1941.

The strength of the Battalion at the end of the year was 1,740.

CHAPTER IV.

THEN CAME CONSCRIPTION AND THE BLITZ

JANUARY, 1942

January, 1942, and training was now to become more of an advanced nature, embracing more field work. It had been arranged that on January 18th, 1942, Number 2 and 4 Companies of the 1st (Exeter) Bn. should attack the defences of Tiverton, which was the Headquarters of the 20th Battalion. Brig. W. H. Brooke, the Group Commander, was to direct the Exercise, No. 2 Company, under the command of Major H. J. Wiltsher, was to attack from the south-west of the river, and No. 4 Company, under the command of Major P. A. B. Cherry, were to attack from the east of the river.

Full reconnaissances had been carried out by the attacking forces. Orders were issued, and everyone was looking forward to a further interesting exercise, particularly as it was to be carried out during the daytime.

On Friday, 16th January, 1942, the Exercise was cancelled. After all the hard work which had been carried out, particularly by the attacking forces, it can be clearly understood that there was much disappointment.

The strength of the Battalion now began to decrease. This was partly due to the fact that a number of volunteers had to be released because of their civil work, others were discharged for personal reasons, and there was still the usual drain of fellows leaving the Battalion to join the Forces.

The end of January brought about a very big change in the conditions of service in the Home Guard. The Government now decided to bring in conscription. A certain time limit was given to all serving members of the Home Guard to leave if they so desired, but, by and large, only a very small percentage took advantage of this offer.

The first announcement of conscription was broadcast on the 19th January, 1942. After that it was published in the Daily Press and came out in Southern Command Orders on the 11th March, 1942.

The method was for the Labour Exchange to direct suitable men into the Home Guard but before they could move the ceiling strengths of each Battalion had to be settled by Higher Command. It was then found which Battalions required conscripts and those which did not.

Many Battalions were, in fact, over the ceiling strength set down by Higher Command, but this Battalion's strength was at that time 1,740 and the ceiling strength was laid down at 2,200.

When all this was settled the Labour Exchange commenced directing men into the Battalion but it was until June that the effect of conscription began to show itself in the strength of the Battalion.

FEBRUARY, 1942

In February, Capt. M. Thacker, M.C., who was originally a Sergeant in No. 2 Company, and was transferred to No. 1 Company as a Platoon Commander and then promoted to Second-in-Command in that company, removed to London and was transferred to 'F' Zone, London Home Guard. Captain Thacker's loss was felt not only by the Company but by the Battalion, he having been one of its most enthusiastic and efficient members. This left a vacancy for Second-in-Command of No. 1 Company which was filled by Lieut. R. W. Bell, who was promoted to Captain.

It is worthy of note that during this month Regimental Sergeant Major F. Howe was awarded a certificate of merit. This was the first certificate received by the Battalion and there is no doubt that Howe was not only one of the most popular but one of the most worthy members of the Battalion to receive it.

MARCH, 1942

In early March the subsistence allowance was altered so that in future there was to be no payment for less than 5 hours continued duty, 1/6 for over 5 and under 8 hours, 3/- for over 8 and under 15 hours, and 4/6 for over 15 and under 24 hours.

Up to this time the University College of the South West, O.T.C. Home Guard were members of the Exeter 1st Battalion, but in Battalion Orders dated 31st March, 1942, they were all transferred to the S.T.C. Home Guard, University College. This meant a drop of 124 in the strength of the Battalion. University College Home Guard, although formed into a unit of their own, still came into the defence scheme for Exeter.

APRIL, 1942

Operation Orders No. 4 were now issued. The role of the Battalion at that time was to defend the city against: —
  a. Paratroops.
  b. Airborne landings of troops.
  c. Seaborne invasion.
but the defended perimeter was the same except for a few minor details, and was still known as the Blue Line to which I have already referred.

In the defended area the Battalion was responsible for the manning of nineteen road Blocks and the immobilisation of 138 petrol pump stations.

Lieut. Hichisson, Battalion Intelligence Officer, was kept very busy sometimes unnecessarily, because of the many alterations, some of them unimportant, in the defence line, due to the fact that there were so many changes in the local Army Commander and that each new Commander had different ideas to the previous Commander.

"B" COMPANY

The Company passing the Saluting Base after Church Parade at the Odeon

Major A. P. Young, M.C. the Company Commander

Company Officers

Company Sergeants

"B" Company passing Saluting Base after Cathedral Service

Except for finishing off certain defence works it can be considered that by this month the bulk of the trenching and wiring was completed. The lay-out was as follows.

No. 1 Company held a line from Countess Weir Roundabout, inclusive to the Swing Bridge along the Canal to Double Locks, then right following Clapperbrook to Alphington Bridge. Thence the line of the Alphinton Brook as far as Balls Farms and on to the Quarry on the crest of Dunsford Hill, including Pocombe Bridge Road Blocks. This was No. 1 Company's right flank.

No. 3 Company then took over from the right of Pocombe Bridge following a line of Barley Lane as far as the Reservoir, then across Old Okehampton Road, Exwick Road, then past Cleve House, finally moving North-East to Exwick Mills.

No. 6 (G.W.R.) Company held a line beginning from just north of St. David's Station covering a line from the South Devon Railway Bridge to the south of St. David's Station, northwards to Cowley Bridge exclusive.

No. 2 Company took over at Cowley Bridge and followed a line roughly parallel with Wreford Lane, crossing Stoke Woods Road and from thence following a line S.E.E. across Stoke Hill at Mincing Lake Bridge on to Mile Lane, Barton Lane, with the right flank on the north side of Pinhoe Road.

The sector between Pinhoe Road exclusive and Countess Weir Roundabout exclusive was to be held by the Royal Marines on 'Action Stations.'

Battle Headquarters were fixed for all Companies and Platoons with first aid positions either in the same Headquarters or in close proximity. The Battalion arranged a shuttle pigeon service with outlying areas.

The Battalion Transport Company had now been detached from the Battalion and had been formed into a Motor Transport Company coming directly under the command of the Royal Army Service Corps. All the men belonging to the Transport Company and others suitable for transport work were transferred out of the Battalion and the Battalion now had the further task of organising a Transport Platoon in H.Q. Company.

On the 25th/26th April, 1942 the City was visited in some strength by the Luftwaffe and considerable damage was done, mainly by fire. There were some casualties amongst the civilian population but the Battalion generally suffered lightly. Many members of the Battalion voluntarily turned out to do work in the City and on the Sunday following the 26th April, there were organised parties of Home Guardsmen working in various parts of the City, excavating amongst the damage, in most cases looking for people who were thought to be missing.

The Battalion Headquarters in the Drill Hall, Bedford Circus, were damaged but fortunately, the damage was of such a nature that it could be repaired, and these repairs were actually commenced the following week.

As a temporary Headquarters the Battalion Commander took over No. 2 Bedford Circus. All records were saved.

During this month P. Westlake was appointed Second Class Warrant Officer on his appointment as Company Sergeant Major, No. 3 Company, vice C.S.M. Coram who resigned.

W. L. Lovell was appointed C.S.M. H.Q. Company.

MAY, 1942

The old City had already suffered in three serious raids towards the end of April and it was naturally the hope of the citizens that Hitler had done his worst but, unfortunately, for Exeter this did not prove to be correct. On the night of May 4th/5th, 1942, Hitler decided to blitz the City and as this was during the time he was concentrating on Cathedral Cities it would appear that the Cathedral was the attraction. The City was dive-bombed as far as dive bombing is possible with bombing planes and many high explosives, together with thousands of incendiaries, were showered down. Much damage was done, but it is not the purpose of this book to record those details but to confine itself to the Battalion.

Before the 'All Clear' had sounded many Home Guardsmen were already out and about, helping wherever possible, and if only it were possible to get these men to talk, many incidents could be related of the help which was given by the members of the Battalion to those people who had suffered and were suffering. One of the serious incidents from the Battalion point of view was the fatal injury sustained by the Commanding Officer, Lt.-Col. F. J. C. Hunter. He had been fire-watching at his home in West Avenue and was outside his shelter when he was very seriously wounded by a high explosive bomb which almost completely demolished his home. Mrs. Hunter, who was in the shelter and uninjured, immediately ran for help and contacted Lieut. Rainbird, a Platoon Commander in No. 2 Company. Seeing the serious nature of the injuries Mr. Rainbird endeavoured to get hold of an ambulance or stretcher but without success, and finally decided, with the help of another soldier, to carry the Colonel to the Wrentham Hall First Aid Section on the only thing available, a door which had been blown down. Worthy of record here are the words given, without solicitation to the writer, by a person who was actually in Wrentham Hall when Col. Hunter was brought in: "Col. Hunter," his tribute runs, "was, in spite of his injuries and the pain he was suffering, the bravest man that I have met and was most cheerful throughout the short time that he was in the first aid station before being taken to hospital. Lieut. Rainbird, too, was amazed at the cheerfulness shown by Col. Hunter. This should be a fitting record of the general spirit of the members of the Battalion. Unfortunately, Col. Hunter's injuries proved fatal within two days. He was buried at Exmouth on May 8th and his funeral was attended by the Divisional Commander, Group Commanders of South and East Devon Groups and many Officers and other ranks of the Battalion. The Senior Officers of the Battalion acted as bearers. His loss was

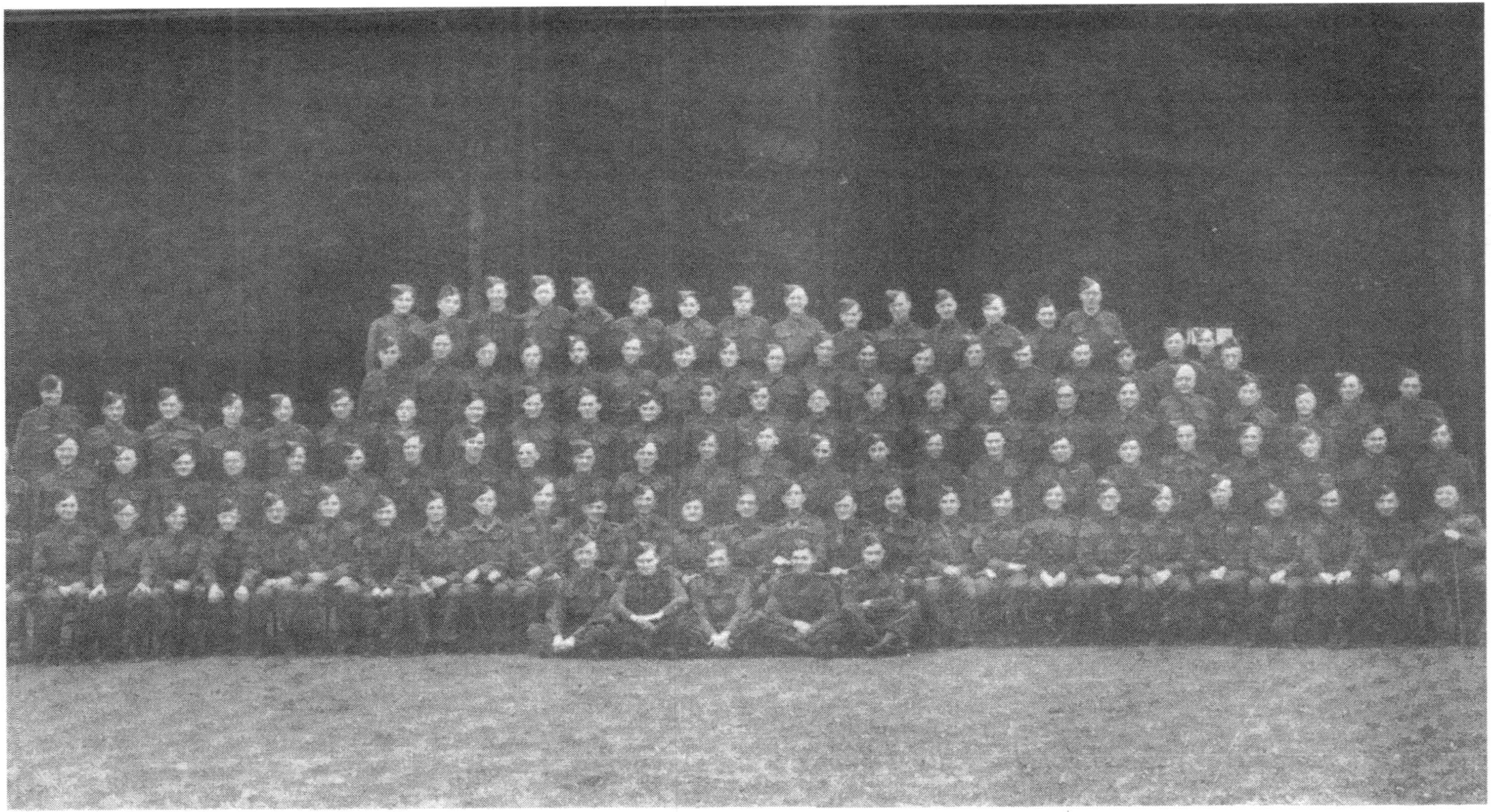

"B" Company

greatly felt throughout the Battalion; he was an original member, having first held the appointment of Transport Officer.

The Battalion Headquarters, Drill Hall, Bedford Circus, received a direct hit as a result of which three of the Guard were killed and one seriously injured. These men died as much on duty for their country as a soldier who is killed on the battle field and their deaths are honoured in the Battalion. The Battalion also suffered casualties of some of the members who were not actually on duty and their loss is also grieved. The names of all the casualties suffered by the Battalion through enemy action are recorded in the back of this book.

Battalion Headquarters was completely destroyed both by H.E.'s and fire and all records, Battalion Stores and Battalion Equipment were lost. This was a terrific blow, but as can be seen by the ensuing record, even this was not sufficient to damp the spirits of the members of the Battalion. Many days were spent by volunteers in digging out the bodies of the H.Q. Guard who had been killed and during that process much equipment was recovered but none of it was of further use. The help given by members of the Battalion to the Old City was amazing. Traffic control duties were undertaken, fire fighting, furniture removing, clearing debris from the streets, and in this connection an important job was done in clearing Castle Street to enable new batteries to be taken to the telephone exchange in order to get the telephone service in working order. Transporting homeless pople to rest centres — salvaging safes from bank vaults, rescuing trapped people, salvaging furniture. Many deeds of heroism were carried out during the blitz and have never been recorded or recognised but the men themselves have a great satisfaction in knowing that they carried out a worth while job.

Lieut. H. J. Ferguson was Orderly Officer on this tragic night, and it is recorded that, throughout the whole of the blitz, he remained at his post and was one of the first to come out to help where help could be given. Cpl. A. H. Hopkins was the Orderly Corporal and both this Officer and N.C.O. were eventually honoured by His Majesty the King for devotion to Duty.

No. 4 Company Headquarters, whilst not receiving a direct hit, were so seriously damaged that they could not be used again. More important still, was the amount of kit and equipment which was lost. This Company had, through their own efforts, contributed to a Company Fund sufficient money to purchase motor cycles and vehicles to make them more mobile than was possible with the equipment issued. This has already been recorded but through the blitz most of this self-obtained equipment and rolling stock was lost. Although all efforts were made no compensation could be obtained. One would expect this to be a heart-breaking blow. Whilst it was a serious handicap it was not long before the Company was again reorganised, under the new Company Commander, Capt. Fayermen, and later Major A. G. Fry — Major P. A. B. Cherry having transferred to another Battalion — and the Company very soon became as efficient as ever it was before the Blitz.

Both No. 1 and H.Q. Companies had their headquarters with the Battalion at the Drill Hall, Bedford Circus, and here again, all company records and equipment were lost.

No. 2 Company Headquarters in Old St. James School behind St. James Church were lucky. The church hard by was completely burnt out. One place where it joined the Company Headquarters also caught fire, but a party of volunteer members of the Company, by forming a chain of buckets and getting on to the roof of the building, were able to prevent the fire from spreading to the Headquarters. Although this operation was started at approximately 4 a.m. it was not until after 7 a.m. that all danger of the fire spreading to the Company Headquarters was removed. There was one amusing incident during the fire fighting which can be recorded. A call was made for tea and Quartermaster Sergeant W. F. H. Payne, who was in the Headquarters, announced that whilst he had tea, sugar and milk, there was no gas with which he could boil the water. One volunteer with bright ideas promptly took up the kettle on the end of a long iron pole and put it through the door of the church right into the fire — this kettle boiled quicker than any kettle has ever boiled before and the workers duly received their drinks.

Nos. 3 and 6 Companies were fortunate in having suffered no damage.

There now commenced a most difficult and worrying time. All Battalion and three Company records had gone but members of the Battalion enthusiastically and conscientiously came forward and gave all the help they could. As a result of this, together with the great help given to the Battalion by members of the Devon Territorial Association, it was not many months before complete Battalion records were again in being. The recovery was a magnificent one. If anything, the experiences of the blitz were beneficial because, instead of going back, the Battalion went forward to become more effiicient than ever.

The last Battalion Orders before the Blitz were issued on the 2nd April, 1942 and, owing to the Blitz, no further orders were issued until the 20th May, 1942, and these were issued by Major J. W. Western, O.B.E., T.D., acting Officer Commanding.

A tribute to Lt.-Col. F. J. C. Hunter was published in these orders and it is worthy of repetition as it voiced the opinion of every member of the Battalion: —

"All ranks of this Battalion are aware of the grievous loss it has sustained as a result of enemy action on the 5th May, by the death of Lt.-Col. F. J. C. Hunter. He was appointed to the command on the 25th August, 1940, and has worked hard and with great enthusiasm to bring the Battalion up to its present state of efficiency. He will long be remembered by all who served with him. His funeral took place at Exmouth on the 8th May and was attended by the Divisional Commander, and Group Commanders of the East Devon and South Devon Groups, as well as by many Officers, Warrant Officers, N.C.O.s and O.R.s of this Battalion.

"His service to the Battalion, given so ungrudgingly and with such cheerfulness, should be an inspiration to us to give of our best in the days to come.

"We also deeply deplore the loss of other valuable lives which can ill be spared and the sympathy of all ranks goes out to those who have suffered bereavement. Many members of the Battalion have had to bear distress and inconvenience owing to the destruction of their homes, etc., and I, as Acting Commanding Officer, offer my sincere sympathy to them, hoping that ere long many of their difficulties will be satisfactorily solved.

"With regard to the future, I am relying on the support of all ranks to carry on to pull together once again. Our role is to meet the invader and annihilate him, and we must, therefore, be prepared."

CHAPTER V.

FIRE WATCHING—"VOLUNTARY"

MAY, 1942

In the changes of command made necessary by the death of Lt.-Col. F. J. C. Hunter, Major J. W. Western, O.B.E., T.D., carried on as acting Battalion Commander, pending the appointment of a new Commanding Officer.

Major H. J. Wiltsher, commanding No. 2 Company, was acting Second-in-Command of the Battalion. Capt. W. H. Hoyt, Second-in-Command of No. 2 Company assumed acting command of the company in the absence of the Company Commander.

For the first few days after the blitz Battalion Headquarters were located as a temporary measure in an office in the D.T.A. Building, but on May 20th, 1942, the Battalion took over the Drill Hall, Normandy Road. This was, however, very inadequate, and it meant working under extreme difficulties. Not only was there insufficient offices but the Drill Hall was generally at least half full with stores.

Major A. P. Manson, the Secretary of the D.T.A. Association did everything was possible to help us and soon obtained a house called Fonthill at Matford Lane into which were put H.Q. Company, No. 1 Company, Machine Gun Company and the Motor Transport Company. Serious congestion naturally occurred in this place and it was quite obvious to everyone that some drastic action would have to be taken.

No. 4 Company, who had also lost their Headquarters, took over some rooms in a house named Shenley in Barnfield Road.

Capt. R. Bullard who had been Second-in-Command of No. 3 Company relinquished his appointment, with effect from 5th July, 1942, and Capt. J. Samuels was appointed Second-in-Command of this Company in his place.

JUNE, 1942

In Battalion Orders, dated 17th June, 1942, Capt. G. H. Vooght, Establishment and Catering Officer, and Lieut. F. Johns, Battalion Accountant, resigned their commissions, having reached the age limit for the Home Guard. Vooght, who had served the Battalion as Establishment Officer since its early days, decided also to resign from the Home Guard altogether and it was with regret that the Battalion heard that he was leaving. Lieut. Johns, with great generosity agreed to continue his service in the Home Guard as Battalion Accountant with rank of S./Sgt., and he carried on until the disbandment of the Home Guard. The writer would record at this stage his great appreciation of the support given to him by S./Sgt. Johns.

At this time it was arranged that, as from the publication of these orders, the Machine Gun Company should cease to be known as such and would be designated No. 5 Company.

Capt. C. A. Songhurst, M.M., now relinquished his appointment as Assistant Adjutant and was appointed Battalion Weapon Training Officer.

The early days after the Blitz were most difficult but somehow or other the Battalion and Companies managed to collect their personnel together, reorganise their records and make the first step towards regaining pre-blitz efficiency, in spite of the great inconveniences existing.

On the 11th June, 1942, the first man was directed into this Battalion by the Ministry of Labour under the compulsory enrolment order and from now onwards the strength of the Battalion was to increase quite substantially.

On June 18th, the Battalion Headquarters moved from Normandy Road to a suite of rooms at Higher Barracks. Although the accommodation was still inadequate there was one benefit and that was that we were allowed to use the Parade Ground for training and, having regard to the fact that so many recruits were to be enrolled, this certainly helped the Weapon Training Officer in his organisation and work.

At the end of June the strength of the Battalion was 1,540 but by the end of July it had increased to 1,870, and even this was not the eventual peak strength.

Owing to the blitz a considerable amount of extra work was thrown on the Adjutant's shoulders and although nobody could have been more willing or more efficient there is a limit to what one man can do, obviously with all the records to be re-constructed and the training for the Battalion reorganized something had to be done to relieve him of some of the detail work, it was therefore decided that an Assistant Adjutant should be appointed, the choice fell on S./Sgt. D. A. Thorne, Intelligence Sergt. for No. 2 Coy., and a better choice could not have been made. Thorne was immediately promoted 2nd Lt. and at once took over his new duties. This officer carried out his many duties in a most efficient manner and those of the Battalion who came in contact with him will remember him for his courteous manner, and his attention to detail.

JULY, 1942

On July 20th Battalion Headquarters took over the Priory Drill Hall, Colleton Crescent, as their Headquarters. This was a big step forward. The Battalion now had all the necessary facilities to enable it to carry out its functions of training and operations.

H.Q. Company and No. 5 Company were allocated rooms in the same building. No. 4 Company moved into Fonthill, Matford Lane.

On July 10th, Capt. Bawden was attached to the Battalion as Quartermaster. This enabled Capt. F. H. Dakyns to concentrate on his job as Adjutant.

Round about this time there was a strong move to make Home

Guardsmen carry out fire watching. This suggestion was very unfavourably received, it being quite rightly felt that members of the Home Guard had already done their share of hard work in preparing defences, they had trained hard to make themselves efficient and they had done their duties such as patrols, guards and picquets at their own Headquarters.

There was no one who had done as much as the Home Guardsmen.

This Battalion was always ready to help in every way when there was something to be done and no one to do it but they resented the suggestion that they alone, of all the voluntary services, should be picked out for more compulsory duties.

Brig. Gilmore, the local Military Commander, called a meeting of the Home Guard Officers at the Guildhall and he certainly heard some very strong views on the matter. As a result of this meeting the Brigadier decided that the question of compulsion should be cancelled and the Battalion was then asked whether they would be prepared to do some voluntary fire watching. After further meetings with the Invasion Committee it was eventually agreed that the Battalion should fire watch the Royal Devon and Exeter Hospital on condition that the other voluntary services would fire watch the City Hospital. The Battalion kept its promise by supplying 15 men per night at the Hospital for a year and there were many expressions of gratitude for the efficient and confident manner in which the service was carried out.

The higher authorities, after a year, cancelled the fire watching at the hospital by the Battalion because they fully appreciated that this work was being done in addition to all the other work and duties which the members of the Battalion were carrying out.

In July it was decided to form a Pioneer Platoon to be attached to the H.Q. Coy. Lieut. A. Beech was the first Officer to command this new unit, but soon after its formation he moved out of the City, and the command was take over by Lieut. W. E. H. R. Howell, previously with No. 2 Coy., who remained with the unit, to do very good work, until disbandment. Never a job of work of any description, but found this Platoon cheerful, willing and capable.

In Battalion Orders dated 22nd July, 1942, Major J. W. Western, O.B.E., T.D., was appointed to command the Battalion with the rank of Lt.-Col. The appointment of Major H. J. Wiltsher as Second-in-Command of the Battalion was confirmed, as was also the following changes brought about by the change in the command of the Battalion: —

Capt. W. H. Hoyt, to command No. 2 Company *vice* Major H. J. Wiltsher; Lieut. A. P. Young, M.C., Second-in-Command of No. 2 Company, *vice* Captain W. H. Hoyt. Another change also took place at this time. It was in the command of No. 4 Company. Capt. H. G. Fayerman, T.D., who had taken over the Company from Major P. A. B. Cherry, died suddenly and Lieut. A. G. Fry was appointed acting Company Commander. Lieut. E. Curtis was appointed acting Second-in-Command.

AUGUST, 1942

Early in August a suggestion was made by Major-Gen. Michelmore at a conference with Home Guard that a Home Guard Royal Engineers Section should be formed in Devon, the personnel to be taken from the skilled engineers in the areas.

Capt. C. R. M. Frost, the original No. 3 Company Commander, re-entered the Home Guard and was entrusted with the organisation of a Sapper Platoon, which was to be part of the 1st Battalion. The approved strength to be three Officers and 60 O.R.s Capt C. R. M. Frost was attached to 203 Brigade Staff as Liaison Officer, Lieut. W. S. Hodges was appointed to command the Platoon with 2nd Lieut. R. Johnson as Second-in-Command.

Intensive weapon training was carried out by the members of this Platoon under the instruction of the Battalion Training Staff and after passing out they carried on with their Technical Training, in the process of which they received valuable help from Major Griffin and his Officers of the 101st Field Company Monmouthshire R.E.s

Eventually the Platoon strength was increased to 150 men and five Officers and during their career they gained considerable experience in all types of engineering work and demolition, including bridge building in conjunction with U.S. Army Engineers who were stationed in this part of the country at the time. The erecting of The Bailey Bridge was one of their outstanding accomplishments and their record in the erection of this type of bridge compared very favourably with the regulars.

This was the only Sapper Coy. (R.E. Unit) in the Home Guard and every man in the Company was proud of that fact.

On the 27th August, 1942, Capt. W. H. Hoyt was promoted to Major, Lieut. A. P. Young, M.C. and Lieut A. G. Fry to Captain.

During August, 1942, the Sector Commander decided that a Sector Signals unit should be formed and he gave the task to Lt. J. Forsyth who was immediately appointed O.C. Sector Signals. Forsyth having formed the Battalion Signals Platoon had the necessary qualification and in his own energetic way he soon had a live unit under his control and in full training. As their operational roll would have been in Honiton with the Sector Commander they naturally spent some of their training time in that town. Lt. W. V. Bristow took over command of the Battalion Signals Platoon.

At the end of August the strength of the Battalion was 2,120 which shows the increase due to compulsory service.

SEPTEMBER, 1942

On Sunday, September 13th, 1942, a Battalion Exercise was an enemy force of approximately 300 men had landed in this country and were believed to be preparing for a swift attack on Exeter. The bounderies were Double Locks to Exwick Mills inclusive, and zero hour was 10.30. 'Cease Fire' was at 16.00 hours.

There was to be a truce between 13.00 and 14.00 hours during which time neither side was supposed to move from the positions they were holding at 13.00 hours, and the men were to partake of their haversack rations.

The defence under the command of Major L. G. Coles comprised Nos. 1 and 3 Companies in their static defence line, No. 4 (Mobile) Company, No. 5 (Machine Gun) Company in Reserve, and Battalion Intelligence Section and Signals Platoon.

The attack was under the command of Major W. H. Hoyt and consisted of the whole of No. 2 Company supported by H.Q. Reserve Platoon and a part of the Transport Platoon.

The Commanding Officer, Lt.-Col. J. W. Western, O.B.E., T.D., directed the Exercise and the Second-in-Command, Major H. J. Wiltsher, was Chief Umpire.

The real purpose of the Exercise was, in addition to general training, to test out Nos. 1 and 3 Companies defence positions in daylight.

The main attack took place through the village of Ide, and there is no doubt that many useful lessons were learnt. There was an excellent turn-out. Everyone worked very hard and conscientiously, and the members of both the attacking and defending forces considered that they had done a very good job of work, and they must have enjoyed themselves because the weather was definitely fine.

This was one of the first occasions the Battalion used the network telephone communications which was an arrangement between the Home Guard and the Post Office, officials it was of great assistance.

There was a general feeling after the Exercise that information was lacking but as this subject was one of the objects of the Exercise, it gave an opportunity of bringing to the notice of everyone concerned this most important form of training.

The training of the recruits was now being carried out under the supervision of Capt. C. S. Songhurst, M.M., at Higher Barracks, and owing to the compulsory enrolment he had, at one time, as many as 700 recruits, all in different stages of training. It must be realised that this was a tremendous task to be carried out in spare time and Capt. Songhurst and his Training Staff are to be congratulated on their work and the results of their efforts.

This elementary training of recruits was a great help to the Companies. It meant less interference with their specialised training which was being carried out by Platoons and Companies, and when recruits were eventually posted to the Company Commander he was able to post them directly into their Platoons and Squads.

OCTOBER, 1942

During this month of October, Capt. Fry was promoted to Major and Lieut. Curtis to Captain.

On October 10th/11th a very ambitious Exercise was directed by Brig. Gilmore, the Local Brigade Commander, whose headquarters at that time were at Higher Barracks. The Exercise commenced at 17.00

Saluting the Battalion Flag at the Presentation

hours on October 10th when the Battalion, took up "Action Stations," supported by the Marines, holding a line along the Bypass from Pinhoe to Countess Weir. The attack was undertaken by a part of the 103 Brigade supported by Marines and the remainder of the Brigade were held in reserve some distance out from Exeter, ready for counter-attacking.

Shortly before 18.00 hours on the night of October 10th British planes acting as the enemy, dive-bomber the City and shortly afterwards the Battalion received a message that Exe Bridge had been destroyed and that all traffic was being diverted *via* Countess Weir and Exe Weir Bridges.

The destruction of the bridge was later confirmed by No. 1 Company and casualties were dealt with by the local A.R.P. Personnel. Petrol stations blown up and a Platoon Headquarters badly damaged. No. 1 Company were compelled to evacuate their Headquarters, Cowick Street Railway Bridge was demolished, water, gas and sewer mains were destroyed. All these emergencies had to be met, thus exercising the ingenuity of those in command. During the Exercise it was reported that an enemy plane had crashed on Stoke Hill. A patrol was sent out by No. 2 Company to investigate and although they found the fake burnt out plane they were unable to trace any of the crew.

It is well at this stage to explain that all the damage described was fake damage, arranged by the Director through his Staff. For instance, as a simple explanation, when Exe Bridge was blown up, messages by runner or D.R. from Battalion Headquarters to the other side of the river had to be taken by an alternative route, but it gave the defence commander very real indications as to the dislocation that would be caused if such an incident had actually happened. By 19.27 hours information was beginning to arrive at Battalion H.Q. as to the whereabouts of the enemy. At various times during the night they were located at Axminster, Halberton, Topsham, Farringdon and various other places around Exeter. Cowley Bridge was destroyed and the Countess Weir Bridge was open to light traffic only. The outlying Battalions of the Home Guard were now beginning to report clashes with the enemy and some of their defended areas were being overrun.

The first clash with the enemy by the 1st Battalion was at Mill Lane Post which was held by a section of No. 1 Company. No. 2 Company reported the approach of the enemy on its right flank but there was no actual combat. At 04.30 hours on the 11th October an order was given to put all road blocks into position. At 07.21 hours No. 1 Company reported Ide occupied by the enemy.

At 08.30 hours the Director intimated that Battalion Headquarters was on the point of being surrounded and it was decided by the Commanding Officer that Headquarters should be moved to No. 2 Company's Headquarters at St. James Road. This movement was completed within 30 minutes. At 10.32 hours the enemy began infiltrating along Hamlin Lane and into the Polsloe Bridge area. They were also reported at Quay Lane and eventually occupied the old Battalion Headquarters at Colleton Crescent. At 12.30 hours the Chief

Umpire reported that the enemy had reached his objective which was, as we found out afterwards, a line drawn approximately through the centre of Exeter on the south side of Sidwell Street — High Street. The Director of the Exercise now decided that the British relief column should counter attack and the order was sent out. The relief column entered the City *via* Stoke Hill, Old Tiverton Road, in their armoured cars and jeeps. They first of all cleared the enemy from the locality of Sidwell Street and gave covering fire to the attacking troops who were by this time following up the retreating enemy with their mobile guns along Sidwell Street.

This was a most instructive exercise but would probably have been more interesting if those taking part had known more of the general scheme. It however, gave both the Home Guard and the civilians some idea of what would happen if the real enemy had in fact attacked Exeter. Everything was carried out throughout the night in accordance with 'Action Stations,' all food being drawn and cooked, and the members of the Battalion had plenty to eat.

In Battalion Orders No. 39, the Commanding Officer published his appreciation of the manner in which all ranks had conducted themselves during the exercise, with special commendations from the Fortress Commander.

H.Q. Company was again re-organized and was now to comprise, Machine Gun Detachment, Signals Platoon, Sub-Artillery Platoon and Transport Platoon. Capt. F. W. Frost was appointed Second-in-Command of this Company in addition to his duties as Staff Machine Gun Officer.

On October 24th a special Church Parade was ordered under Company arrangements.

The same orders published the relinquishment of his appointment with the Home Guard of Major H. M. Enefer, one of the original members of the Battalion. He had done a considerable amount of work especially in the early days. His job as Transport Officer had been a particularly difficult one but he carried out his duty efficiently. He carried with him the good wishes of the Battalion.

Once again an alteration in H.Q. Company had to be recorded, the Sector Signals Platoon, Sapper Platoon and Infantry Records Section being added to the strength of this Company.

It will no doubt be interesting to publish here an extract of an order issued, as to the definition of the duty of the Home Guard:

1. A member of the force becomes 'on duty' at the time he reaches the place of assembly (*e.g.*, H.Q., a post or rendezvous, etc.), as may have been, or may be, assigned to him by a superior officer, or when he begins to perform such duty without being required to report to a place of asseembly. A member will come 'off duty,' when he is dismissed by a superior officer on the completion of the duty, or any part of the duty, assigned to him, or, where no superior officer is present, when he has completed the duty he has been ordered to perform.

2. The words 'in uniform' have been omitted from the definition. Whether a man is in uniform or not is not usually material to the

question, whether he is on duty, but in all cases where a member of the Home Guard will come in contact with the general public in the exercise of his powers under the Defence Regulations, he should be in uniform.

During the end of November a 'Battle for Fuel' exhibition was held in the foyer of the Odeon Cinema, Exeter, and the Battalion arranged a display of their arms and equipment to make the exhibition more interesting from the public point of view.

It is interesting to note that during this month the Red Cross Penny-A-Week-Fund was commenced in the Battalion. The amounts collected at various times will be noted later in this record.

DECEMBER, 1942

On the 31st December there was published in Battalion Orders a Special Order of the Day by Major-General Michelmore, D.S.O.,

On the 20th December, 1942, a Church Parade was held at the Odeon Cinema, Exeter, by kind permission of the Manager, Mr. C. Gwilliam. The Battalion paraded at St. Luke's College Ground under the command of Lt.-Col. J. W. Western, O.B.E., T.D., and marched to the Cinema. The march was headed by the Band of the Devonshire Regiment by kind permission of Brig. Gilmore. The Band also supplied music for the service. A collection was made for the Prisoners of War Fund which amounted to a grand total of £30 18s. 6d. This was most gratifying. The Service was taken by the Battalion Padre, the Rev. Preb. E. Reid, M.A.

All training ceased during the week 22nd December — 29th December inclusive, but guards were continued as usual.

The Commanding Officer sent his greetings to all ranks of the Battalion for Christmas and the New Year.

M.C., T.D., A.D.C., Commander 77th Infantry Division, Home Forces, in which he expressed his good wishes for the New Year to the Commanders and all ranks in the 77th Infantry Division area.

Capt. Bawden, the Quartermaster, now left the Battalion on being posted to the Reception Depot, Pioneer Corps, and Capt. Davies joined the Battalion and took up duty as Quartermaster.

The year 1942 ended in somewhat the same manner as it had begun. Training was intensive but more advanced. The Battalion had, however, gone through a very difficult time owing to the 'blitz' and it is a great credit to all ranks that it should have reached the efficiency it did reach at the end of this year, in spite of the hard blow which it had received.

The enemy had not made any invasion of this part of the country, either by sea or by air and the Home Guardsmen feels that the existence of the Home Guard was probably a deterrent.

The strength of the Battalion at the end of December, 1942, was 2,120.

CHAPTER VI.

THE FLAG

JANUARY, 1943

The opening of 1943 saw particular attention being paid to training in Battle Drill. This training was very much different to anything else that had taken place and although it needed concentration in the early stages, it was certainly a change and was entered into with enthusiasm by all ranks.

It is to be noted with regret that the names of Pte. J. W. Dooling, of the Signals Platoon, and Platoon Sergeant F. G. Vincent, of No. 3 Company, were published in Battalion Orders No. 1 dated 6th January, 1943, as having been killed by enemy action. These two Home Guardsmen were killed when the Hun carried out a tip-and-run daylight raid on Exeter a short time before, and when a bomb fell very close to Battalion Headquarters. The loss of these two volunteers was felt throughout the Battalion.

On the 3rd January, 1943, an Exercise called "Gervase" was carried out. The general idea was that the Hun had landed a large number of paratroops followed by gliders, in certain parts of Devon and the Battalion was ordered to 'Stand To.' On Sunday morning they were ordered to 'Action Stations,' all posts to be manned. The A.R.P. Services and the Housewives co-operated and fake casualties of all kinds were arranged so as to exercise the medical service and the stretcher bearers. No. 4 Company, under the command of Major A. G. Fry, provided the enemy with No. 3 Company, under the command of Major T. Greenslade, in the defence, and the Exercise, which was during the day time, proved very instructive. It was particularly gratifying to find the Civil Defence Services taking part, as there was no doubt that if German paratroops had actually landed and made an attack on Exeter, the assistance of these Civil Defence Services to the Home Guard, would have been most important.

C.T.M. Bell was appointed C.S.M. No. 6 Company.

The Commanding Officer and Second-in-Command attended a conference of the Invasion Committee at the Castle on January 8th. The purpose of this meeting was to discuss the functions of the Civil Defence on 'Action Stations.'

No. 4 Coy. held a very successful Social at the Battalion Drill Hall on January 20th. This was attended by the majority of the Company, and there was no doubt that everybody thoroughly enjoyed themselves.

The Commanding Officer attended an Army Commanders' Conference at the Castle, Exeter, on January 21st.

On January 23rd a very successful Smoking Concert was held by No. 1 Coy. at the Shakespeare Road Hut.

On the 24th January, 1943, Capt. F. W. Frost, who had been Second-in-Command of H.Q. Coy., was relieved of his duty in order to concentrate on his role of Battalion Machine Gun Officer. Lieut. S. W. Down, who had previously been in command of No. 3 Platoon, No. 2 Coy., was appointed Second-in-Command of H.Q. Coy. and promoted to the rank of Captain.

On the 29th January, the Director General of the Home Guard, Lord Bridgeman, held a conference at the Higher Barracks, which all Commanding Officers and Senior Officers attended.

No. 2 Coy. held a Social on Saturday, 30th January. This concert was preceded by a Children's Party at which all the kiddies received presents.

On the 31st the Sector Commander, Lieut.-General E. A. Osborne, C.B., D.S.O., East Devon Sector Commander, held a conference at the Drill Hall, Ottery St. Mary, for all Commanding Officers and Company Commanders. No doubt all who were present will remember the very inclement weather which prevailed at the time.

FEBRUARY, 1943

On Sunday, 7th February, the Deputy Sector Commander held an all-day conference at Battalion Headquarters.

On the 8th February, 1943, Lieut.-Gen. E. A. Osborne, C.B., D.S.O., gave a talk to all Officers and N.C.O.s of the Battalion on the Exeter Defence Scheme. There was almost 100% attendance for this lecture which was very much appreciated by all concerned.

On the 14th February, the 'Bampfylde' Exercise was held, and this was a similar Exercise to 'Gervase,' but in this case the defending Company was No. 1 Coy., under the command of Major L. G. Coles.

A Battalion Church Parade was again held at the Odeon Theatre by kind permission of the Manager, Mr. C. Gwilliam, on Sunday, 21st February, 1943. In this case each Company marched to the Cinema independently on a time programme, and the service was taken by the Battalion Padre, the Revd. Preb. E. Reid. The salute at the march past after the Service was taken by Lt.-Gen. E. A. Osborne, C.B., D.S.O.

In Battalion Orders No. 7 dated 17th February, was published a note on security, the Commander-in-Chief having expressed his satisfaction with the high standard of security discipline throughout the Home Forces in which was included the Home Guard.

In Battalion Orders No. 8 a compliment was published from the Zone and Sector Commanders on the turn-out and march past of all companies at the Church Parade the previous week.

MARCH, 1943

Some very good Training Films were displayed at the Odeon Cinema, Exeter, and the whole Battalion attended. It was the general opinion that this was a very instructive and enjoyable form of training.

During the following days, up till May 16th, a certain amount of rehearsal was put in hand for the ceremony of the Presentation of the Flag.

March, 1943, brought forth other items of interest to the Battalion. The first one was a Services' Night at the Odeon Cinema on March 12th, and the artistes were all members of the Battalion. The management of the Odeon Cinema very kindly invited a large number of members of the Battalion to the Cinema, where they not only enjoyed the full programme of films, but also the programme of entertainment given by the members of the Battalion.

Another item was a Special Concert which was held, by kind permission of the Directors of the Odeon Theatre, at the Odeon Theatre, on March 21st. The proceeds of the Concert, after expenses were paid, were devoted to the Battalion Commander's Fund. Special artistes were engaged, and the Band of the Devonshire Regiment, by kind permission of Major W. L. Sparkes, supplied a most excellent programme of music. The Battalion is indebted to Major Sparkes and the Band for their great help and support. As a result of this Concert £60 was handed to the Commanding Officer's Fund.

The last item of interest was the fact that during this month Home Guard women auxiliaries cooked food for the members of the Battalion on exercises for the first time, and it was very much appreciated, especially by the Company Commanders because it freed the men who would normally have done the cooking to do the fighting.

W. V. Bristow was appointed Battalion Signals Staff Officer on March 7th, 1943.

MAY, 1943

On Sunday, May 16th, an armed parade and march past of the Home Guard was held in Central London to celebrate the 3rd anniversary of the Home Guard and this Battalion were ordered to send one Sergeant to take part in the Parade. Sgt. S. R. Pooley of No. 1 Company was selected from this Battalion and duly went to London for the Parade.

The 16th of May was a great day for the Battalion, and it received the greatest honour it had received during its existence. The Civic authorities presented a Flag to the Battalion.

Some time previously Lt. E. A. R. King of No. 1 Company had suggested to the Battalion Second-in-Command, that it would be a good idea if a Flag could be presented to the Battalion and that he could arrange for one to be given.

On receiving Major H. J. Wiltsher's whole-hearted support he went ahead and the Battalion eventually received a communication from the Mayor and Corporation of the City, that they, the Civic Authorities, would be greatly pleased to present the Battalion with a Flag.

This offer was naturally most readily accepted and arrangements were immediately put in hand to make the Presentation Ceremony well worthy of the occasion.

Major H. J. Wiltsher, Second-in-Command, was in charge of the arrangements for the Parade and was assisted by the Adjutant, Captain F. H. Dakyns.

The Padre blessing the Flag at the Presentation

Permission, first of all, had to be obtained from Gen. Sir Charles Maynard, Colonel, the Devonshire Regiment, who very soon replied, supporting the idea and agreeing that the Flag should bear the crest of the Devonshire Regiment. He considered that the Battalion, being part of the County Unit, was in close alliance with all other Battalions of the Devonshire Regiment, and it was his opinion that any step which might help to strengthen the ties of this alliance should be encouraged.

The actual presentation was arranged to coincide with the celebration of the 3rd anniversary of the Home Guard which was to be held on the 16th May, 1943.

All companies marched to the County Ground, St. Thomas, Exeter, independently and after the Officers had fallen out and handed the Companies over to the Company Sergeant Majors, R.S.M. Howe formed the Battalion up in three sides of a square.

The dress was Battle Order without haversacks and gas capes.

After the Battalion had paraded the Battalion Second-in-Command, took over command and all officers took post.

The Commanding Officer, Lt.-Col. J. W. Western, O.B.E., T.D. awaited the arrival of the distinguished guests.

We were favoured by the presence of the Devonshire Regiment Band, who played appropriate music throughout the ceremony.

On the arrival of the Right Worshipful the Mayor of Exeter, R. Glave Saunders, Esq., accompanied by the Sheriff, Col. J. Mac D. Latham, M.C., Officer Commanding Devon Sub District, and Lieut.-Gen. E. A. Osborne, C.B., D.S.O., Officer Commanding East Devon Sector, the Battalion were brought to attention and gave the General Salute, whilst the Band played a part of the National Anthem.

The Battalion were then brought back to the Order.

On the fourth side of the square had been placed a table at which stood His Worship the Mayor, the Sheriff and the Town Clerk on the one side, and the Battalion Padre, the Rev. Preb. E. Reid, on the other.

After the Padre had blessed the Flag it was presented by the Mayor to the Commanding Officer who thanked the Mayor on behalf of the Battalion.

The Flag Party, which consisted of Lieut. E. A. R. King, Flag Bearer, No. 1 Company, and Sgts. E. L. Clarke (E. Coy.), C. T. Lane (D. Coy.) and L. Morgan (B Coy.), had formed up in front of the Battalion and now marched in quick time to the Commanding Officer, Lt.-Col. J. W. Western, who handed the Flag over to the Flag Officer. Lt. King then ordered the Party to 'Present Arms.' The Battalion was next brought to the 'present' by the Second-in-Command, and the band played the regimental march. After the Battalion was brought back to the 'slope' the Commanding Officer saluted the Mayor and marched back to his position in the front of the Battalion, the Flag Party was then given the order to 'Troop,' and they slow marched round the inside of the three sides of the square in front of the Battalion and on the Flag approaching each Company, the Company Commander gave the order to 'present arms' to the Flag. Finally the Flag Party saluted the Mayor on passing him at his stand in front of the table and resumed their position in front of the Battalion. After this the Battalion marched round the County Ground past the front of the stand where a platform had been erected and where the Right Worshipful the Mayor of Exeter, took the Salute.

The Battalion were now the proud possessors of their own flag, and a very beautiful flag it is, being made of pure silk, hand embroidered, very similar to the colours presented to Regular Battalions. The 1st Battalion were, in fact, the first Home Guard Battalion to have received a flag of their own and I believe they were still the only Battalion to have a flag when the Home Guard was 'Stood Down.'

The Battalion is indeed grateful to the Mayor and the Civic Authorities for their very kindly thought and for the honour they have extended to the Battalion in making this presentation and this record would not be complete without including a copy of a letter which the Commanding Officer received from the Right Worshipful the Mayor of Exeter.

"It was very gratifying to all of us to witness the splendid display last Sunday and we are more than repaid for the trouble and cost of getting the Flag. Everyone present was struck by the smart appearance of the men, hardly distinguishable from members of the Regular Army and the way that all the items followed without a hitch. It was a day we shall all remember when this tragic war is only an unpleasant memory."

Following upon this Parade the Commanding Officer, Lt.-Col. J. W. Western, issued a Special Order of the Day and this record again would not be complete without a copy.

"I desire to express my warmest thanks to all ranks for the splendid way they turned out for the Battalion Parade on Sunday last. It was, to say the least, a magnificent demonstration of the progress of the Home Guard and I have been extremely proud to receive congratulations from among the quarters, both civil and military, on the manner in which the whole of the proceedings were carried out. No one will, I feel, begrudge a special word of praise to the Flag Party, whose trooping could not have been surpassed by very highly trained regular soldiers.

"I am very grateful indeed to Officers and O.R.s for the keenness and enthusiam they displayed. In conclusion, I should like to quote a few words of a memorable speech made by the Prime Minister after Dunkirk. 'We shall not flag or fail, we shall go on to the end.' Let the inspiration given us on Sunday last, therefore urge us to carry on with cheerfulness and determination until the enemy has been completely crushed."

By the graciousness of the Gaumont British Picture Corporation, one of their cameramen took a newsreel of the whole proceedings and this was shown to the public at the Gaumont British cinema during the following week, as part of the general news. It was a very memorable record of the ceremony of presentation and the original film was handed to Lt.-Col. H. J. Wiltsher sometime later, he, having by that time, assumed command of the Battalion.

The film is an imperishable record of the 1st (Loyal City of Exeter) Btn. Devon Home Guard.

Now to continue the Parade. The Companies, having marched past and saluted the Mayor, continued their March outside the County Ground, where they were dismissed by companies so that they could all return to the ground to join their ladies who had been invited to the Presentation.

Members of the Battalion then gave demonstrations in the use of the various weapons issued to the Home Guard and this again was very successful and enjoyed by all present, except for one incident. One Company gave a demonstration in an attack on a defended position erected on the ground. The Commander of this attack decided that he would use smoke bombs from a mortar, but as we were not issued with smoke bombs for firing, he arranged at the proper time for smoke cannisters to be set alight around the defended position. The wind was blowing towards the grandstand and consequently the smoke percolated into the stand itself. This was not serious, but, unfortunately, one of the smoke cannisters had been incorrectly marked as smoke, whereas it was in fact later found to be practice gas, and a lot of people suffered some effect, although not serious, from this gas. The Battalion regretted very much the inconvenience caused to those people who suffered, but an investigation clearly proved that the marking on the cannister was for smoke and entirely different to the marking which one finds on a practice gas cannister. No blame could, therefore, be attached to anyone.

It is certain that everyone went away both from the Presentation Parade and the demonstration very satisfied with the whole proceedings and the City have expressed, in the words of the Mayor, their pride in their own Battalion of the Home Guard.

The Flag has been kept in safe custody since that day and has only been taken out for ceremonial parades. After the war it is to be handed over to the Mayor for safe custody.

CHAPTER VII.

DRILL—WITH A DIFFERENCE

On the 22nd May there was a Service March Past through Exeter for the 'Wings for Victory' Week, and to this Parade the Battalion sent a detachment of approximately 500, all ranks. The Parade formed up in Pinhoe Road, and the Battalion contingent was under the command of Major H. J. Wiltsher. All branches of the Services took part and the column moved off at 15.00 hours, passing through Sidwell Street to the Saluting Base at the Guildhall where Group Captain Woodhall, accompanied by the Mayor of Exeter, took the Salute. On then, down Fore Street, over Exe Bridge to the Hele's School playing ground, where each detachment was formed up and dismissed independently. Tea was provided for all those taking part.

The weather was decidedly bad as it was raining most of the time and all those who took part got thoroughly wet but the members of the Battalion were quite satisfied that they had done a good job of work and had enhanced the name of the Battalion.

During this month the Odeon Cinema was booked for the showing of Training Films. Companies marched independently to the Theatre on a time schedule, the films were instructive and an interesting form of training.

On the evening of the 22nd May, 1943, was held an Officers' Mess Dinner at which the ladies were invited. The Dinner was served in the Drill Hall at Battalion Headquarters and was a farewell to the Commanding Officer, Lt.-Col. J. W. Western, O.B.E., T.D., on his retirement. There was a full muster of officers with their wives and ladies and a very successful evening was enjoyed by all.

Special guests at dinner were Major-General A. P. Dawson, O.B.E., A.D.C., R.M., Lieut.-Gen. E. A. Osborne, C.B., D.S.O., Col. H. D Goldsmith, C.B., D.S.O., D.L., Major W. L. Sparkes, Devonshire Regiment, Lieut.-Col. P. C. Bull, D.S.O., T.D., Col. W. H. Brooke, C.B.E., M.C., D.L., Major R. C. Cumming, O.B.E.

The Second-in-Command, Major H. J. Wiltsher, proposed the farewell toast to the Commanding Officer during which he drew the attention of all to the amount of national Work which Col. Western had done throughout his lifetime, having joined the 1st Rifle Volunteers in 1896, and had a total service of 35 years before joining the Home Guard.

Col. Western suitably replied, on the completion of which, Major Wiltshire presented to him, on behalf of the Officers, two silver salvers suitably inscribed.

The toast of the Battalion was given by Lt.-Gen. E. A. Osborne and this was replied to by Col. Western.

Major W. H. Hoyt proposed 'The Ladies' in reply to which Mrs. Western, wife of the Commanding Officer, gave a very interesting talk.

BATTALION STAFF.

Commanding
Officer
Lt. Col.
H. J. Wiltsher,
O.B.E.

2nd in Command
Major
W. H. Hoyt

The Adjutant
Capt. F. H. Dakyns

The Quartermaster
Capt. H. F. Davies

The Padre
The Rev.
Preb. E. Reid, M.A.

The toast of 'The Guests' was given by Major L. G. Coles and was replied to by Major-General Dawson.

We were very much favoured by the presence of the Devonshire Regiment Band, by kind permission of Major Sparkes, who played throughout the evening.

Capt. S. W. Down acted as Mess President.

In Battalion Orders No. 21 dated 26th May, 1943, Lt.-Col. J. W. Western relinquished command of the Battalion as from Sunday, 30th May, 1943.

Lt.-Col. Western joined the Home Guard at the end of September, 1940, had been Assistant Adjutant, and then Second-in-Command of the Battalion before taking over command.

In the same Battalion Orders, Major H. J. Wiltsher assumed command of the Battalion as from Monday, 31st May, 1943, with the rank of Lieut.-Col. Lieut.-Col. Wiltsher was one of the few who had attended the meeting called on May 30th, 1940, by Major Anstey, the first Detachment Commander, when a skeleton organization of what was then known as the Detachment, was arranged.

He was, at that meeting, appointed Company Commander, No. 2 Company, and remained with that Company until taking over the appointment of Second-in-Command of the Battalion on the death of Lt.-Col. F. J. C. Hunter.

The Commanding Officer received a visit from Lord Fortescue, G.S.O.1, H.G.

On June 1st, 1943, S./Sgt. L. Rey, was promoted 2nd Lieut. and appointed Administrative Officer. Most members of the Battalion will remember this officer for the enthusiastic manner in which he carried out his duties and his willingness at all times to assist anybody in need of help, whether on the question of records or on the Social side. Very little took place without this Officer having something to do with the arranging. The compliments received by the Battalion on many occasions because of the way in which the records were kept was due to the efficiency and keenness of Lieut. Rey.

JUNE, 1943

On June 4th No. 1 Company held a most successful Smoking Concert at the Constitutional Club. The Commanding Officer was present with the Second-in-Command, and complimented the Company on their efficiency. Major Coles, the Company Commander, in proposing the health of the Battalion and the Commanding Officer, quite rightly stressed the loyalty which No. 1 Company had always shown towards the Battalion.

Round about this time, a Man-Power Board was formed at the Ministry of Labour, and the Commanding Officer accepted an invitation to be a member of this Board. The main idea was to sort out the various types of men so that those unfit for Home Guard duty could be released for Civil Defence work and, where possible, men could be released from Civil Defence work to make up the strength of the Battalion. Further to this, it was expected that the Labour Exchange would be able to direct still more men to one of the Services, but the sum result was that very few men were either directed or exchanged.

Battalion Orders dated 16th June, 1943, notified the change of title of one of the H.Q. Company specialist Platoons. The R.A. Platoon was in future to be known as the Sub-Artillery Platoon.

On June 20th the Sector Commander inspected the Wireless Links of all Battalions.

It is worthy of note that Battalion Orders dated 30th June, 1943, announced the first issue of a decoration other than a certificate to a member of this Battalion. Lieut. Henry John Ferguson, No. 1 Coy. was made a Member of the Most Excellent Order of the British Empire, (M.B.E. Military Division). Lieut. Ferguson gained this high award for outstanding devotion to duty during the "Blitz" of May, 1942, when he was Orderly Officer at Battalion Headquarters and when those Headquarters were destroyed. Lieut. Ferguson joined the Battalion at the formation and had been an officer for two years. Just after the 'Blitz' he had been awarded a certificate for gallantry and there was no doubt that he carried with this award the good wishes of all the Battalion.

On Thursday, 1st July, 1943, the Battalion received a signal honour in the visit of the Colonel, the Devonshire Regiment, Major-General Sir Charles Maynard, K.C.B., C.B.E., D.S.O. He visited Battalion Headquarters accompanied by Major W. L. Sparkes, and was introduced to the Commanding Officer and the Senior Officers of the Battalion. He complimented the Commanding Officer on the efficiency of the Battalion.

On Saturday, 3rd July, No. 2 Coy. held a very enjoyable Social Evening in the Drill Hall at Battalion H.Q. During the evening Major Young, the Coy. Commander, proposed the health of the Battalion to the which the Battalion Commander replied.

On Wednesday, 7th July, the Commanding Officer and the Sector Commander visited No. 4 Coy.'s Headquarters to watch the Platoon training.

On Sunday, July 11 an exercise, similar to "Bamfylde" and "Gervase" was held, the defending Company this time being No. 2 Company, under the command of Major A. P. Young, M.C.

Early in the summer the Battalion had formed a Cricket Club, under the Chairmanship of Major A. G. Fry, and on September 12th they ran a very successful dance at the Drill Hall, Colleton Crescent. The object was partly social and partly to raise funds, and in both they were successful.

On the 14th July, 1943, Lieut. M. C. B. Hoare of No. 2 Coy. was appointed Battalion Press Officer in addition to his other duties as Platoon Commander, and here again the Battalion owes this Officer a debt of gratitude for all the good work which he has done.

On Wednesday, 21st July, the Commanding Officer and Sector Commander visited No. 1 Coy. during their Platoon training.

On Saturday, July 24th, the Commanding Officer inspected Hele's School Cadet Coy.

On Tuesday, July 27th the Commanding Officer inspected No. 3 Company of the Army Cadet Force at St. Thomas's.

AUGUST, 1943

On the 8th August, Lt.-Gen. E. A. Osborne, C.B., D.S.O., presented the Territorial Efficiency Medal to Pte. Rosenberg of the Signals Platoon.

On the 13th August, the Battalion took part in an Exercise directed by the G.O.C. South West District, which was called the 'Hay' Exercise, and commenced at 20.00 hours on the 13th August, and finished at 21.00 hours on the 15th August. It was understood that from 21.00 hours on the 13th until 15.00 hours on the 14th, only a limited number of the Home Guard could be available, but for that period, the Commanding Officer, Second-in-Command, the Adjutant, and the Captain A. & Q. were on duty. At 15.00 hours on the 14th, the whole Battalion were turned out at full strength.

The Exercise was an ambitious one. The Battalion Commander, commanded the Battalion and also acted as an Umpire, and problems were set so as to exercise both the operational and the A. & Q. side of the Battalions taking part. A Battle Report was kept by Battalion Headquarters of the progress of the enemy, and this was tabulated to a small degree.

Lieut. Hichisson, the Intelligence Officer, and his Staff were kept very busy throughout the night and, like everyone else in the Battalion, they gained a considerable amount of experience.

The enemy did, in fact, manage to get into the City, but in very weak strength, and as a consequence, they were unable to do any damage. The Exercise finished on an optimistic note in regard to the possibility of enemy troops being succesful if they did attempt to make any attack on this part of the Country.

The Battalion Catering Officer, Lieut. C. H. Spiller, was now to be known as the Battalion Messing Officer. This Officer took on this difficult job when it was first started and after a considerable amount of work he had completed all details, so that whatever happened there would be no fear of the men of this Battalion not getting their full ration of good food, properly cooked.

The Sector Commander, accompanied by the Commanding Officer, visited No. 6 Coy. during their Platoon training.

Preparations were now in hand for the big Demonstration which the Battalion were to give on Dartmoor, and on Sunday, 29th August, the Commanding Officer, accompanied by the Second-in-Command and the Adjutant, and those Staff Officers who had a job of work to do, spent a whole day on Dartmoor, laying out the ground and making the necessary plans.

SEPTEMBER, 1943

Battalion Orders No. 32, dated September 1st, confirmed the promotion of Captain A. P. Young, M.C., O.C., No. 2 Company to Major, and Lieut. L. C. Duncan, Second-in-Command, No. 2 Company to Captain.

On September 15th, the Commanding Officer held a Conference of all the Officers detailed for duty for the Dartmoor Demonstration.

On September 26th, Brigadier Wyatt, M.C., T.D., Sub-District Commander, called on the Battalion Commander.

OCTOBER, 1943

On October 2nd, the Commanding Officer, with the Company Commanders, proceeded to Salisbury for a Camouflage Course. This turned out to be most interesting and instructive.

On the 3rd October, 1943, the Battalion gave a demonstration of all weapons on the Warren House Range, Dartmoor. A very ambitious programme was arranged down to every detail, and the various squads taking part had trained well and truly for their task.

In the first place we have to thank the Sector Commander, General E. A. Osborne, for his great assistance in allowing us the necessary transport, and as a result of his help we were not only able to take all those taking part in the demonstration, but also approximately 600 from the Battalion as spectators.

The distinguished visitors were Brig. R. J. P. Wyatt, the Sub-District Commander, General E. A. Osborne, the Sector Commander, a Colonel from the U.S. Army, with other American Officers, and a number of Home Guard Battalion Commanders, together with a small representative party from other Battalions.

Picquets were set out at various points as a safety precaution to prevent any civilians walking into the danger area. Lieut. Burvill was in command of these picquets.

Lieut. W. V. Bristow, the Battalion Signals Staff Officer arranged all the communications which were carried out by the Battalion Signals Platoon under the command of Lieut. Campion.

Lines were laid to the various points which in some cases were over half a mile away, and wireless was also provided.

The ammunition dump was under the control of the Battalion Ammunition Officer, Lieut. Ellis. The First Aid Section was under the command of Sgt. Horwood and the Medical Officer was also on parade.

Lieut. Finn the Sub-Artillery Staff Officer was responsible for the Sub-Artillery demonstration.

Lieut. Sykes, Transport Officer was responsible for all transport including the em-bussing and de-bussing both ways. All troops, after being debussed, came under the command of the R.S.M. F. Howe, who paraded them and marched them to the spectators rendezvous.

Every man was ordered to bring a haversack ration, but arrangements were made by the Messing Officer, Lieut. C. H. Spiller, for tea to be made and at the midday break, every man was issued with half a pint of tea.

Readers will no doubt be interested in the details of the demonstrations which took place. Four men were detailed to attack a building as a battle patrol. All the correct movements, including the clearing of the building, were carried out, and live 36 grenades were used. The commentary was by Captain Nickels.

The Battalion Bombing Officer, Lieut. C. A. Thomas gave a demonstration in the use of the S.I. (Sticky Grenade), and here again the commentary was by Captain Nickels.

The third item was an attack by a Battle Platoon, the demonstration being under the control of the Adjutant, Captain F. H. Dakyns, the Battle Platoon being under the command of Lieut. Crouch of "D" Company, from whom the Battle Platoon was supplied. Briefly the intention was to show a Battle Platoon in attack under Battle inoculation and during the whole of the attack two Bren Guns fired live rounds interposed with tracer, over the heads of the attackers. In the path of the attackers, the Explosives Officer, Lieut. Elwell, let off land mines which he had previously prepared.

The Platoon was split up into three squads and the O Group, White Flag, No. 1 Squad a Blue Flag, No. 2 Squad a Green Flag, and No. 3 Squad a Red Flag.

All camouflage was closely practised and every protection both from view and danger was carried out and it was for this reason that one man in each of the groups carried a flag so that the spectators whilst not being able to see the approaching troops were able to follow the exact movement of each squad or the O group.

At a certain point the attackers came under heavy fire (represented by increased bursts from the Brens) and the whole Platoon went to earth and the Platoon Commander moved forward with his O Group to decide on his final attack.

He decided on a left flanking attack and eventually reached the building and carried his objective.

Lieut. Crouch and his Platoon are to be congratulated on the excellent manner in which this demonstration was carried out and this short record does not by any means give full credit for their work.

The break for feeding took place after this demonstration and then followed demonstrations by the Lewis Guns in the charge of Lieut. Holland, who also gave the commentary.

The E.Y. Rifle followed and six men, under Sgt. Prout, demonstrated the use of this weapon with 36 grenades, as an anti-personnel weapon, it was most effective. The commentary was by 2nd Lieut. Thomas.

The Northover Projector was demonstrated by two teams using first 36 grenades and then dummy S.I.Ps. It was impossible on a place like Dartmoor to use the real S.I.Ps. The commentary was by Lieut. Holland.

A very effective demonstration by the Browning Machine Guns under the command of Lieut. Ezard followed. They demonstrated all phrases of this weapon including "Beaten Zones," Traversing and Swinging Traverse. To those who have never seen a heavy Machine Gun in action before, it must have been most impressive. The marksmanship was excellent. The commentary in this case was by Captain Frost.

A demonstration was then given by two teams under the charge of Lieut. Rainbird on the Spigot Mortar. A special movable target had been fitted up, but unfortunately the marksmanship was too good and the targets were hit and destroyed too early. The idea of the firers was to just miss the targets as the burst of the shells could easily be seen by the spectators.

A demonstration in the Smith Gun under the command of Lieut. Johns followed. Here again the marksmanship was 100 per cent., the target being hit in every case. The American Colonel was so much intrigued with this weapon that he asked to be allowed to fire, and his wish was naturally granted. Lieut. Finn was the commentator in this case.

All the persons mentioned above deserve the highest credit for their keenness and enthusiasm and the hard work which they had put into the arrangements but there is one officer who has not yet been mentioned, and that is, the Weapon Training Officer, Captain C. S. Songhurst, M.M.

When the Commanding Officer first of all decided to run this demonstration he picked on the Adjutant, Captain F. H. Daykns and Captain Songhurst to make all the arrangements and left it to them. They were responsible for all details and the fact that the whole demonstration went off from beginning to end without a hitch is due entirely to their efforts, combined with the co-operation which was given to them by all the Officers and men, who had volunteered to help, including the Battalion P.S.Is., Sgts. B. Budd and T. Williams.

The Commanding Officer said a few words over the loud speaker afterwards and thanked everyone taking part for the grand work which they had done.

Both General Osborne and Brig. Wyatt complimented the Battalion very highly.

It was fortunate that the weather was fine and the general opinion afterwards was that more such demonstrations should be given and that if possible more spectators, including those outside the Home Guard, should be allowed to attend.

A Battalion Church Parade was held at the Odeon Theatre on Sunday, October 10th, 1943. Again the Companies marched to the Theatre independently on a timed programme and the Service was conducted by the Revd. Preb. E. Reid, Honorary Chaplain to the Battalion. The lessons were read by the Commanding Officer and the Second-in-Command.

After the Service the Battalion formed up in Old Tiverton Road and marched past the Saluting Base which was on the Odeon Theatre steps, where the Salute was taken by the Sector Commander, General E. A. Osborne, accompanied by the Commanding Officer.

The Band of the Devonshire Regiment, by kind permission of Major W. L. Sparkes, provided the music for the Service and played outside during the march past. There was a very good attendance of visitors.

Battalion Orders No. 39 dated October 20th, 1943, confirmed a change in the Company titles. Up to this time Companies had been numbered, 1, 2, 3, 4 and 6, but from now onwards they were to be known as A, B, C, D and E; H.Q. remaining as before.

For some time there had been rumours, followed by instructions,

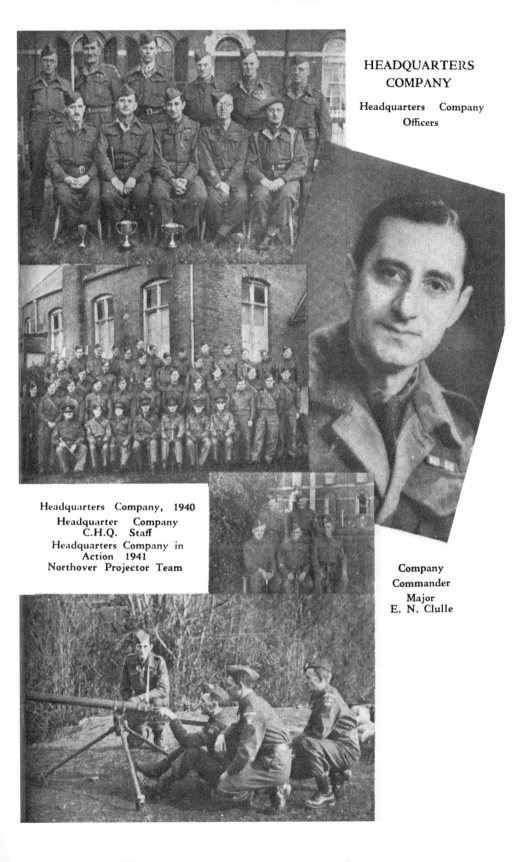

HEADQUARTERS COMPANY

Headquarters Company
Officers

Headquarters Company, 1940
Headquarter Company
C.H.Q. Staff
Headquarters Company in
Action 1941
Northover Projector Team

Company
Commander
Major
E. N. Clulle

that a First Aid Competition was to be run by Devon Sub-District which Command included practically the whole of Devon. It was finally arranged that, by competition, each Battalion should choose its best Company First Aid Squad, and this Battalion held their Inter-Company Competition on Friday, October 22nd. The result was a win for "C" Company, who were chosen to represent the Battalion at the Sector Competition, which was to be held later.

In continuance of the Battalion policy of encouraging the social side, No. "C" Company held a very enjoyable Social at the Battalion Drill Hall, Colleton Crescent, on Saturday, October 23rd.

The confirmation of Major Hoyt's appointment as Second-in-Command of the Battalion was published in Battalion Orders dated October 27th, 1943.

On October 29th, the Sector Commander held a meeting at the 1st Battalion Headquarters for all Battalion Commanders.

The Final of the Sector First Aid Competition took place at the Battalion Drill Hall, Colleton Crescent, on Sunday, October 31st. No. 3 Company, representing the Battalion, did not win but they put up a very creditable show. The Hall was prepared by the Battalion Camouflage Officer, Lieut. Bilsborough, and was made to represent a field and a hedge. This was very well done.

NOVEMBER, 1943

The officers of the Battalion held a Dance in the Drill Hall, Battalion Headquarters, on the 5th November, 1943. This was most successful. It was organised to enable the ladies to take part in some of the Battalion's activities.

The Band of the Devonshire Regiment played appropriate music and Mr. C. Gwilliam, Manager of the Odeon Theatre, brought along a cabaret party which gave a varied programme.

During the interval the film which had been taken of the Presentation of the Flag by the Gaumont British Picture Corporation, was presented to the Commanding Officer, Lieut-Col. H. J. Wiltsher, by Lieut. Forsyth.

This is another record in the exploits of this Battalion.

On November 5th the Army Commander held a Conference at the Castle, Exeter.

On November 8th, 1943, the Devonshire Regiment Band gave a most excellent concert in the Civic Hall, Exeter, the proceeds of which were equally divided between the Devonshire Regiment's Comforts' Fund and the 1st (Loyal City of Exeter) Bn. Devon Home Guard Welfare Fund. A varied repertoire of operas, descriptive pieces, etc., were played by the Band and the Concert was enjoyed by all those present.

As November 11th was Armistice Day the Commanding Officer, accompanied the Mayor and his party to both the City and the County Memorials, where wreaths were laid by different authorities.

The H.Q. Company carried out an Exercise on their Defended Home, which was the Castle, and Brigadier Brooke, the Deputy Sector Commander, in addition to supervising the Exercise with the Commanding Officer, carried out a survey of the various defensive positions in conjunction with the Commanding Officer's "Plan B."

Battalion Orders No. 43, dated November 17th, set out an extract from a speech made by the Prime Minister at the Mansion House Dinner on the 6th November, 1943, and this is worthy of being copied in a Home Guard record.

"We cannot, however, exclude the possibility of new forms of attack on this island. We have been vigilantly watching for many months past every sign of preparation for such attacks. Whatever happens they will not be of a nature to affect the final course of the war, but, should they come, they will naturally call for the utmost efficiency and devotion in our Fire Watchers and Home Guard, and also a further display of the firmness and fortitude for which the British Nation has won renown. This is no time to relax in all our precautions or discourage our splendid auxiliary services."

In the House of Commons on the 11th November, 1943, the following question was put to the Prime Minister: "If, in view of the recent increase in the number of air raids in this country, and especially in London, and the proximity of the enemy, you will make it clear that the duties of the Home Guard and Fire Guards are still of great national importance, and encourage them in the performance of their duty."

The Prime Minister's reply was as follows: —

"Sir, His Majesty's Government attach the highest importance to the work of the Home Guard and Fire Guards, who have played, and continue to play, so important a part in our Home Defences. In my speech at the Mansion House on Tuesday last, I gave reasons, why, in my opinion, this is no time to relax all our precautions, or discourage our auxiliary services. On the other hand, I have asked that steps should be taken to ease up as much as public safety allows, the strain upon efficient members of the Home Guard, who are working long hours."

Another Church Parade and Carol Service was held at the Odeon Theatre, the service being taken by the Padre and a collection was in aid of the Royal Devon and Exeter Hospital, and the Orthopaedic Hospital.

As a result of this service the Commanding Officer was able to hand over approximately £7 to each of these Hospitals.

"E" Company held a Social at the Assembly Hall, Cowick Street, on Friday, November 26th, and, as usual with this Company, it was very successful and was enjoyed by all.

On Sunday, November 28th, the Sector Commander, General Osborne, directed an Exercise at Exe Bridge at which "C" Company, practised the manning of their Defended area, under "Plan B."

It is with regret that another casualty has to be reported. On the 30th November, 1943, 2nd Lieut. H. B. Blackbourne, Second-in-Command of the Transport Section, was involved in a serious accident whilst proceeding home by car, after having been on duty all night at the Royal Devon and Exeter Hospital Fire Picquet. This Officer was conveyed back to the Hospital and it was many months before he recovered from his serious injuries.

During this month, Operation Orders were issued by Lieut-Col. H. J. Wiltsher, which were to be called "Plan B," and which conformed to "Defence in Depth."

This meant a considerable amount of extra work for Company and Platoon Commanders, but it was all very cheerfully carried out.

DECEMBER, 1943

On December 12th, 1943 "D" Company took part in a local Exercise.

More social events took place on Saturday, December 18th—"B" Company running a dance at the Drill Hall, Colleton Crescent, whilst "A" Company held a Social at the Constitutional Club, Heavitree.

All training was cancelled for a period from the 24th December to Sunday, January 9th, 1944, to give the members of the Battalion the opportunity of celebrating Christmas in the best method possible under War conditions, and also to give them a well earned rest.

During the end of this month "C" Company held their annual Smoking Concert, and during the proceedings the Company Commander, Major T. Greenslade, D.C.M., spoke of the loyalty of the Battalion as the essence of good soldiering. The Battalion Commander, Lieut.-Col. H. J. Wiltsher, replied by stressing the necessity for continued training. The evening had included a concert party and was a very successful one, and before the end Major Greenslade presented Pte. E. Patton with an inscribed plaque for his good work in connection with the rescue of a horse at Cowley, and Captain J. Samuels presented the Company Commander with a framed drawing of the incident.

On Friday, December 28th, the Officers of the Battalion had a Get-Together Night at the Officers' Mess.

This brings us to the end of 1943. From the number of Exercises conducted by higher authority it will be seen that greater interest in the training of the Home Guard was being taken by those authorities and that such training was more on the lines of the operations which the Battalion were likely to take part in, if the Hun had attempted an invasion.

The training was to be more specialised, and we were now concentrating in such things as "How to prepare a house for defence," "Street fights" and "Clearing a house occupied by the enemy." The members of the Battalion will remember the many problems which arose and had to be prepared for in dealing with their own particular "defended home." The burnt out Ackland Hotel will be remembered as the place used for House clearing and also the badly damaged House on the Topsham Road which was selected for the final test for the "Bull Trophy." These few remarks will bring back memories, memories of hard work well done but also some amusing incidents of which there were many. Some models of houses were made to help in this form of training and these were very useful on wet nights. The Sub-

Artillery and Machine Gun Platoons were also kept busy in their particular problems which were many and varied, and for which there training was suitably arranged by Lieut. Finn and Captain F. W. Frost.

Another big stride forward was the fact that every man was being taught his own individual job and there is no doubt that the Battalion were fit and ready to undertake any serious job of work which might come along.

The news was beginning to brighten and the prospect of peace in 1944 was being seriously suggested.

It was realised, however, that a danger period was still ahead, the invasion of Europe by the Allies was still to come and it was quite readily thought that this might be a suitable opportunity for the Hun to attempt some dirty work on this Country.

Relaxation, therefore, of training, in at least the early part of the coming year, was not foreseen or contemplated.

The strength of the Battalion at the end of December, 1943, had shrunk to 1,555.

CHAPTER VIII

BATTLE INOCULATION

JANUARY, 1943

The first item of interest in 1944 was contained in Battalion Orders No. 1, referring to a letter which had been received by the Commanding Officer from Major-General Sir Charles Maynard, K.C.B., C.M.G., D.S.O., late Colonel of the Devonshire Regiment, in which he wished the Battalion every success in 1944. Since the General's visit to the Battalion, he had relinquished his appointment as Colonel of the Devonshire Regiment.

The year started off with more social events, and on Wednesday, January 5th, "D" Company held a very successful "Social" and Dance at the Battalion Drill Hall.

On Saturday, January 8th, "C" Company held a Social at the Battalion Drill Hall, and here again there was a very good attendance and a successful evening was enjoyed by all present.

BATTLE INOCULATION was arranged for all Companies. This was something very personal to the Adjutant, Captain F. H. Dakyns, who was responsible for all arrangements, and who made sure that it was as near the real thing as possible. Companies sent either one or two Platoons at a time to Digby's Quarry, where they were formed up into squads and given a patrol task to carry out. All this was carried out in the hours of darkness, and in the course of the patrol they came across various trip wires, bearing tin cans or bells, which at the slightest touch to the wire would set up a noise, which was the signal for two Bren Guns to open fire, with live ammunition, including tracer, over the heads of the patrol.

Each patrol was given a finishing task. They had to take up a position actually in the centre of the Quarry where they would engage the enemy with Sten and rifle fire; the enemy being represented by life-size targets set up on the Quarry face and illuminated at the last minute by the headlights of a stationary car parked on the other side of the Quarry.

Throughout the whole operation, in addition to the inoculation from Bren Guns, Lieut. Elwell set off land mines, thunder flashes, and, as a finale, 69 Grenades. There is no doubt that this is a very excellent form of training. It gave the men the training to carry on with their task under fire and in the midst of a considerable amount of noise, and taught them to keep their heads down and to take whatever cover was possible, and, what was very important, it taught them the steadiness to engage the enemy after having completed the patrol and whilst being fired at by Bren Guns and grenades. The Adjutant was always sure of a full turn out on these occasions which proved the interest of the men. It was arranged that as far as possible, every Officer, N.C.O. and man should go through this Battle Inoculation

Test. As it all had to be done during the early months of the year, whilst the nights were dark, it meant that the Adjutant and his staff had to spend two or three evenings a week on this form of exercise. The instructors were as keen as if they were actually taking part. Everybody in the Battalion had at least the chance of going through this inoculation and there cannot have been very many who missed it.

One night we were honoured by a visit from Alderman F. P. Cottey, C. J. Newman, Town Clerk, Alderman Tarr, and Lieut.-General E. A. Osborne, C.B., D.S.O., and other Battalion Commanders. The Patrols operating that night were in excellent form and the visitors expressed themselves very freely on the excellent work carried out by the Battalion.

All through the winter months the Adjutant carried out a series of lectures to the Companies on tactical subjects.

On Sunday, January 30th, the U.S. Army First Aid gave a demonstration in the Drill Hall, Colleton Crescent. This was very well attended by the First Aid Sections of the Battalion, and it was most instructive, especially to see the equipment carried by the U.S. Army First Aid parties.

The Civic authorities had now organised and opened the Royal Albert Museum as an Allied Services Club, and as a special recognition, invited the Home Guard to use the Club, when in uniform.

A record should be made at this stage of the total Red Cross Penny-A-Week Fund collection, which had been made by the Battalion up to date. The total amount was £116 4s. 3d., a very worthy effort.

Early this month "E" (G.W.R.) Company were reorganised as a L.A.A. Troop. The training responsibility was taken over by the local A.A. Brigade, but the alteration in the role of this Company threw a tremendous amount of work on the Company Commander, Major C. R. Panes, and his staff. In order to be certain that reliefs would be provided throughout the 24 hours, almost every man in the Company had to be trained as a gunner, but, fortunately, in the event of any ground operations only 25 would have been required, to man the guns, and the remainder would have reverted to their original role of infantrymen.

FEBRUARY, 1944

On Sunday, February 5th, "C" Company attended St. Andrew's Church, Exwick, for the morning Service, under the command of Major T. Greenslade, D.C.M. The collection, which was for the Merchant Navy Comforts' Fund, amounted to over £10.

On Sunday, February 13th, an order was received that the Battalion were to cease supplying a Fire Picquet at the Royal Devon and Exeter Hospital. The main reason was because the Battalion were to concentrate on more specialised training. Most of the men who had been doing the Fire Picquet were somewhat disappointed but they realised that their time was to be fully occupied.

On Sunday, February 13th, Devon Sub-District ordered the Battalion on an "Action Stations" Exercise.

BATTALION HEADQUARTERS
Battalion I.O. and Staff

Battalion Signals in
Operation

Battalion Signals Platoon on Parade

Capt. C. A. Songhurst, M.M. The W.T.O.
with his Staff. Also the R.M.'s on parade

The Sector Commander, General Osborne, had always been very interested in the organisation of the Home Guard Intelligence Sections, and to that end he asked Lieut.-Col. P. C. Bull, D.S.O., T.D., the Sector Training Officer, to arrange a demonstration, to take place at the Battalion Drill Hall, Colleton Crescent, on Sunday, February 20th. This demonstration was called "Right and Wrong," and it was attended by the other Battalion Commanders of the Sector, and all the Battalion Intelligence Officers and Sections. Lieut. Hichisson, the 1st Battalion Intelligence Officer, and his Section, carried out the demonstration under the direction of Colonel Bull. The right way to run an Intelligence Office was first demonstrated, and then the wrong way. After the demonstration was completed, questions were asked and answered and General Osborne summed up the whole proceedings.

The Officers' Mess held a Dinner, to which the Ladies were invited, at the Rougement Hotel, Exeter, on Tuesday, February 22nd, 1944.

The Mess President, Captain S. W. Down, was responsible for all the arrangements and there is no doubt that it was due to his untiring efforts that the evening was such a complete success.

The Battalion was honoured by having a number of distinguished guests, amongst them being Sir Robert Greig, former Chairman of the Scottish Board of Agriculture, Lieut.-General E. A. Osborne, C.B., D.S.O., Brig. R. J. P. Wyatt, M.C., T.D., and others.

Officers of the Battalion had felt for a long time that they should show some appreciation of the help which they had received from their wives during the four years that the Home Guard had been in existence and all those present did their best to see that the ladies enjoyed themselves.

Brig. Wyatt proposed the toast of the Battalion, during which he not only said some complimentary things about the Battalion and the Home Guard, but also told the story of the old Sergeant-Major, proudly wearing the South African War ribbons, who gave his age as 45 when enrolling in the Home Guard.

Another story was against the Home Guard. The speaker whilst on an Exercise tackled an N.C.O. on a certain course of action which should have been taken and asked him what line he was going to pursue. The N.C.O. replied that he thought about making himself a cup of tea.

He complimented the Battalion on its efficiency.

Col. Wiltsher stressed, in his reply, the fact that the work which the Home Guard had done during the Blitz on Exeter, was not as widely appreciated as it might have been but he assured everyone present that the whole Battalion was prepared and ready to do any job which might come along.

He thanked the guests for joining us, with a particular word of thanks to the ladies.

Sir Robert Greig, made a very interesting speech, praising the Home Guard for what they had done. He informed the company that he himself had enrolled by concealing his age, and that he had, because of that and pressure of work, resigned from the Home Guard every year but still remained. He recalled the time when he was deputed to carry out a certain task of authority and when he explained the difficulty for a private to do the job he was given three stripes.

General E. A. Osborne in a very short speech commended the Battalion for the spirit which permeated their duties.

Lieut. A. M. Hichisson, Intelligence Officer, gave a toast to The Ladies, which was replied to by Mrs. M. C. B. Hoare. There were musical interludes, and when the evening broke up, there were expressions of satisfaction from everyone.

On Wednesday, February 23rd, the General Officer Commanding A.A. Southern Command met the Commanding Officer and Major Panes at "E" Company H.Q. where he talked to the Officers of this Company.

Training Films were again shown to the Battalion at the Odeon Cinema.

On February 25th we were honoured by a visit from Col. Amory, D.S.O. who gave us an interesting and instructive lecture on his experiences in the Middle East where he won his D.S.O. He told us many things about the peculiarities of the Hun, and his visit, which was arranged by General Osborne, was much appreciated.

On Sunday, February 26th, 1944, the Battalion paraded by companies and marched to the Odeon Cinema, where films of training interest to the Home Guard were shown. This was not our first experience of training films but it was the kind of training which was always enjoyed.

MARCH, 1944

On Sunday, March 5th, 1944, the Battalion paraded in St. James' Football Ground, and then set off on a route march of approximately five miles, before starting the Battalion Commaander, Lieut.-Col. H. J. Wiltsher, presented a certificate to Cpl. A. H. Hopkins of "A" Company, who had been commended for brave conduct whilst on duty at Battalion Headquarters during the Blitz of May 4th/5th, 1942. This was a special recommendation, and entitled Hopkins to wear the Oak Leaf Emblem.

After this ceremony the Commanding Officer marched the Battalion off by way of Blackall Road, New North Road, Cowley Road, Cowley Bridge, and then along the Tiverton Road, turning into Stoke Woods where a halt was made for food. During the march out, an opportunity was taken to give all ranks some experience in marching with their respirators on.

Early in the morning all Company Messing N.C.O.s and cooks, under the command of the Battalion Messing Officer, Lieut. C. H. Spiller, had proceeded to Stoke Woods, where fires were built and the food cooked under active service conditions. The excellent meal, served up to the men, was thoroughly enjoyed. The march home was by way of Pennsylvania, Rosebarn Avenue, past the Triangle, Old Tiverton Road where the Commanding Officer took the Salute. The Companies then marched off independently under the command of the Company Commanders.

There was a general call for more route marches but, unfortunately, time would not permit, owing to so many commitments for special training.

Battalion Orders No. 11, dated March 15th, published the special recommendation for brave conduct to Cpl. A. H. Hopkins of "A" Company.

Up to the 8th March, 1944, "C" Company alone had collected £40 for the Red Cross Penny-A-Week Fund. This Company deserves a special commendation for this wonderful effort.

The Commanding Officer now decided that all Companies should spend one Sunday on a Manning Exercise. This involved turning out the whole Company as on "Action Stations," and included, in addition to the manning of the Defended Homes as in "Plan B," the transference of all stores from the normal Company H.Q. to Battle H.Q., and of all ammunition from the peace time dumps to battle dumps, including issuing such ammunition down to Platoons. Casualties were detailed and dealt with in accordance with the arrangements between the Home Guard, Civil Defence, and the hospital authorities. Casualties were transported by the Civil Defence to the main hospital after having received first aid. During this Exercise the Commanding Officer set the Companies and Platoons certain tasks without any preparation and as a test of reaction to sudden emergencies it proved highly successful. All the Exercises meant a tremendous amount of work but everybody realised the necessity for the action taken especially as it had never been done before. They brought to the notice of the Company and Platoon Commanders certain weaknesses, in Company or Battalion organisation and particularly in regard to transport. These were put right.

"D" Company, were the first on the list for this manning exercise, and theirs took place on Sunday, March 12th. This Company, forming the Mobile Reserves, were given various tasks outside the "B Plan" area, which gave them practice in em-bussing and de-bussing and taking up defended positions in strange country.

On Tuesday, March 14th, all the Battalion Staff Officers took part in Battle Inoculation at Digby's Quarry.

"A" Company's Manning Exercise took place on Sunday, March 19th, 1944.

On March 21st, Lieut.-Col. H. J. Wilsher gave a talk to Exeter Rotarians at their luncheon, and, after giving his listeners a brief history of the formation of the L.D.V., assured them that they could depend on the Battalion to do what was necessary in the event of any trouble breaking out.

APRIL, 1944

During the beginning of April, a special check was made on security. Officers were reminded that they must, at all times, carry their A.F.B. 2606, and all ranks their National Registration Identity Cards.

The Manning Exercise for "C" Company and the University College of the South West Company took place on Sunday, March

26th, and on the same day the Commanding Officer arranged an exercise for the Battalion Intelligence Section and the Signals Platoon.

From Tuesday, March 28th, until Sunday, April 2nd, this Battalion was visited by the Travelling Wing sent down by Southern Command. Certain personnel from the Battalion were detailed to form classes for this instruction, which was very beneficial to the Battalion, as it included street fighting and house-to-house clearing. Those taking part returned to their Companies, and passed on what they had been taught to the other members of the Company.

"B" Company's Manning Exercise took place on Sunday, April 2nd, and during this week they took the opportunity of carrying out night exercises. "B" Company were put through Battle Innoculation at Digby's Quarry under the Adjutant and his Training Staff on the night of Wednesday, April 12th.

The Manning Exercise for the H.Q. Company was held at their Battle H.Q. and Defended Home, The Castle, Exeter, on Sunday, April 23rd. There was an excellent turn-out and the opportunity was taken to revise some of the Defence Positions which were not altogether satisfactory.

MAY, 1944

A serious message was received from the Commander, East Devon Sector Home Guard, General E. A. Osborne, C.B., D.S.O., and published in Battalion Orders No. 18, dated May 3rd, 1944, so that the message could be brought to the notice of all members of the Battalion, and it is well worthy of repetition in this record: —

"To Home Guardsmen of the 1st Battalion. Some of you are being, and more of you will be, called upon to carry out certain duties which are of real importance at the present time. To many, the performance of these duties will involve some degree of hardship and inconvenience. I am confident that, in spite of this, there will be no Home Guardsman in the Battalions of this Sector who will fail to parade for, and carry out, their tasks 100 per cent. There is no blinking the fact that any man who attempts to shirk any duty at this moment is failing his country, bringing discredit to his unit, and, what is far worse, is letting down his comrades and Allies who are fighting this battle."   E. A. OSBORNE,

Commander East Devon Sector, Home Guard.

Lieut.-Col. P. C. Bull, D.S.O., T.D., who was one of the Sector Training Officers, and the one interested in this Battalion, very kindly presented the Battalion with a solid silver tankard to be the prize for an Inter-Platoon Competition in the following subjects: —House Clearing, Patrols, Defended Areas. Col. Bull, had not only been a great friend to this Battalion, but had always been ready to help us in every way possible, and the writer of these notes would here express his sentiments of gratitude and appreciation.

The Competition was entered into in the most enthusiastic manner. Each Company first of all ran its own eliminating contests and the winning Platoons then conformed to the arrangements for the final, which were made by the Adjutant, Captain F. H. Dakyns.

Pontoon Bailey
Bridge

A pause
between
work

Box Girder
Bridge

Captain
C. R. M. Foot
The Company
Commander

SAPPER COMPANY

Bailey Bridge

Independent umpires were detailed to judge the final contest and one Platoon from each of "A," "B," "C" and "D" Companies took part.

The winners of the contest were No. 2 Platoon, "B" Company, with 100 marks out of a possible 120. This was undoubtedly a magnificent effort and the Platoon Commander, Lieut. E. R. Stanton, is to be complimented on the way in which he had trained his Platoon.

Unfortunately, on the day the Trophy was presented by Col. Bull, Lieut. Stanton was ill, and the Company Commander received the trophy for him. The conditions laid down by Col. Bull were that the trophy should be the personal property of the Platoon Commander of the winning Platoon, and Lieut. Stanton has something which will remind him of the time he spent in the Home Guard.

This record would not be complete without some reference to our associations with our Allies from America. By this time most of them have left the Country to carry out the task for which they had been training so hard, but during their stay, from those who were stationed in Exeter we received nothing but close friendship and help. Col. McGowan commanding a U.S. Cavalry Regiment and with him Lieut.-Col. Leigh and Lieut.-Col. Burke were stationed at Topsham Barracks for approximately two years and during that time we got to know each other very well. Certain articles required by the Battalion for training, were readily handed over and in return we were able to help in many ways. Our experts in Grenades, Lieut. Elwell and Sgt. Prout sectioned some of their grenades and shells much to their delight. The feeling by the Americans towards the Battalion was clearly shown one Sunday morning when three Sergeants from the Battalion paid a visit to Topsham Barracks and arrived on the Drill Square where Col. McGowan was about to take the salute of his Regiment in a march past, the Colonel seeing the three Home Guard Sergeants invited them to join him at the Saluting base. This kindly gesture was much appreciated not only by the Sergeants but also by the Battalion, who quite rightly considered it an honour. Col. McGowan and his Regiment left Exeter to complete their training at the Battle School from whence they proceeded to France on or about D-Day. They carried with them the good wishes of this Battalion. The next arrival was an Infantry Regiment Commanded by Col. Byrne, their stay in our midst was a short one but the Commanding Officer proved to be as co-operative as Col. McGowan and was always ready and willing to help us in every way. Capt. Taylor, U.S.N., stationed at Counters Weir, is another who has the problem of the friendship of the U.S.A. and the Bristish Isles in his mind and who is prepared to make the effort to foster the necessary good feeling. The writer has been honoured by being a guest at Capt. Taylor's Mess and fully appreciates his hospitality; they have all given the impression that they appreciate the value of and the work done by the Home Guard, and this Battalion appreciates the hand of friendship they extended to us.

On the 12th May, the "Exeter Express and Echo," published an article on the forthcoming celebrations of the fourth anniversary of the Home Guard, and, with apologies to the writer of that article, a part of it is repeated here as it so well expresses the spirit of this Battalion.

"The people of this ancient City are not unmindful of the duties and exertions which these men have been called upon to share since that far off day in 1940 when Mr. Eden signalled the call to arms. Britain's part-time army have given of their precious time in the fulfilment of duties and details, specialised tasks, unexpected demands, all in the main, with a grand spirit. You may be sure there have been grouses and grumbles—the Britisher has a trait that way—but you can equally depend upon it, that 'when a man's a-grumbling, he's a-getting on with the job' "

The G.O.C. Southern Command, Lt. Gen. W. D. Morgan, C.B., D.S.O., M.C., and the Commanding Officer, Lt. Col. H. J. Wiltsher, O.B.E.

CHAPTER IX

FOURTH ANNIVERSARY AND OPERATIONS—
"STAND DOWN"

MAY, 1944

14th May, 1944, was another hall mark in the record of this Battalion. It was the fourth anniversary of the formation of the Home Guard and arrangements were made by the Battalion to celebrate the occasion in the appropriate style. We were very highly honoured on this occasion by the presence of Lieut.-Gen. W. D. Morgan, C.B., D.S.O., M.C., G.O.C. Southern Command, who had kindly consented to be with us on this memorable occasion.

The Battalion paraded under the command of Lieut.-Col. H. J. Wiltsher on the Exeter School Ground at 10.00 hours and marched off headed by the Band of the Devonshire Regiment, and carrying the Flag which was presented by the City. Lieut. E. A .R. King was again the Flag Officer, and the Flag Sergeants were Sgt. E. L. Clarke of "E" Company, Sgt. C. T. Lane of "D" Company, and Sgt. L. Morgan of "B" Company. The route was via Magdalen Road, South Street and Broadgate to the Exeter Cathedral, where a special service was held. When General Morgan arrived he was met by Lieut.-Col. Wiltsher and General E. A. Osborne, and was duly escorted into the Cathedral.

We were also greatly honoured on this day by the presence of the Right Worshipful the Mayor of Exeter (R. Glave Saunders, Esq.), the Sheriff of Exeter (Alderman W. O. Wills), in their robes, and by other distinguished guests.

The Dean of Exeter, Dr. Carpenter, in his sermon said, amongst other things, that it could be claimed for the Home Guard that it had defended our island home against the enemy.

The Battalion Padre, the Rev. Preb. E. Reid, M.A. read the lesson and Lieut.-Col. H. J. Wiltsher read the King's special message to the Home Guard. This record would not be complete if the King's message was not repeated: —

The Home Guard Birthday message from The King, their Colonel-in-Chief, May 14th, 1944. "The fourth anniversary of the Home Guard falls in a year when the duties assigned to you have a very special importance. To the tasks which lie ahead the Home Guard will be enabled to make a full contribution. I know that your greatly improved efficiency, armament and leadership render you fit in every way for the discharge of these tasks. The burden of training and duty depending as it is on the needs of war, cannot fail to fall with greater weight on some than on others. To that great number of you who combine proficiency and enthusiasm in the Home Guard, with responsible work of national importance in civil life, I would send a special message of thanks and encouragement.

"To all of you I would like to express my appreciation of your past service, and my confidence that you will continue to carry on with the same spirit of patriotism that you have always shown, until the day of Victory."

After the service the Battalion paraded on the Palace Grounds, under the Command of Major W. H. Hoyt. The ground was used by us for this parade by the kind permission of the Lord Bishop of Exeter, and it can be stated here that the Bishop conferred a signal honour on the Battalion because this was the first and only time that an armed body had been allowed to parade in his grounds.

Lieut.-Col. H. J. Wiltsher had a very interesting and gratifying conversation with General Morgan whilst the Battalion was being paraded.

When the Battalion had formed up in mass with the Flag Party in the centre, the Commanding Officer escorted the G.O.C. Southern Command to the Palace Grounds, where the General, after having been introduced to the Second-in-Command and the Adjutant, inspected the Battalion and was introduced to the Company Commanders.

Col. Wiltsher escorted the General out of the Palace Grounds and then handed him over with his party to Lieut. A. Elwell, who escorted the General to the Saluting Base outside the Guildhall whilst the Commanding Officer rejoined the Battalion for the march past. The route taken was from the Palace into South Street, turning right into High Street, past the Guildhall.

After completing his Salute, Lieut.-Col. H. J. Wiltsher handed over the Battalion to Major W. H. Hoyt, and joined the General, the Mayor and the Sheriff on the saluting base. The salute was taken by both General Morgan and the Right Worshipful the Mayor of Exeter.

When the Battalion had passed London Inn Square, the Companies marched off independently and the Company Commanders joined the Commanding Officer in the Mayor's Parlour where they were again introduced to the G.O.C. Southern Command, Lieut.-Gen. W. D. Morgan, C.B., D.S.O., M.C. and were able to have a more intimate conversation with him. It was a very kindly thought on the part of the Mayor (Mr. R. Glave Saunders) to extend this invitation to the Senior Officers of the Battalion and it was very much appreciated.

Before leaving General Morgan expressed to the Commanding Officer his delight at the excellent and smart turn-out and complimented him on having an efficient Battalion.

This was followed up by a personal letter from General Morgan which is repeated here: —

"I was very glad to meet you and your Officers on Sunday, and for the opportunity of seeing the men of the 1st Battalion on the occasion of the fourth anniversary of the Home Guard. I was very much impressed with the good turn-out, smartness and bearing of the Battalion on Parade and during the march past. I was also very pleased to hear from you of the keenness in training and the support which you have received from all ranks over the past difficult years.

"I shall be grateful if you will convey this message together with my good wishes to your Battalion."

This letter was framed and hung in the Officers Mess as a tribute to all members of the Battalion who had so worthily earned praise from such high authority.

The Commanding Officer, on the 18th May, issued a Special Order of the Day to all ranks giving a copy of the letter.

The Gaumont British Newsreel Corporation, sent their newsreel cameraman to Exeter especially for the occasion and a full newsreel was taken. This film was shown in the news at the Gaumont British Cinema, Exeter, during the following week and was very much appreciated by all ranks. The newspaper reports stated that the film was enjoyed by packed houses who applauded the smart turn-out of Exeter's citizen army.

The first showing of the Film was attended by the Commanding Officer with many other Officers of the Battalion and the distinguished guests were Brig. R. J. P. Wyatt, General E. A. Osborne, His Worship the Mayor of Exeter (R. Glave Saunders, Esq.), The Lord Bishop of Exeter, the Sheriff and many others.

The actual film has been presented to the Commanding Officer by Lieut. Phillips, on behalf of the Gaumont British, at a meeting which was held at Bn. Headquarters during the early part of August. This is another record of the Battalion's work which will go down to posterity as the film will eventually be presented to the civic authorities for safe keeping.

This might be an appropriate time to record a period of operational duty carried out by the Battalion faithfully and zealously and, although no actual contact was made with the enemy, there is no doubt that great credit is due to all members of the Battalion for the efficient and zealous manner in which all orders were carried out and all duties performed.

The operations commenced on the 24th April, 1944, when an order was received that all vulnerable points were to be manned and inlying picquets established at Battalion and Company Headquarters. Every man was ordered to do 48 hours per month and as a consequence all training was cancelled for the time being except that training which could be carried out in conjunction with the operational duties.

The order was received with a certain amount of excitement.

No-one knew in the early days for what purpose these orders were issued but when D-Day came along it was fully realised and appreciated because it made the Home Guardsman feel that he was, in fact, a part of the tremendous operations which were being carried out under the command of General Montgomery. The Home Guardsman's job was not only to guard vulnerable points but also to safeguard the communications of the invading forces.

This Battalion was responsible for such vulnerable points as North Bridge, Staffords Bridge, Cowley Bridge, South Devon Bridge, and St. David's Station, and it was the practice of each Company to carry out these outlying picquets for one week and for the other Companies to supply the inlying picquets at their Headquarters. Each 24 hours a Company Commander was on duty remaining at Battn. Headquarters with a Staff Officer and the Orderly Officer from the early evening until midnight or after and it was part of the duty that either he or his Staff Officer visited all picquets.

The Signals Officer, Lieut. Bristow, arranged for land lines to be laid from all outlying picquets to Battalion Headquarters so that in the case of trouble, immediate contact could be made.

The average strength of each outlying picquet was one N.C.O. and five men, and the average strength of the inlying picquets was approximately one Officer and 30 O.Rs. All leave was cancelled and no excuses were taken for absence except illness on a doctor's certificate and it is to the credit of the Battalion that there were no absentees without reasonable excuse.

The picquets were eventually taken off on the 1st July and there was an expression of regret and in some cases disappointment, but it was felt by the higher authorities that the expected danger or perhaps counter thrust by the enemy had receded and that it was not fair to keep men on duty any longer than could possibly be helped, having regard to the fact that they had their daily work to carry out.

During the operations the Commanding Officer took the opportunity of moving the inlying picquets from one part of the City to another as reinforcements and in order to get them exercised in mobility.

JULY, 1944

July 2nd, 1944 was a red letter day for the Sapper Company. Brig. H. G. Pyne, M.C., C.R.E. Southern Command paid them a visit and after inspecting the Company watched them at work in all branches. The Company paraded under the Command of Capt. C. R. M. Frost, supported by Lieut. W. S. H. Hodges and Lieut. A. J. M. Hodges.

It was very unfortunate that it started to rain hard during the morning, this meant that the work had to be carried out under cover.

The Brigadier was not only delighted at all he saw but was surprised at the efficiency of the Company and he complimented them highly. In addition to the Officers, C.S.M. H. Prince was congratulated for his efficient and untiring work, the merits of which could be clearly seen during the demonstration.

On July 2nd, 1944, the Sector Commander, Lt.-Gen. E. A. Osborne, C.B., D.S.O., directed an Exercise which was called 'Exercise Otter,' and its main purpose was to test the task Companies of the 20th and 3rd Bns. Lt.-Col. W. H. Brooke, C.B.E., M.C. and Lt.-Col. H. J. Wiltsher were Assistant Directors and the Chief Umpire was Lt-Col. P. C. Bull, D.S.O., T.D. Officers of the 1st, 3rd and 20th Bns., not taking part in the Exercise, acted as Umpires. D (Mobile) Company of the 1st Battalion commanded by Major A. G. Fry, took up a defensive position near to Four Firs, Woodbury, and

Sapper Company—Brig. Pyne, M.C. inspecting Company

it was the task of the Companies from the 3rd and 20th Bns. to contact and destroy them.

Gen. Osborne in addition to being the Director also commanded the attacking Companies. Unfortunately it poured with rain throughout the whole of this Exercise but that did not deter all ranks taking part from showing every enthusiasm for the job which they had in hand and the exercise proved of great value to the two task units who were being tested, this being their first major exercise since their formation.

The Sector Commander stated quite frankly afterwards that all the troops performed very well and that although lessons were to be drawn from the Exercise, they had been noted and would be acted upon. The Exercise commenced at 10.45 hours and was completed at approximately 15.00 hours. No break was allowed for food, the exercise taking place as far as possible under 'active service' conditions, the men having to fight and feed at the same time.

It was very gratifying to see the spirit of the men when the Exercise was completed and they were ready to embus for home. They were wet through to the skin but very cheerful at having completed a good job of work.

Major Fry, commanding "D" Company, 1st Battalion had not forgotten to make arrangements for his men to be supplied with hot tea on the completion of the Exercise, and it would not be out of place in this record to compliment all the personnel of No. 4 Company on the magnificent spirit which they showed under trying conditions.

In Battalion Orders Dated 5th July, 1944, was published an extract from a supplement to the London Gazette on Friday, 2nd July, 1944, which read as follows: —

"The King has been graciously pleased on the occasion of the celebration of His Majesty's Birthday to approve the award of the British Empire Medal (Military Division) to Colour-Sergeant Walter Frederick Herbert Payne, Exeter Home Guard."

Colour-Sergeant Payne has already been mentioned in this record and had been serving as Quartermaster-Sergeant with "B" Company since July, 1941. He had seen service in three wars and was the proud possessor of many campaign medals, his first campaign being in South Africa. He was a great soldier and was popular with all ranks,, both on duty and on the sporting field and the good wishes of the Battalion went to him in the honour which he had been awarded.

The funeral service for Captain Pullen took place at the Countess Wear Church on Thursday, 13th July. Captain Pullen had been one of the original members of the Battalion, and was a Lieutenant in "A" Company until he was called up to join the Army. He was killed on active service and the funeral was attended by the Commanding Officer, Major L. G. Coles, his H.G. Company Commander, and other members of the Battalion.

Exeter City held their "Salute The Soldier" Week from July 8th to July 15th, 1944. Lieut.-Col. Wiltsher was invited to become a member of the Committee, which was under the Chairmanship of Alderman Vincent Thompson. Their target was £750,000 to equip and clothe five Battalions of the Devonshire Regiment and one Airborne Battalion. This Battalion threw themselves into the programme wholeheartedly. The week opened on Saturday, July 8th, with an impressive parade through the City of Exeter, by many units representing all Services. The Battalion supplied a contingent of 150, commanded by Major T. Greenslade, D.C.M., O.C. "C" Company, and Second-in-Command, Captain Curtis, 2 i/c "D" Company. The march was from Pinhoe Road, through Sidwell Street, past the Guildhall, where the Mayor and Lieut.-Gen. W. D. Morgan, C.B., D.S.O., M.C., took the Salute, and the march terminated at the County Ground, St. Thomas.

Prior to this, Lieut.-Col. H. J. Wiltsher had been invited to lunch with the Mayor and General Morgan, and other City dignitaries and members of the Committee at the Mayor's Parlour, and during the after-lunch speeches the Sheriff gave the toast of the Devonshire Regiment coupling it with the name of the 1st (Loyal City of Exeter) Battalion Devon Home Guard, to which Lieut.-Col. Wiltsher replied.

This record is only concerned with the items which were performed by the 1st Battalion and is naturally not a record of the whole week.

On the evening of Saturday, 8th July, the Battalion held a tournament at the St. Luke's College Playing Fields. The tournament had been arranged by the Second-in-Command, Major W. H. Hoyt, assisted by representatives from each of the Companies, and the public were invited to attend free of charge. The programme consisted of a cavalcade representing the Battalion from the early days of the L.D.V. to the present time. This was certainly a source of great interest to those present.

Our Sub-District Commander, Brig. R. J. P. Wyatt, was with us and made the opening speech. After that a demonstration of Arms Drill under the R.S.M. was given. The members of this parade were all volunteers and were from the various companies in the Battalion, and they gave what was undoubtedly a most magnificent demonstration of Arms Drill, first on the orders of the R.S.M. and secondly without any order at all. Every movement was carried out perfectly and they very rightly received congratulations from all sides including one, which was a very generous one, and that was from the Royal Marines.

Then followed Machine Guns in action by H.Q. Company, bridge building by the Sapper Company, and an attack on an enemy post by No. 1 Platoon "A" Company, supported by Sub-Artillery.

The defence consisted of members of "D" Company.

There was a surprise item which was very realistic. A number of booby traps had been arranged by Lieut. Elwell and Sgt. Prout. They were placed in various positions on the ground, under seats and under souvenirs, and three members of the Battalion representing British Tommies very realistically set them off showing to the public not only the danger of booby traps but also the danger of carelessness.

The 22nd (S.R.) Battalion Home Guard gave a display on their A.A. Guns and to finish up the programme the Royal Marines gave a gymnastic display.

Interposed with the various events, there was a Tug-of-War competition won by "A" Company. The "Salute the Soldier" Week committee had kindly given War Savings Certificates for the winners and War Savings Stamps for the runners up.

There were very good reports of this demonstration and the general opinion was that the Battalion had put up a very fine show, which was thoroughly enjoyed by everyone of the 4,000 people there.

Again we were favoured by the Band of the Devonshire Regiment who played selections throughout the whole demonstration.

We were also honoured by the presence of the Mayor, R. Glave Saunders, Esq., the Sheriff, Alderman W. H. Wills, Mr. A. C. Reed, M.P., the Chief Constable, and General E. A. Osborne, the Sector Commander.

The credit for this show goes to Major W. H. Hoyt, Lieut. A. Elwell, who acted as Marshall, Lieut. L. Rey, Organising Secretary, Captain and Adjutant, F. H. Daykns, who gave a lively and detailed commentary, together with all those other officers from the Companies who so kindly gave their help.

On Sunday, July 9th a Drumhead Service was held at the Cathedral at 15.00 hours. The 1st Battalion sent a contingent of Platoon strength under the command of Lieut. M. C. B. Hoare ("B" Company) Second-in-Command, Lieut. R. E. V. Harris ("A" Company).

The contingent formed up with the contingents of the other services in Bury Meadow and marched to the Cathedral via Queen Street and High Street. The Service was held outside the Cathedral and was conducted by the Bishop of Exeter, assisted by the Dean.

It had been left to Colonel Wiltsher to supply the programme for Wednesday, July 12th and he had arranged for the 102nd Infantry Regiment, United States Army, who were stationed at Topsham Barracks at that time, to supply the Indicator Parade in the morning to give a full Battalion Parade with their Divisional Band through the City in the afternoon, and a Band Concert in the evening. Also Col Byrne, the Commanding Officer, had promised to speak at the Indicator Parade in the morning. Unfortunately, however, at the last minute these people were ordered to move and the R.A.P.C. found the parade for the indicator, Lieut-Col. Wiltsher inspected the Parade, and made the speech from the indicator platform. The main point of his speech was that the citizens were being asked to contribute £750,000 to send their own troops to Berlin and no provision had been made for their return journey. He, therefore, asked that the amount should be made up to a million pounds, allowing £250,000 for the return journey.

On Friday, July 14th, the 1st Battalion (Loyal City of Exeter) Devon Home Guard supplied the troops for the ceremonial march to the Indicator Board, approximately Platoon strength, under the command of Lieut. T. E. Davey, "D" Company, Second-in-Command, Lieut. W. Kemp, "D" Company. The march was as usual from Bury Meadow, and the inspection was carried out by Lieut-General E. A. Osborne, C.B., D.S.O., Commander, East Devon Sector H.G. supported by Lieut.-Col. H. J. Wiltsher. General Osborne spoke from the platform and appealed for support for the War Savings.

Altogether the week was a successful one and the final figure was just over £900,000.

The members of the Battalion had done a fine job of work and they received many congratulations on the show which they had put up.

During July it was decided to hold a special Signals classification test to enable members of the Signals Platoon to be tested and examined by personnel from the Royal Corps of Signals. This Battalion was the first in the Sector and probably from a much larger area, to send their Signals personnel for this test. 16 were sent and 16 passed, and were then entitled to wear the Signals Crossed Flags. This was a great effort and a greater compliment to Lieut. W. V. Bristow who was not only the Signals Platoon Commander but also the Battalion Signals Staff Officer. It was the culminating point of the hard work which he had put into his job, he being responsible for the training of the Battalion Signals. I know he considers that these results amply repaid him for all his work.

The Sector Commander sent his congratulations on this most excellent result to Lieut- Bristow, including in those congratulations the Instructor and the candidates themselves.

The Commanding Officer, in passing on his own congratulations, expressed his appreciation of the fact that the Battalion was the first in the Sector to obtain Cross Flags on this classification test.

The Commanding Officer granted the Battalion a period of leave from training from Monday, August 7th to Sunday, August 13th, inclusive.

On the 30th July, 1944, the Battalion held an inter-company patrol competition to pick a patrol to represent the Battalion in a Sector inter-Battalion competition. The Machine Gun Platoon of H.Q. Company supplied the winning team and they had the honour of representing the Battalion in the East Devon Sector competition. Although unsuccessful in winning this inter-Battalion competition, their efforts were worthy of the occasion.

In June a handsome silver cup had been presented to the Commanding Officer by L/Cpl. F. J. Chudley, a member of H.Q. Company. This Cup was to be called the Chudley Cup (Efficiency) and was to be awarded monthly to the Company scoring the most points in proficiency and efficiency. The first winner which was for the month of July was "A" Company and they are to be congratulated.

AUGUST, 1944

On August 13th the Battalion Drill Squad gave a demonstration in arms drill to the Cadets at Honiton Camp and there is no doubt that the Cadets and all those present were very much impressed with the display.

Round about this time the Daily Press were probably anticipating official instructions, as it turned out quite prematurely. One paper or more would one day "Stand Down" the Home Guard, and another paper the next day would deny it. This was all very perturbing to the Home Guardsmen who were reading these notices in the paper and was certainly not conducive to help the organisation in any way.

On the 30th August an official letter was issued definitely stating that it was necessary that the Home Guard should continue to take the place of the Regular Forces until all dangers were past but suggested that this time might be near.

On August 14th, Lieut.-Col. H. J. Wiltsher paid an official visit to the Cadets in Camp at Honiton.

"A" Company spent a very enjoyable week-end at Honiton, commencing on August 23rd. They had borrowed an American Camp just behind the Town and on Saturday evening approximately 60 all ranks proceeded by train to Sidmouth Junction and then marched to Honiton, approximately 7 miles. The cooking was done by Company cooks and a very enjoyable Saturday evening was spent. On Sunday the Volunteers fired on the Honiton Range and after partaking of another well cooked meal they returned to Exeter by train in the early afternoon. The Parade was purely voluntary but if there had been another opportunity the number of Volunteers would undoubtedly have been much greater. Major L. G. Coles, the Company Commander, was with his Volunteers throughout the week-end, and undoubtedly felt very gratified that the Company had been able to put on such a good show.

The Blitz on Exeter in May, 1942 was good cause for the discontinuation of the inter-company Miniature Range Competition and owing to increased training it had been difficult to reinstitute this competition, but about this time Capt. F. W. Frost was instructed to make all the necessary arrangements for the competition to be re-started and the first shoot for the Hunter monthly Cup and the Company Commanders' Aggregate Cup took place on August 25th. The result was a win for "D" Company, who also took the aggregate cup.

Another source of encouragement to the Home Guardsmen was started by the inauguration of a special course of musketry which would enable Home Guardsmen to qualify for a marksman's badge, i.e., crossed guns. The course was undoubtedly a stiff one, for men who had no time to train from the physical point of view. The final phase was quite exhausting; the men had to advance 300 yards firing at targets at various intervals and finishing up by firing from the hip at close range. There were, however, many keen and enthusiastic members of the Battalion who were only too anxious to put into practice what they had learnt, and a number of the Battalion began to qualify week by week. The first two tests took place generally on the Prince of Wales Road Range but the remaining three tests were carried out either at Honiton, or on one of the other Ranges in close proximity to Exeter. Unfortunately, "Stand Down" Orders were received before all members desirous of going through the course could be given the opportunity.

The Chudley Efficiency Cup for August was again won by "A" Company.

SEPTEMBER, 1944

On Friday evening, September 1st, "D" and "E" Companies met at "D" Company's Headquarters in a Miniature Range and Darts

Match. The result is not important but good comradeship was most evident in the meeting of these two Companies and a very successful evening was enjoyed by all.

On Sunday, September 3rd, the Battalion marched to the Odeon Theatre by Companies, where another Battalion Church Parade was held. The Battalion Honorary Chaplain, Revd. E. Reid, conducted the Service and Brig. W. H. Brooke, C.B.E., M.C., accompanied by the Commanding Officer, took the Salute from the Odeon Cinema steps, when the Battalion marched past under the command of Major W. H. Hoyt, the Battalion Second-in-Command.

This Church Parade was held at the express wish of His Majesty The King, who had asked that the Day should be set aside by the whole country as a special Day of Prayer.

The Chudley Efficiency Cup for September was won by "A" Company.

On Wednesday, September 6th, the Right Hon. Sir James Grigg, K.C.B., K.C.S.I., M.P., Secretary of State for War, broadcast to the nation, that compulsory drills and training for the Home Guard should be discontinued, and that any operational duties still required for the Home Guard should be on a voluntary basis. These arrangements were to take effect as from Monday, September 11th, 1944. As a result of this, the Commanding Officer issued a Special Order that the Battalion would now only be expected to parade on the second and fourth Sundays of each month but that all Home Guard picquets were to be continued as usual.

The general feeling in the Battalion was one of surprise that any alteration could have been thought of before the war was over; it seemed to suggest a rather too optimistic view. Most Home Guardsmen would have liked to have remained in harness until the end of hostilities.

The Secretary of State for War, in his broadcast, thanked the Home Guard for what they had done and told them that perhaps soon even voluntary duties would be discontinued.

It was now decided that when "Stand Down" was ordered, all clothing and equipment would have to be withdrawn but later, an order stated that Home Guard volunteers would be allowed to retain their battle dress and boots and again later still it was directed that they would be allowed to retain certain other items such as greatcoats, etc.

A pamphlet entitled "Instructions for the Standing Down of the Home Guard" was issued so as to enable Commanding Officers and their Staffs to formulate a plan and to be ready to put it into operation when the order for "Stand Down" was given. Somewhere or other it was generally accepted that the final "Stand Down" parade would be round about the end of October although the order for "Stand Down" had not been issued. Arrangements were, in fact, in hand for the final parade of this Battalion to be held on that date but these were eventually cancelled.

There will be more of this on the appropriate date.

Another Challenge Cup which was allowed to become dormant as a result of the blitz was the Officers inter-company miniature

The Commanding Officer with the Batt. Staff Officers, R.S.M. and R.Q.M.S.

range competition. Each team was to consist of four officers. This re-organised shoot was fired off on October 13th and resulted in a win for Battalion Officers.

OCTOBER, 1944

It is with regret that a record now has to be made of the death of one of the Battalion's early enthusiastic members, Major H. Enefer, who died on October 18th, 1944. Enefer's service had already been referred to previously in this book, but too high a value cannot be set on the work so cheerfully and efficiently carried out by this Officer for the good of the Battalion and the Home Guard in general.

Major Enefer was buried at the Higher Cemetery and the funeral was attended by Lieut.-Col. H. J. Wiltsher, the 1st (Exeter) Bn. H.G., Lieut.-Col. F. Horobin, Commanding the M.T. Column, and many other Officers.

In Battalion Orders No. 42 dated 18th October, was published the fact that the Home Guard may be allowed to retain certain articles of clothing. This information had been published in the daily papers sometime previously and had led to a misunderstanding because some volunteers were under the impression that the clothing was to become their property at once. This had, therefore, to be put right in a Battalion order when the Home Guardsman's attention was drawn to the fact that clothing would not become his personal property until the disbandment of the Home Guard. This was a very necessary precaution because the possibility of a call-up in the future had always to be faced.

"A" Company retained possession of the Chudley Efficiency Cup.

H.Q. Company had arranged for their final Social to take place at Holloway Street Drill Hall on Saturday, October 21st. There was a very good gathering of members of the company and the entertainment provided by a concert party was thoroughly enjoyed by all. The Commanding Officer was present and spoke a few words to the assembly during which he thanked them for their loyalty and congratulated them on their efficiency.

Major E. N. Clulee, the Company Commander, complimented the members of the Company on the fact that although they were all specialists, they were able to hold their own with the field companies in all competitions. He thanked the company for their loyal support.

On Sunday, October 22nd, 1944, two photographs of interest to the Battlaion were taken. One was of all the Officers of the Battalion and the other was the Battalion Staff Officers. In addition to these photographs all the Companies had made their own arrangements for company photographs to be taken to form a very fitting record for the future.

On October 27th, 1944, Orders were issued by the Commanding Officer that "Stand Down" would commence on October 1st, and was to be completed by December 31st, and that the ceremonial Parade was fixed for Sunday, December 3rd. This order was received by most of the members of the Battalion with a great deal of disappointment. It was well-known and realised that the Home Guard would have to "Stand Down" sometime or other but even so that did not lessen the blow for those who had worked so hard and so loyally towards the efficiency and well-being of the Battalion.

The arrangements based on the instructions for the "Standing Down" of the Home Guard were now put into operation and most of the arms and equipment had been returned by the end of the year, together with all papers, pamphlets, etc., which were collected from Company Headquarters to be stored at Battalion Headquarters.

The members of the Battalion were reminded that they were only "Standing Down" and that they should hold themselves in readiness to report as quickly as possible should they be called up.

Friday, October 27th, was the date chosen by "C" Company for their final gathering and this took the form of a dance at the Drill Hall, Colleton Crescent. A most enjoyable evening was spent by all especially the ladies, and C.S.M. Westlake and his Committee are to be congratulated. Lieut-Col. Wiltsher, in a short speech, paid tribute to the mothers, wives and sweethearts of the members of the Company and also to the womenfolk of the Home Guardsmen, assuring them that when their menfolk said they were on Home Guard duty they were always telling the truth.

Major T. Greenslade, D.C.M. spoke very feelingly of the fact that this was their last social and that they were soon to be "Stood Down." He recorded the wonderful spirit which had always prevailed since the days of 1940 when he was with them in their country lane patrols in all weathers. Captain Samuels made an appeal for the Red Cross and the collection amounted to £7 3s. 6d. bringing the Company's total to over £70. A grand effort.

Early in October the Commanding Officer received a letter from the Dean of Exeter, Dr. S. Carpenter, inviting the Battalion to a service in the Cathedral in order to give the Dean and the Cathedral a chance of expressing, on behalf of the whole City, their sense of gratitude to the Home Guard for a long and faithful service. As a result of meeting between the Dean and the Commanding Officer a service was arranged for Sunday morning November 19th, 1944.

During this month all the Officers of the Battalion entered Miniature range shooting competition for a Trophy presented by Lieut. A. M. Hichisson. This was eventually won by Capt. S. W. Down, 2 i/c H.Q. Company with a total score of 176.

NOVEMBER, 1944

On November 11th the Commanding Officer, joined the Mayor, the Sheriff and Major W. L. Sparks, representing the Devonshire Regiment, at the brief memorial service at the City War Memorial Northernhay. Lieut.-Col. Wiltsher placed a wreath on the War Memorial as a token of remembrance from the 1st (Loyal City of Exeter) Bn. Devon Home Guard.

From there he accompanied the Mayor to the County Memorial in the Cathedral Close and then on to the Devonshire Regiment Chapel in the Cathedral, where a short service was conducted by the Dean, Dr. S. Carpenter.

At the invitation of the Mayor of Exeter, Mr. Vincent Thompson,

the Commanding Officer returned to the Mayor's Parlour, at the Guild-
hall, where he presented to the Mayor a photograph of the Battalion's
Flag which the Civic authorities had presented to the Battalion. This
photograph was taken by Mr. A. W. Walburn, F.R.P.S., of Topsham,
and a copy of it was not only on view at the Royal Photographic
Society exhibition in London, but was reproduced in "The Year's
Photography," the official publication of the Royal Photographic
Society.

Col. Wiltsher reminded the Mayor that the Flag which was the
City's gift to the Battalion was very highly prized and he hoped that
the photograph would form an interesting addition to Exeter's records.

The Mayor gratefully accepted the photograph and said the sacrifice and time which the Home Guard had given for the very necessary
purpose had not been always fittingly recognised by the War Office.
He hoped however, that they would remember that the country as a
whole appreciated what they had done. In due course the Mayor
hoped to see the Exeter Battalion's Flag in an honoured place in the
Guildhall.

On Sunday, November 19th, the Battalion paraded in Old Tiverton Road, under the command of Lieut.-Col. H. J. Wiltsher, to attend
the morning service at the Cathedral to which they had been invited
by the Dean. The march to the Cathedral was by way of Sidwell
Street, High Street and Broadgate to the Cathedral and the Battalion
was headed by the Band of the Royal Marines.

The Flag was carried by the Flag Officer, Lieut. E. A. R. King,
escorted by the three Colour-Sergeants.

The lesson was read by the Battalion Padre, the Rev. Preb. E.
Reid. The Dean based his sermon on two words from St. Matthew
—"Well done," and a part of the sermon might be repeated here as
it is a very appropriate description of Home Guardsmen: —

"We thought of the Home Guard with no less respect and
admiration but with a different kind of admiration, as of men somehow nearer to ourselves, giving hours of their time to the monotonous
work of being drilled, learning to use weapons and marching night after
night, facing the cold and the wet. There were the men we knew and
met in the morning. When we went into the bank, office or shop,
there they were—civilians, alert, cheerful, efficient, courageous, courteous. The Home Guard lived in a world not of ships or barracks,
but in their own parishes. There they were ready for whatever might
come. They were not actually called upon to fight, at least, on any
considerable scale. The enemy did not come. Why did the enemy not
come? Because the Home Guard were there."

The Dean also paid a tribute to the wives and ladies of the Home
Guardsmen.

The Battalion was honoured by the presence of the Mayor, the
Sheriff, Mr. A. C. Reed, M.P., Mr. J. Whiteside, the Clerk to the
Justices, Lieut.-General E. A. Osborne, C.B., D.S.O., Brig. R. J. P.
Wyatt, M.C., T.D., Col. F. W. Dewhurst, R.M., Brig. W. H. Brooke,
C.B.E., M.C., D.L., Lieut-Col. P. C. Bull, D.S.O., T.D., Lieut.-Col.
E. W. Booth, O.B.E., M.C.

The Salute was taken by the Mayor and Lieut-Col. H. J. Wiltsher at the site of the Lower Marker, Fore Street.

Also on November 19th, had been arranged a parade for the G.W.R. Home Guard, Southern Command, and other districts, at Weston-Super-Mare. This was to be a "Stand Down" ceremony. "E" (G.W.R.) Company were released by the Commanding Officer from the Cathedral Service in order to attend this Parade.

Major C. R. Panes, O.C. "E" Company had been greatly honoured by having been appointed Officer to command the Parade, which was approximately 2,000 strong, and after the Cathedral Service, Lieut-Col. H. J. Wiltsher, accompanied by the Adjutant, immediately proceeded to Weston-Super-Mare, to witness the Parade and the March Past.

The Final for the Officers' Individual Shoot for the John Bond Cup, presented by Lieut. A. M. Hichisson, was held at Battalion H.Q. on the evening of the 13th November. This Trophy was won by Captain Down, 2 i/c H.Q. Company, and he is to be congratulated on the excellent score which he put up.

On the 14th November, Col. Mulock, G.S.O.I., South-West District who had always been very helpful to the Battalion, called on the Commanding Officer to say goodbye. Col. Mulock was retiring to civilian life, and complimented the Battalion, during his conversation with the Commanding Officer, on its efficiency.

On the 16th November, the Commanding Officer was honoured by an invitation from Major-General Campbell, through Col. F. W. Dewhurst, Commander of the Marines at Exton, to attend a Marine Officers' Dance at Exmouth. Col. F. W. Dewhurst, R.M., had had many close connections with the Commanding Officer, and the Battalion, in his capacity as Fortress Commander.

On the 17th November, Brig. R. J. P. Wyatt called at Battalion Headquarters to say goodbye to the Commanding Officer. Brig. Wyatt had been for some time the Devon Sub-District Commander and this Battalion came under his command we owe to him a debt of gratitude for his help and consideration during the close association. Brig. Wyatt complimented the Battalion on its efficiency.

Some months previously to November there had been a great desire amongst the Battalion for the Darts Competition to be re-opened, the competition having been allowed to lapse after the blitz. The Battalion had, in the old days, been presented with a most handsome Darts Trophy called the "Templeman Cup," by Major T. J. W. Templeman, and Capt. C. R. M. Frost now presented another silver cup to be called the "Frost Cup." The "Templeman Cup" was for a knockout competition and the "Frost" Cup was now allocated for a league competition.

Lieut. Phillips of No. 4 Company agreed to arrange both of these competitions and the result was that every Wednesday the Company teams met at the Drill Hall, Colleton Crescent, when the league and knock-out games were played.

The finals took place on Wednesday, November 8th, 1944 and the "Templeman Cup" was won by "C" Company, and the "Frost

Cup" by "E" Company. Lieut-Col. H. J. Wiltsher presented the C. R. M. Frost Cup in the absence of the donor, and Major T. J. W. Templeman presented the "Templeman Cup."

Both the Colonel and Major Templeman took the opportunity of thanking Lieut. Phillips and his assistants for the wonderful job which they had made of organising these two competitions and the players and supporters for their general support. A happy evening concluded with refreshments and some music.

In Battalion Orders No. 47 dated November 22nd was published a special message to all ranks from the Commanding Officer in which he thanked the members of the Battalion who paraded for the Special Cathedral Service on the 19th November and drew attention to the final parade on the 3rd December, especially inviting all families and friends of the Battalion to watch the parade and help to give the Battalion the reception which it so thoroughly deserved after 4½ years of hard work and ungrudging service.

The same Battalion Orders gave notice of the three men who had been chosen to represent the Battalion at the General Parade in London on December 3rd. These were:—P. H. Kendall, D.C.M. of "A" Company, A. L. White of "E" Company, and D. S. Redfern of "B" Company. They were congratulated by the Commanding Officer in having been selected for this honour, in Battalion Orders No. 48.

"E" Company's smoking Concert for members of the Company was held at the Recreation Hall, St. Thomas, on Friday, November 24th. Some good talent was provided and everybody thoroughly enjoyed themselves.

There were a number of speeches, the first being one by Mr. Worth, the District Traffic Superintendent of the G.W.R. He complimented all members of the Company on the wonderful spirit which had enabled them to not only carry on their civilian jobs as railway men, especially during the hard days both before and after "D" Day, but because they had also given up their spare time to make themselves efficient as Home Guardsmen.

The Commanding Officer, Lieut.-Col. H. J. Wiltsher, praised them for their efficiency, and thanked them for their loyalty to him and their Company Commander, Major Panes, and he expressed a wish that they would continue their wonderful spirit of comradeship after the War.

Major Panes expressed the thoughts of all when he said how sorry they all were that the Home Guard was finishing. He considered it an honour to have commanded them since the formation of the Company in 1940.

On Saturday, November 15th, 1944, "B" Company held a final social at their own Headquarters at which the Commanding Officer attended. Here again a very enjoyable evening was spent by all those present, but for some reason or other the organisers had decided that there were to be no speeches and the Commanding Officer did not, under the circumstances, have an opportunity of passing on his thanks to the Company, to which he was so much attached, having regard to the fact that he had been their first Company Commander. This was rectified after the Final Parade on the 3rd December when, after the Commanding Officer had dismissed the Battalion, "B" Company reformed, and at the request of the Company Commander, Major A. P. Young, M.C., Lieut.-Col. Wiltsher, spoke to the Company for a few minutes, during which he reminded them that through their efficiency he had been called to Battalion first as Second-in-Command and then to take command, that was a "B" Company honour. He went on to thank them for their loyalty and friendship which he hoped to retain always. Major Hoyt, the Second-in-Command of the Battalion also a late "B" Company Commander, said a few words of thanks to all ranks of the Company.

In Battalion Orders No. 48 dated November 29th was published the following letter received from the Commander, East Devon Sector: —

"As the majority of the final 'Stand Down' parades will be held on the 3rd December, there are many of these Parades which I shall not be able to attend. I want to thank all ranks of the Battalions in the Sector for their loyal support and efficiency. To put it in one sentence the Home Guard has done a wonderful job, and done it really well.

I hope most sincerely that the spirit of comradeship and service to country and unit which has been so marked in the Home Guard will continue in some form or the other in our towns and villages. After these $4\frac{1}{2}$ years of serving together you know how pleasant it is to belong to an organisation of men working together for an object of national importance. Try and hold together and do not revert to a mass of individuals. Further, you will become local organisations which will have a great influence for good in many things concerning the development for your own communities, and that of the nation as a whole.

For myself, these last two years of intimate connection with the Devon Home Guard is probably the last episode of my soldiering life. I shall always look back on my time with the Home Guard with particular pleasure, and remember the grand spirit which imbued all ranks serving under me during those years."

(*Signed*) E. A. OSBORNE, Colonel
Commander East Devon Sector Home Guard.

Also was published a special message to all ranks from the Commanding Officer, and this is repeated here: —

"Our final parade is now very near and I take this opportunity of recording in Battalion Orders my thanks to all members of the Battalion present and past for their loyal and devoted service to the Battalion and all its officers. I have been greatly honoured at having been in command of this Battalion and such a grand lot of fellows. You will stand down knowing that you have been a member of a Battalion which is second to none, that this is because of the tradition which you yourselves have built up over the last four and a half years. That tradition must not be allowed to disappear. The friendships which we have all made must not be allowed to be broken, and our sense of duty to the country must be kept alive. It will be needed in the difficult years of peace to come.

You have all practised self-sacrifice throughout the years of war, we must not lose what we have gained by that sacrifice, by ignoring the problems of peace, which are our problems. We have it in our hands to make the new world a world fit for heroes, some of whom have been members of this Battalion before joining the Forces. We have a duty to them, let us see that we carry it out.

There is always a possibility of a call up in the future, and I know that I can depend on all of you, should the call come, and that you will be ready to undertake any job of work with the same willingness which you have shown in the past. My last message to you is that whilst physically you will be inactive, your thoughts should be with those who are still carrying on the struggle in foreign parts. We would have wished to have continued to the end with them but greater minds have decided otherwise—we must, therefore, continue to do so in spirit.

Once again I say 'Thank You' for a job of work well and truly done. We were honoured by being allowed to wear the Badge of the Devonshire Regiment with its motto 'Semper Fidelis" (Ever Faithful); you accepted that trust and have upheld it, you will, I know, continue to uphold it."

DECEMBER, 1944

On Friday, December 1st, "D" Company held their final social, which took the form of a Dance at Battalion Headquarters.

There was a very good attendance of members of this Company with their wives and ladies, and the whole evening went off with a swing. Captain E. Curtis, Lieut. Phillips and the Committee are to be congratulated on their arrangements.

During the evening, the Commanding Officer spoke a few words to the assembly, congratulating the Home Guardsmen on their keenness and enthusiasm reminding them that although they had not been in operation, they had been chosen for an important role and that he was quite satisfied that they would have fulfilled that role if the opportunity had arisen.

Major A. G. Fry, the Company Commander, also spoke to his Company, expressing his thanks for their co-operation and loyalty to him and informed them that he had considered it an honour to have been in command of "D" Company.

The 3rd December, 1944, the day of the Battalion's Final Parade arrived wet and stormy, and right up to the last minute it was very doubtful whether those on parade were going to get wet or not. Fortunately, although it remained very windy the rain kept off until the parade was completed.

The Battalion paraded in full strength in Pinhoe Road with the head of the column at St. Mark's Church. At 10.30 hours sharp the Battalion marched off under the command of Lieut.-Col. H. J. Wiltsher. The route taken was Sidwell Street, High Street, Fore Street, Cowick Street, on into the County Ground, St. Thomas, where the Second-in-Command of the Battalion, Major W. H. Hoyt, took command, whilst the Commanding Officer proceeded to report to His Worship the Mayor

(Alderman Vincent Thompson), and the Sheriff (Alderman F. P. Cottey).

When the Battalion was in the ground the Commanding Officer escorted the Mayor to the Saluting Base for the march past, the Salute being taken by the Mayor, and Lieut.-Col. H. J. Wiltsher.

After the march past the Battalion formed up in three sides of a hollow square, with the Battalion Flag in the Centre.

A special invitation had been issued to ex-L.D.V. and H.G. members who paraded under Lieut. Ferguson, M.B.E., himself an ex-Home Guardsman, on the right of the square.

When the Battalion formed up the Commanding Officer read the message from His Majesty the King.

The Mayor then spoke to the Battalion conveying to them the thanks of the Citizens for the great service they had given since the inception of the L.D.V. He particularly mentioned the fact that the first Commanding Officer was his close friend and partner, the late Major A. Anstey.

He went on to point out that there was always an element of regret in the Standing Down of any military force, and that one could not but feel it that day, but as the value of the service you have rendered to the realm (continued the Mayor), and as to the greatness of the sacrifice you have made for your fellow citizens, there can be no question. It will be your proud privilege to remember to the end of your days that for four long years you and others like you, as free men and volunteers, have borne a full share of the defence of your Country. He reminded them that in the period that lay ahead it was for the country to buckle down to the hard and long task of restoring trade and especially that freedom which had so much to do with making them what they had been as Home Guardsmen of the City of Exeter.

Lieut.-Col. H. J. Wiltsher in his final speech to the Battalion, said the Parade marked the end of 4½ years of wonderful comradeship and that their thoughts must be both sad and proud. Sad, because it was the end of a wonderful period of service, and proud because they belonged to a Battalion that was second to none, and it was they who had made it so by their devotion to duty, by their loyalty to their officers and by the time and work they had given for the good of the country entirely unpaid.

He reminded them that the Battalion was held in high esteem by the Civic authorities, who had honoured them so greatly in May, 1943 by presenting them with the flag which was on parade that day.

Their memories went back to the dark days of 1940 when many of them on parade that day tramped the country lanes, kept observation in lonely spots and guarded vulnerable points during the hours of darkness—all this in their own clothes, with a stick, an old revolver or a shot gun as their only arms. They had made great sacrifices— sacrifices worthy of the men of the City of Exeter and of the Old Country. Now they could do nothing but look back on those days with satisfaction . . .

They had been honoured to wear the Badge of the County Regiment, the Devonshire Regiment; they could, with pride, say to that Regiment, "we have upheld its honour and its great tradition. The motto of the badge of the Devonshire Regiment and also of the City of Exeter was 'Semper Fidelis' (Ever Faithful); he complimented them on having honoured that trust and kept it untarnished.

The Commanding Officer drew their attention to the Devonshire Regiment Flag which was also flying in front of him. This emblem had been made in H.M. Dockyard at Malta in 1939 for the 2nd Battalion of the Devonshire Regiment, and was flown from the Battalion Headquarters all through the siege of Malta. It has been sent to Major W. L. Sparkes, O.C. Regimental Depot Party for safe keeping and he had loaned it to the Battalion for this occasion.

This was a link between the 1st (Exeter) Bn. H.G. and the Devonshire Regiment and it was appreciated that this flag, which commemorated the trials and hardships which the 2nd Battalion underwent in Malta during the dark days of the siege, was flying in this, the final parade.

Lieut.-Col. Wiltsher finished by thanking his personal staff, mentioning the Second-in-Command, Major W. H. Hoyt, the Adjutant, Captain F. H. Dakyns, the Quartermaster, Captain F. Davies, all the Company Commanders and everyone on parade for their great loyalty, efficiency and capacity for hard work.

He also thanked the Sector Commander, Lieut-General E. A. Osborne, for his great personal help and the Mayor and Corporation of the City of Exeter, for the great interest they had taken in the Battalion.

After these speeches, Lieut.-Col. Wiltsher presented certificates of Service to the following relatives or friends of personnel killed by enemy action whilst serving as members of the Battalion: —

Lieut. Phillips on behalf of Mrs. Burgess for SIDNEY HENRY BURGESS;

Mrs. Dale for HERBERT FRANCIS DALE;

Mrs. Dowling for JOHN WILLIAM DOWLING;

Miss Greenslade, Matron Dr. Barnado's Home, Exeter, for EDWIN HAROLD HUBBARD who spent his early days at the Home;

Mrs. Keith for HAROLD FREDERICK KEITH.

The Chaplain, the Rev. Preb. E. Reid, M.A., led short prayers and all present joined in singing the Hymn, "O God our Help in Ages Past."

The National Anthem was played by the Band after which the Commanding Officer gave the order to all ranks to remove headgear, and called "Three Cheers for H.M. The King."

The Officers "fell out" and the Commanding Officer dismissed the Battalion.

"A" Company's final social took place on Saturday, December 9th, at the Battalion Drill Hall. This took the form of a smoking concert, and there was an enthusiastic assembly. The talent was supplied by members of the Company and an enjoyable evening was spent.

The Commanding Officer took the opportunity of thanking the Company for their loyal support and complimented them on their efficiency.

Major L. G. Coles, the Company Commander also spoke to the Company, and expressed his thanks for the way in which they had co-operated with him from the very early days and he expressed a wish which had been expressed by others at different times that their wonderful spirit should not be allowed to die, but should be continued in the Old Comrades' Association, of which he was the Chairman.

Captain Bell, Second-in-Command of the Company proposed the health of the Company Commander and said "no finer gentleman could have commanded the Company."

"A" Company Officers, with the Company Commander, Major L. G. Coles, in the chair, held a successful Dinner at the Mocha Cafe, Cathedral Close on December 11th, at which there were many guests, including the Commanding Officer, Second-in-Command, the Adjutant, the Padre, and the Company Commanders. The organisers of this ight are to be congratulated on their most excellent arrangements.

There were many speeches in a light vein which contributed to the success of the evening.

On the 13th December the Officers' Mess held a Dance at the Battalion Headquarters to show their appreciation of the support given by their womenfolk during the last four years. Excellent music was provided and entertainment was supplied by Mr. Herbert Aldridge and Miss Alice Coty who journeyed especially from London to appear. Capt. E. Curtis, Mess President, proposed the toast of the ladies to which Mrs. Wiltsher replied.

Major L. G. Coles proposed "the City of Exeter," replied to by the Mayor.

The Sheriff, Mr. F. P. Cottey, gave a toast to the Battalion which was replied to by the Commanding Officer, Lieut.-Col. H. J. Wiltsher.

It was unfortunate that the weather was very foggy and this undoubtedly kept a number of people away. At the same time, however, a very good evening was enjoyed by approximately 150.

In the London Gazette dated Tuesday, December 12th, 1944, it was recorded that His Majesty the King had been graciously pleased to appoint the Commanding Officer, Lieut.-Col. H. J. Wiltsher to be an Officer of the Military Division of the Most Excellent Order of the British Empire.

The Regimental Sergeant-Major, F. Howe, got the Battalion W.Os. and Sergeants together in the Drill Hall at Battalion Headquarters on the evening of the 16th December for a final social.

Very excellent entertainment was supplied by the members of the Battalion and the result was an enjoyable evening.

At the beginning of the evening, the R.S.M., on behalf of all those present, congratulated the Commanding Officer on having been awarded the O.B.E. and, in a short speech later the Commanding Officer told the Sergeants that it was due to their keenness, loyalty and disregard of personal comfort which had been the means of making

Officers' Mess Dinner, 31st January, 1945

the Battalion the efficient force that it was, as a result of which the higher authorities had awarded this high honour to him.

He reminded them that the honour belonged to the Battalion and that he was the one selected to receive and wear it. He thanked all those present for the friendship which they had not only shown to him but to all others in the Battalion.

He reminded them that the Battalion had a good esprit de corps and he hoped the spirit and comradeship would be carried on in the Old Comrades' Association.

The health of the R.S.M., F. Howe was drunk with enthusiasm and there is no doubt that in spite of his efficiency and the fact that he was a sticker for discipline, he was most popular amongst all the N.C.Os.

From Wednesday the 6th December until Wednesday, 13th December, the Gaumont Cinema displayed in the News Item the film taken of the Battalion's Stand Down Parade and on Tuesday the 12th December, the Gaumont British extended an invitation to the Commanding Officer, Lieut.-Col. H. J. Wiltsher, the Second-in-Command, Major W. H. Hoyt, and other Officers of the Battalion and their wives to attend the Gaumont Cinema in the evening to see the film.

Also present at the invitation of the Gaumont British was the Mayoress, Mrs. Anstey, the Sheriff and the Deputy Mayor and others.

The Sappers decided to hold their final evening, a smoking concert, on Thursday, December 28th, 1944, at the Recreation Hall, St. Thomas, and again this resulted in an enjoyable evening.

The Commanding Officer, Lieut.-Col. H .J. Wiltsher, with the Second-in-Command, Major W. H. Hoyt, Major Greenslade, the Padre, the Adjutant and others were the guests of the evening.

After Lieut. Hodges had proposed the Toast of the Battalion the Commanding Officer replied by complimenting the Sappers on their efficiency which had been proved by the fact that Brigadier Pyne, C.R.E., Southern Command had visited them, watched them at their work, and had sent a very complimentary letter to Capt. Frost.

There was no doubt, said the Commanding Officer, that this was the only complete Sapper unit in the Home Guard in this country. The Battalion were proud to have such a unit in their ranks. He asked them to carry on in the Old Comrades' Association the same spirit of enthusiasm which they had displayed so excellently in the Home Guard.

Capt. Frost spoke to the assembly thanking them for all they had done and for their keenness, enthusiasm and loyalty, especially mentioning C.S.M. Prince. During the evening, Capt. Frost handed over Rifle and Sten Gun Trophies to Corporals Edwards and Ketell, and L/Cpl. James, and there was a special silver tankard presented to C.S.M. Prince for his untiring work.

The N.C.Os. and men presented Capt. Frost with a silver cigarette case and an illuminated brochure.

CONCLUSION

This brings us to the end of 1944 and the end of the last chapter. The 31st December was the final day for the Stand Down of the Home Guard. From that day onward all the members of the Home Guard were free from all duties and it is quite certain that many of them were disappointed and were going to miss their evenings out with their comrades.

From the last day of the year the Commanding Officer was to carry on on his own, with the Adjutant, Capt. F. H. Daykns, the Quartermaster, Capt. Davies, Lieut. L. Rey, and a storekeeper and typist and there was plenty to do in checking the arms and equipment which by this time, had been collected by the Battalion from the Companies.

All the arms and equipment were carefully laid out in Holloway Street Drill Hall by Companies, so that, in the event of a "Call up," the re-issue could be made without any confusion and in the least possible time.

In most of the "Stand Down" Orders, there is a suggestion of the possibility of a call-up, and the Commanding Officer therefore decided that all small arms and equipment, including Company stores, which had to be kept by Battalion, should be laid out in the Drill Hall, Holloway Street, in such a manner that it would be a simple matter for the members of each Company to file in and take up their kit without confusion. This task was carried out by Quartermaster Captain Davies with great efficiency, and it was a sight worth seeing. Captain Davies is to be complimented on this job of work, which was carried out and completed in the usual Davies manner, which is thoroughness.

On January 8th a letter was received at Headquarters detailing the Adjutant, Capt. F. H. Dakyns to report to a holding unit. Thus was another intimate link with the Battalion broken. Capt. Dakyns had served the Battalion as Adjutant most loyally since July, 1941 and the writer of this book would record his own feelings of gratitude for the way in which Capt. Dakyns discharged his duties as Adjutant and for the most loyal manner in which he had supported him since he had taken over command of the Battalion. Capt. Dakyns left the Battalion with the good wishes of everyone and with an expression of hope that he would be given another appointment well worthy of his efficiency and capabilities.

Previous to this Capt. Dakyns had been presented with a wallet from the Officers of the Battalion as a token of esteem and regard.

The Old Comrades' Association was now a live organisation, due to the untiring efforts of the Chairman, Major L. G. Coles, the Secretary, Lieut. L. Rey, the Treasurer, Cpl. E. Bale, and the Committee. The first Annual General Meeting had been held, during which Lieut. Col. H. J. Wiltsher was elected first President.

On January 26th, a large number of the Battalion Officers met at the Royal Clarence Hotel, for a Dinner, which had been arranged by a Committee, comprising Major W. H. Hoyt, Second-in-Command, Captain Curtis, Mess President, Lieut. G. M. Phillips, Vice-Mess President, Lieut. King and Lieut. Hodges.

We were greatly honoured by the presence of the G.O.C., Southern Command, Lieut.-General W. D. Morgan, C.B., D.S.O., M.C., the Sector Commander, Lieut.-General E. A. Osborne, C.B., D.S.O., Brigadier W. H. Brooke, C.B.E., M.C., D.L., Lieut.-Col. Spincer, O.B.E., T.D., R.A., Captain Taylor, U.S.N., Major B. N. Gibbs, the Army Commander's Personal Assistant, and Major W. L. Sparkes of the Devonshire Regiment. Colonel Booth, O.B.E., M.C., R.A.P.C., and Major Manson, M.C., were unable to accept their invitations owing to illness.

The evening was thoroughly enjoyed by all those present and there was a general feeling that, although the Home Guard had "Stood Down," and would in the near future be disbanded, there should be more such occasions. General Osborne very kindly proposed the toast of "The Battalion," coupling with it the name of the Commanding Officer, Lieut.-Colonel H. J. Wiltsher. He referred to that time when, in common with the citizens of Exeter, the Battalion was under fire, and when it had lost its Commanding Officer, and other members. He quite frankly stated that the Battalion had become first-class in every way, and had done its duty with conspicuous success.

The Battalion, said General Osborne, had two great characteristics namely, discipline and smartness, and it always rose to the occasion in a most efficient way. He went on to say that when he first took over the Sector he had the impression that the Senior Officers of the Battalion were Bolsheviks! Judging by the present war—"The Russians were then only 65 miles from Berlin"—it seemed that that was the type needed. He complimented the Battalion on the fact that it was found from the top to the bottom that the Officers always led and would not ask anyone to do anything they would not do themselves. He then made special reference to the Commanding Officer for whom, he said, he had always had great respect. He had found him to be an excellent Commanding Officer. He said that he could not put it more highly than to say how delighted he was when Lieut.-Col. Wiltsher was awarded the O.B.E., which was not only a tribute to himself, but an honour to the Battalion. He closed by saying that he hoped the Old Comrades' Association would retain the spirit of co-operation which had existed in the Battalion, pointing out that such a body would always be of value to the City, of which he knew all members of the Battalion were justly fond, and proud.

Colonel Wiltsher replied to the toast, by first of all thanking General Osborne for the way in which he had proposed it and for the very nice things he had said about the Battalion and himself personally. He drew the attention of all those present to the fact that such words, coming from an officer of the vast experience and high rank as General Osborne were indeed high praise. The Colonel went on to tell the Officers present that they were the ones responsible for the Battalion being worthy of such high praise and that because of the work which they had put into their jobs, he, as Commanding Officer, had been singled out for the receipt of the O.B.E. He commented on the loyalty and friendship of the officers of the Battalion and thanked them for the support which they had always given to Battalion H.Q. He drew attention to the fact that, during the long "Stand To" in April, 1944, which was before and during D-Day, he had given an order that every man should parade 48 hours monthly, and that he would accept no excuses for absence other than illness. Although the "Stand To" lasted approximately six to seven weeks, no man was reported for being absent. During the course of these remarks, the Commanding Officer mentioned the Old Comrades' Association. He asked them to continue the good work, pointing out that it would be just as important after the war, as it was during the war. "When they ceased to kill, they would have to commence to heal." He thanked General Osborne personally for the great help and advice which he had always given to him, and complimented the General on the way in which he had, on so many occasions, smoothed over the troubled waters. The Battalion was fortunate, he said, in having a Sector Commander of such rank and experience and, more important still, with so much common sense and consideration. The Commanding Officer also said a word of thanks to Brigadier Brooke who was the original Sector Commander, and reminded him of the time, in 1941, when he issued an order that the wiring of the Perimeter of Exeter was to be completed as quickly as possible because the Hun might arrive at any time, forgetting altogether that there were $14\frac{1}{2}$ miles to be wired.

Major Coles very ably proposed the toast of the guests, and, after having referred to General Morgan and Captain Taylor, who were to reply, he suggested that perhaps those of the guests who were not officially on the Toast List might like to say a few words when their turn came. Major Coles, who in addition to being "A" Company Commander, is the Chairman of the Old Comrades' Assoiacation, spoke very feelingly of that body, and drew attention to the good work which they hoped to do in the future, and stressed the facilities which were to be available in the near future. He went on to thank General Morgan for all the help the Battalion had received from the Regular Army.

General Morgan, in replying to the toast of "The Guests" said that he had the obvious and most pleasant duty of thanking the Commanding Officer and all those present for allowing him to come down to the party, and for the very pleasant evening, which had thoroughly enjoyed. He also commented on the delightful service which he had attended with the Battalion a short time before and when he took the salute at the march past afterwards. He congratulated Colonel Wiltsher on having been awarded the O.B.E., and said that he was glad that the Exeter Battalion should have been so recognised as they were deserving of it. General Morgan said he appreciated all the nice things which Major Coles had said about the help given by the Regular Army to the Battalion, and he knew that it had needed a lot of hard work and training to bring the Battalion to such a state of efficiency. They had read about the fanatical German resistance, but we have never had any fear of the result of any German attack since we knew that we were so well represented by such an efficient body as the Home Guard.

Captain Taylor, in a few brief remarks, laid emphasis on the importance of close co-operation between his own country, America, and this country. He felt that as long as America and Great Britain were friendly, there was not much fear of future wars, but, said Captain Taylor, this friendliness must arise from the citizens of the two countries.

The other guests in turn spoke a few words of thanks for a very jolly evening.

On February 3rd, at the Gaumont British Cinema, Exeter, W. J. Forsyth presented to the Commanding Officer the Film of the "Stand Down" parade. The Commanding Officer was supported by the Second-in-Command and the Company Commanders.

There is very little more to be said. Platoons here and there were still holding final social evenings but generally speaking the activities of the Battalion, except for Battalion Headquarters, were finished, and there were only two alternatives to come, one disbandment, and the other the possibility of a call-up. This latter, in view of the progress made by the Russians on the Eastern Front and by the Allied Armies on the Western Front, became more remote every day.

This is the record of the 1st (Loyal City of Exeter) Battalion Devon Home Guard, and I want to say, in conclusion, that every man who has served in the Battalion and conscientiously done his duty, has something to be proud of, something to look back upon. I have received letters from the Commanding Officers of active service Battalions, and without hesitation they all stress the point that they and their men fully realise that it is they who have all the glamour, but they know and admire the efficient hard work which has been caried out at home by the Home Guard.

I would repeat the words of one Commanding Officer of a Devon Battalion who was then serving in Holland: "We have every reason to be proud of you all, and I only hope that you will be able to transmit this realisation to your Officers and men, as I cannot help feeling that perhaps Home Guardsmen occasionally feel that their duties are not being sufficiently appreciated, either by the Fighting Forces, or by the general public, at home. I can assure you that with us this is very far from being the case."

SEMPER FIDELIS—(Ever Faithful)—I have one more word to say. On the evening of Friday, February 16th, 1945, the Old Comrades' Association building, 71, Holloway Street, Exeter, which had been kindly lent to us by the Devon Territorial Association, was officially opened by the Right Worshipful the Mayor of Exeter (Vincent Thompson, Esq., M.A.), accompanied by the Sheriff, F. P. Cottey, Esq., the Chief Constable, A. E. Rowsell, O.B.E., Lieut.-General E. A. Osborne, C.B., D.S.O., and many others. The progress of this Association will form another history in the years to come.

FINIS.

1940.
"STAND TO."

1942.
"STAND UP."

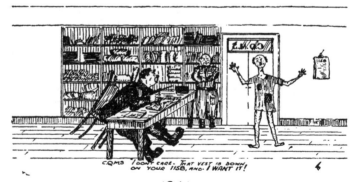

C.Q.M.S. "I DON'T CARE. THAT VEST IS DOWN ON YOUR 1158, AND I WANT IT!"

1944.
"STAND DOWN."

1st BATTALION (Loyal City of Exeter) DEVON HOME GUARD

OFFICERS SERVING WITH THE BATTALION AT "STAND DOWN," DECEMBER 3rd, 1944

Many of these joined the Home Guard in May, 1940. Many of them were Officers before commissions were granted.

Name	Appointment	Date of Home Guard Commission
BATTALION HEADQUARTERS STAFF		
Lieut.-Col. Herbert John Wiltsher, O.B.E.	Commanding Officer	1 2 41
Major William Handford Hoyt ...	Second-in-Command	1 2 41
Capt. Francis H. Dakyns	Capt. and Adjutant	7 7 41
Capt. H. F. Davies	Capt. & Q.M. ...	12 12 42
Major Thomas John Weenbridge Templeman	Liaison Officer ...	1 2 41
Major John N. Watson	M.O.	1 2 41
The Revd. Prebendary Edward Reid	Padre	15 5 41
Capt. Charles Albert Songhurst, M.M.	W.T.O.	1 2 41
Capt. Francis William Frost	M.G. Officer ...	1 2 41
Capt. Cecil Radford Marshall Frost	Liaison Sapper Offi.	14 7 42
Lieut. Wallace Victor Bristow ...	Signals Officer ...	1 6 42
Lieut. Rupert George Burvill ...	Gas Officer	12 4 41
Lieut. Henry Leslie Ellis	Ammunition Officer	26 11 42
Lieut. Arthur Elwell	Asst. W.T.O. ...	1 2 41
Lieut. Bryant Harding	Inst. W.T.O. Staff	1 2 41
Lieut. Alfred Montague Hichisson	I.O.	1 2 41
Lieut. Leonard Rey	Admin. Officer ...	1 6 43
Lieut. Benjamin Roberts	Press Liaison Officer	1 2 41
Lieut. Charles Henry Spiller ...	Messing Officer ...	25 1 43
Lieut. Cecil Alfred Thomas ...	Bombing Officer ...	26 11 42
Lieut. Donald Archer Thorne ...	Asst. Adjutant ...	14 7 42
2nd/Lieut. Charles Ernest Aguilar	Asst. I.O.	10 2 43
2nd/Lieut. William Thomas Kellaway	Second-in-Command Signals Platoon	24 5 44
Lieut. M. C. B. Hoare	Press Officer ...	1 4 42
"A" COMPANY		
Major Lionel Godfrey Coles ...	Coy. Commander ...	1 2 41
Capt. Richard William Bell ...	Second-in-Command	1 2 41
Lieut. George Beattie	Platoon Officer ...	12 4 43
Lieut. Allen Selwyn Exell	" " ...	1 7 41
Lieut. Ralph Edwin Valentine Harris	" " ...	2 9 42
Lieut. Alfred Samuel Bedford Johns	" " ...	1 2 41
Lieut. Ernest Arthur Reginald King	" " ...	1 2 41
Lieut. Daniel Wilder Lanceley ...	" " ...	1 2 41

Name	Appointment	Date of Home Guard Commission		
Lieut. William Thomas Roberts, M.C., T.D.	" " ...	1	2	41
Lieut. Francis Albert Thoday, T.D.	" " ...	1	2	41
2nd/Lieut. Harry Brentano Kilburn	" " ...	15	3	44
Lieut. Alfred Ernest Rogers ...	" " ...	4	2	43

"B" COMPANY

Major Alexander Paterson Young, M.C.	Coy. Commander ...	1	2	41
Capt. Leslie Charles Duncan ...	Second-in-Command	9	4	41
Lieut. Bertram Ayear	Platoon Officer ...	1	7	42
Lieut. Sydney Richard Berryman ...	" " ...	1	8	42
Lieut. Marcus Cecil Bradford Hoare	" " ...	1	4	42
Lieut. Stafford Harold Burt Isaac	" " ...	1	7	42
Lieut. Harry Scott Knight	" " ...	12	4	41
Lieut. Arthur Rainbird	" " ...	28	5	41
Lieut. Eustace Reginald Stanton ...	" " ...	22	10	41
Lieut. Donald Mayfield Wareham, M.C.	" " ...	1	4	42
Lieut. George Algar Williams ...	" " ...	1	12	41

"C" COMPANY

Major Tom Greenslade, D.C.M. ...	Coy. Commander ...	1	2	41
Capt. Julius Samuels	Second-in-Command	12	4	41
Lieut. Frederick James Allen ...	Platoon Officer ...	1	6	42
Lieut. Harry Bennett	" " ...	16	11	42
Lieut. Lawrence Wilmore Campion	" " ...	1	2	41
Lieut. Reginald Samuel Holland ...	" " ...	30	9	42
Lieut. William Hunt	" " ...	1	4	42
Lieut. Ernest Claude Loynes ...	" " ...	1	2	41
Lieut. William Northcott	" " ...	1	2	42
Lieut. Thomas Charles Powell ...	" " ...	1	2	42
Lieut. James Raphael	" " ...	1	2	41
Lieut. Jack Rushmere	" " ...	16	4	42
2nd/Lieut. Frank William Adams	" " ...	12	4	43
2nd/Lieut. Arthur Frederick Thompson	" " ...	12	4	43
2nd/Lieut. George Arthur Redvers Ward	" " ...	19	7	44

"D" COMPANY

Major Arthur George Fry	Coy. Commander ...	1	2	41
Capt. Ernest Curtis	2 i/c Coy	9	6	41
Lieut. Leonard Symons Brewer ...	Platoon Officer ...	12	11	42
Lieut. Jack Bleackley	" " ...	1	2	41
Lieut. Arthur Edmund Crouch, M.M.	" " ...	1	2	41

Name	Appointment	Date of Home Guard Commission
Lieut. Robert Dexter	„ „ ...	1 2 41
Lieut. Jeffrey Fletcher	„ „ ...	1 3 42
Lieut. Fred Hoare	„ „ ...	1 2 41
Lieut. Walter Kemp	„ „ ...	1 8 42
Lieut. H. Alban Peters	„ „ ...	1 2 41
Lieut. Geoffrey Moorhouse Phillips	„ „ ...	1 8 41

"E" COMPANY

Name	Appointment	Date of Home Guard Commission
Major Claud Panes	Coy. Commander ...	1 2 41
Major Basil Livingstone Macassey	Liaison Officer, G.W.R.-H.G. ...	4 8 43
Capt. Leonard Fred Nickels ...	Second-in-Command of Company ...	1 2 41
Lieut. Thomas Edgar Davey ...	Platoon Officer ...	1 2 41
Lieut. Archibald Thomas Drew ...	„ „ ...	1 9 41
Lieut. Albert Alexander Dunn ...	„ „ ...	21 2 44
Lt. Frederick Charles Morgan ...	„ „ ...	4 8 43
Lieut. George Joseph Page	„ „ ...	17 11 42
Lieut. Theodore George Vallance	„ „ ...	19 3 41
2nd/Lieut. Ernest William Clatworthy	„ „ ...	1 7 43

H.Q. COMPANY

Name	Appointment	Date of Home Guard Commission
Major Edward Neason Clulee ...	Coy. Commander ...	1 2 41
Capt. Sydney William Down ...	2 i/c Coy.	1 2 41
Lieut. Edward Henry Ralph Ezard	Platoon Officer ...	1 2 41
Lieut. George Henry Finn	„ „ ...	1 9 41
Lieut. Sydney James Forsyth ...	„ „ ...	12 4 41
Lieut. William Edward Henry Roy Howell	„ „ ...	17 11 42
Lieut. Allan James Harvey Hurst	„ „ ...	1 2 41
Lieut. Bernard W. J. H. Martin, D.S.O., M.C.	„ „ ...	1 10 41
Lieut. George Thomas Richards	„ „ ...	1 2 41
Lieut. Bevis Percival Turner ...	„ „ ...	1 2 41
2nd/Lieut. James Herbert Bilsborough	„ „	20 10 43
2nd/Lieut. John Andrew Blackbourne	„ „ ...	20 10 43
2nd/Lieut. Harry Stephen Hearn	„ „ ...	15 10 43
2nd/Lieut. Willie Messenger ...	„ „ ...	9 11 43
Lieut. Howard William Allen ...	M.O.	6 4 41

SAPPER COMPANY

Name	Appointment	Date of Home Guard Commission
Capt. Cecil Radford Marshall Frost	Coy. Commander ...	14 7 42
Lt. William Samuel Henry Hodges	Second-in-Command of Coy.	14 7 42
Lieut. Arthur John Marcus Hodges	Platoon Officer ...	14 12 42
Lieut. Reginald Thomas Johnson	„ „ ...	14 7 42

MINIATURE RANGE. .22 COMPETITION. INTER-COMPANY
TROPHY PRESENTED BY LIEUT.-COL. F. J. C. HUNTER

TO BE SHOT FOR MONTHLY

Date		Winners
1940 December		No. 3 Cov.
1941 January		H.Q. Coy.
February		No. 3 Coy.

TROPHY PRESENTED BY THE COMPANY COMMANDERS
FOR THE BEST MONTHLY AGGREGATE

HUNTER CUP		COMPANY COMMANDERS' CUP	
Date	Winners	Date	Winners
1941 March ...	No. 4 Coy.	March ...	No. 4 Coy.
April ...	No. 4 Coy.	April ...	No. 4 Coy.
May ...	H.Q. Coy.	May ...	No. 4 Coy.
June ...	H.Q. Coy.	June ...	H.Q. Coy.
July ...	H.Q. Coy.	July ...	H.Q. Coy.
August ...	No. 3 Coy.	August ...	H.Q. Coy.
Sept. ...	No. 4 Coy.	Sept. ...	No. 4 Coy.
Oct. ...	No. 4 Coy.	October ...	No. 4 Coy.
Nov. ...	No. 4 Coy.	Nov. ...	No. 4 Coy.
Dec. ...		No Competition.	
1942 Jan. ...	M.G. Coy.	January ...	M.G. Coy.
Feb. ...	No. 4 Coy.	February ...	No. 4 Coy.
March ...	No. 6 Coy.	March ...	No. 4 Coy.
April ...	M.G. Coy.	April ...	M.G. Coy.
May ...		No Competition.	

Owing to the "Blitz" on Exeter, the Competition was not re-started
until August, 1944.

1944 August ...	"D" Coy.	August ...	"D" Coy.
Sept. ...	"C" Coy.	Sept. ...	H.Q. Coy.
Oct. ...	"B" Coy.	October ...	H.Q. Coy.
Nov. ...	H.Q. Coy.	Nov. ...	H.Q. Coy.
Dec. ...	H.Q. Coy.	Dec. ...	H.Q. Coy.

1st BATTALION (Loyal City of Exeter) DEVON HOME GUARD

OFFICERS WHO WERE SERVING WITH THE BATTALION BUT LEFT PRIOR TO "STAND DOWN," DEC. 3rd, 1944

Name			Appointment	Date			Relinquished Reason
Anstey, A.	...	...	Bn. Cdr. ...	21	8	40	Death.
Dart, J. C. B.		...	Coy. Cdr.	11	9	40	Business reasons.
Paul, R. J.	...	...	Coy. Cdr	27	9	40	Joined R.A.F.
Upright, K. R.		...	Pln. Cdr. ...	4	10	40	Joined R.A.F.V.R.
Searle, W. H. L.	...	2 i/c Coy.	14	10	40	Own request.
Pullen, R.	...	...	Lt.			40	Joined Army, since Killed in Action.
Brigden, J.	...	...	Dep. Pln. Cdr. ...	8	1	41	Business reasons.
Sharland, W.		...	A/Dep. Pln. Cdr. ...	5	2	41	Own request.
Jones, A. E.	...	...	A/Pln Cdr.	3	2	41	Own request.
Kingsland, F.		...	A/Pln. Cdr.	5	3	41	Business reasons.
Row, R. (M.C.)	...	2 i/c Coy.	12	3	41	Joined Army.
Huntingford, C. W.	Pln. Cdr.	19	3	41	Own request.
Wonnacott, R.	...	2/Lt. ...	3	5	41	Joined Army.
Hillard, J.	...	...	Captain ...	17	5	41	Transferred.
Smith, F. W.	...	2/Lt. ...	19	9	41	Own request.
Beadon, J. A.	...	Lt.	30	6	41	Transferred.
Culley, J.	...	...	Q.M. ...	19	9	41	Own request.
Coverdale, H.	...	Adjutant ...	7	7	41	Own request.
Stoneman, G. D.	...	Lt.	4	10	41	Own request.
Comben, H. C.	...	2/Lt. ...	4	11	41	
Trafford, J. B.	...	Lt.	29	9	41	Own request.
Craig, F. D. ...	...	2/Lt. ...	15	9	41	Resigned.
Hill, G. T. R. (M.C., D.F.C.) ...	...	Lt.	15	8	41	Resigned.
Hubbard, F. T. P. ...	2/Lt. ...	8	11	41	Joined H.M. Forces.
Speller, C. E. K.	...	2/Lt. ...	25	11	41	Joined H.M. Forces.
Bullard, R. B.	...	Captain ...	5	2	42	Transferred.
Thacker, N. (M.C.)	Captain ...	26	1	42	Transferred.
Hunter, F. J. C.	...	Lt. Col. ...	5	5	42	Killed by Enemy Action.
Melhuish, C. H.	...	2/Lt. ...	3	2	42	Resigned.
Bolton, H. S.	...	Captain ...	27	5	42	Transferred.
Miller, C. H.	...	Lt.	1	7	42	Transferred.
King, E.	...	...	Lt.	14	6	42	Transferred.
Salter, A. G. ...	...	Lt.	22	5	42	
Vooght, G. H.	...	Captain ...	15	6	42	Age limit.
Johns, F.	...	...	Lt.	15	6	42	Age limit.
Pettitt, W. R.	...	Lt.	1	7	42	Transferred.
Faverman, A. G. (T.D.).	...	...	Captain ...		6	42	Death.
Hand, W. B. ...	...	2/Lt. ...	27	7	42	Transferred.

Name		Appointment Rank		Date			Relinquished Reason
Cherry, P. A. B. ...		Major	...	30	9	42	Transferred.
Fry, S. W.		Lt. ...	...	10	12	42	Transferred.
Enefer, H. M. ...		Major	...	1	9	42	Business reasons.
Tenby, H.		2/Lt.	...	20	5	42	Transferred.
Bawden, M.C. (T.D.)		Capt., Q.M.		21	11	42	Ill-health.
Beach, A.		2/Lt.	...	6	1	43	Transferred.
Turner, B. F. P. W.		Lt. ...	...	31	1	43	Transferred.
Marco, H.		Lt. ...	...	31	5	43	Transferred.
Western, H. J. (O.B.E., T.D.) ...		Lt.-Col.	...	30	5	43	Retired.
Bushop, J. P. ...		Lt. ...	...	15	4	43	Business reasons.
Rackwood Cocks, W.		Lt. ...	...	23	6	43	Ill-health.
Vaughan, H.		2/Lt.	...	1	9	43	Business reasons.
Maw, J. B.		Lt. ...	...	30	8	43	Transferred.
Wakeford, S. J. ...		Lt. ...	...	11	10	43	Transferred.
Woolcott, R.		Lt. ...	...	1	12	43	Transferred.
Horobin, E. F. ...		Major	...	16	2	44	Transferred.
Hodges, L. R. V. ...		Lt. ...	...	15	3	44	Transferred.
Peskett, H. N. ...		Lt. ...	...	1	3	44	Transferred.
Ferguson, H. J. (M.B.E.) ...		Lt. ...	...	12	3	44	Ill-health.
Plant, W. G. ...		Lt. ...	...	3	4	44	Joined R.M.
Roberts, S. F. ...		Major	...	1	2	44	Trans. to M.T. Coy.
Morgan, R. J. ...		Captain	...	1	2	44	Trans. to M.T. Coy.
Towell, W. R. ...		Lt. ...	...	1	2	44	Trans. to M.T. Coy.
Bridges, L. W. B. ...		Lt. ...	...	1	2	44	Trans. to M.T. Coy.
Herbert, F. J. ...		Lt. ...	...	1	2	44	Trans. to M.T. Coy.
Sanders, W. W. ...		2/Lt.	...	1	2	44	Trans. to M.T. Coy.
Burrow, A. ...		2/Lt.	...	1	2	44	Trans. to M.T. Coy.
Lambert, J. F. ...		2/Lt.	...	1	2	44	Trans. to M.T. Coy.
Flack, T. F. ...		Lt. ...	...	1	6	44	Ill-health.
Patterson, W. Y. ...		Lt. ...	...	13	9	44	Transferred.
Beddall, B. S. ...		2/Lt.	...	9	3	41	Joined H.M. Forces.
Turner, B. P. ...		Lt. ...	...	24	9	41	Transferred.
Sykes, L.		Lt. ...	...	6	9	44	Transferred.

Where the Officer left before commissions were granted his appointment only is shewn under the heading of "Rank."

Except for the above, the rank held by the Officer at time of leaving the Battalion is given.

1st BATTALION (Loyal City of Exeter) DEVON HOME GUARD
Members of the Battalion Killed by Enemy Action whilst Serving with the Battalion

Lieut.-Col. F. J. C. Hunter ...	...	...	...	5 5 42
C.Q.M.S. H. F. Keith	...	...	H.Q. Coy.	5 5 42
Pte. F. W. Draper ...	...	...	H.Q. Coy.	5 5 42
Pte. H. F. Dale	...	...	H.Q. Coy.	5 5 42
Pte. E. H. Hubbard ...	...	...	H.Q. Coy.	5 5 42
L/Cpl. H. R. Dimond	...	...	H.Q. Staff	5 5 42
Sgt. S. H. Burgess ...	...	...	4 Coy. ...	5 5 42
Pte. D. R. Hill ...	...	...	4 Coy. ...	5 5 42
Pte. D. H. Bird	...	...	6 Coy. ...	5 5 42
Pte. J. W. Dowling ...	...	...	Signals Platoon	30 12 42
Pln. Sgt. G. F. Vincent	...	...	3 Coy. ...	30 12 42

Members of the Battalion Wounded through Enemy Action whilst Serving in the Battalion

Pte. A. W. French ...	...	...	H.Q. Coy.	5 5 42
Pte. A. Welch ...	...	...	H.Q. Coy.	5 5 42
Pte. A. E. Farley	...	...	H.Q. Coy.	5 5 42

Number of Men who have joined H.M. Forces 811

Number of Men Killed on Active Service 8

Number of Men Wounded on Active Service .... Unknown

Number of Men Awarded Honours: —
  Home Guard ... 31.   H.M. Forces ... 2 M.C.s, 2 D.F.C.s

Approximate Number of Men through Battalion including present Strength 4,500

  Strength of Battalion at "Stand Down" 1,430

FINAL.—The above record regarding members of the Battalion who have joined H.M. Forces is very much incomplete, owing to the difficulty of obtaining information.

1st BATTALION (Loyal City of Exeter) DEVON HOME GUARD
HONOURS GAINED BY MEMBERS OF THE BATTALION

Officer of the Military Division of the Most Excellent Order of the British Empire

Lieut.-Colonel Herbert John Wiltsher ... December 15th, 1944

Member of the Military Division of the Most Excellent Order of the British Empire

Lieut. Henry John Ferguson ... ... June 9th, 1943

British Empire Medal (Military Division)
Colour-Sergeant William Frederick Herbert Payne, June 2nd, 1944

Commendation for Brave Conduct
Corporal Albert Henry Hopkins ... ... September 28th, 1943

Certificates for Good Service

R.S.M. F. J. Howe	February 11th, 1942
Lieut. H. J. Ferguson	January 20th, 1943
C.S.M. O. T. Dare	,, ,, ,,
Sergeant F. G. Prout	,, ,, ,,
Cpl. A. H. Hopkins	,, ,, ,,
Pte. A. R. Jerman	,, ,, ,,
Pte. W. Lang	,, ,, ,,
Pte. W. Stabb	,, ,, ,,
Pte. E. Q. Chick	,, ,, ,,
Lieut.-Col. J. W. Western, O.B.E., T.D. ...	June 9th, 1943
Colour-Sergeant W. F. H. Payne	,, ,, ,,
Sergeant J. Voaden, M.M.	,, ,, ,,
Captain J. Samuels	January 1st, 1944
Sergeant R. B. Newman	,, ,, ,,
Major W. H. Hoyt	June 8th, 1944
Sergeant W. H. Ellis	,, ,, ,,
Sergeant J. M. Jennings	January 12th, 1945
Sergeant F. Johns	,, ,, ,,
Sergeant W. Cummings	,, ,, ,,
Cpl. P. H. Kendall, D.C.M.	,, ,, ,,
Cpl. A. C. Price	,, ,, ,,
Sergeant R. C. Tonkin	,, ,, ,,
Sergeant A. H. Manley	,, ,, ,,
Sergeant E. L. Clarke	,, ,, ,,
Cpl. W. Hook	,, ,, ,,
Sergeant A. B. Mundy	,, ,, ,,
Sergeant F. A. Green	,, ,, ,,
L/Cpl. D. T. Dare	,, ,, ,,

NOMINAL ROLL OF BATTALION
AT "STAND DOWN" *Dec. 3rd, 1944*

BATTALION HEADQUARTERS STAFF

Aguilar, C. E.
Ash, W. R.
Berry, H. W.
Beer, V. S.
Bristow, W. V.
Burvill, R. G.
Bumstead, A. R.
Down, C. A.
Ellis, H. L.
Elwell, A.
Frost, F. W.
Gresswell, W. C. J.
Hart, E. L.
Hartvel, C. L. C. P.
Harding, B.
Heard, A. S.
Hewett, W. H.

Hichisson, A. M.
Hill, E. A.
Howe, F. J.
Hoyt, W. H.
Jennings, J. M.
Johns, H. E.
Manley, W.
Martin, J.
Martin, J. H.
Phillips, G.
Pike, G.
Porter, A.
Pritchard, B. T.
Rayner, S.
Reid, E.
  (Hon. Chaplain)
Rey, L.

Roberts, B.
Elswood-Row, J. A.
Setter, H. E. C.
Songhurst, C. A.,
  M.M.
Spiller, C. H.
Stoneham, J. A.
Templeman, T. J. W.
Thomas, C. A.
Thorne, D. A.
Watson, J.
Whiteside, J.
Wiltsher, H. J., O.B.E.

HELD SUPERNUMERARY TO ESTABLISHMENT

Brooke, W. H.,
  C.B.E., M.C., D.L.
Capel, E.
Oakley-Evans, N. H.,
  M.C.

Gliddon, L. C.
Goldsmith, H. D.,
  C.B.E., D.S.O., D.L.

Manson, E. P., M.C.
Pearce, R. H. C.
Theobald, L.

BATTALION SIGNALS

Adams, S. H.
Ballman, R. H.
Boucher, C. H.
Branch, G.
Buckfield, B. J.
Churchfield, F. C.
Challice, A. L. J.
Derges, H. G.
Dwyer, E.
Galt, E. D.

Grant, A. H.
Green, F. A.
Isaac, A. E. H.
Isaac, R. T.
Jordan, F. J.
Jordan, L. W.
Kellaway, W. T.
Lang, H. S.
Martin, H. J.
Padbury, I. R.

Palmer, J. C.
Potter, J. W.
Richards, A.
Ridewood, C. C.
Rosenburg, B.
Spencer, S. J.
Taylor, C.
Turner, W. H.
Wills, V. E.

"A" COMPANY

Aggett, P. J.
Allen, B.
Andrews, J. R.
Bainborough, N.
Baker, H.
Baker, W. G.
Bastin, A.
Bates, W. J.

Beavis, L. J. J.
Beattie, G.
Bell, R. W.
Beer, A. J.
Beer, A. W.
Beer, F. A.
Beer, L. M.
Belotti, P. F.

Bolton, G. W.
Boneham, H.
Boult, G. E.
Brett, A. H.
Brewer, J. C.
Brown, W. A.
Brown, W. G. H.
Browning, F. R. J.

Browse, H. M.
Cann, A. H.
Cappelaere, R.
Carter, L. J.
Cheeseworth, F. N.
Clements, F. W.
Councer, G. J.
Coombe, J. C.
Coles, L. G.
Coles, F. H.
Cobley, A. C.
Cracknell, J. S.
Cudmore, W. J.
Cullen, C. A.
Cummings, W.
Curtis, W. F.
Dare, E. P.
Dart, W. R.
Davis, T. O.
Densham, A. C.
Dobson, W. A.
Donnison, S. W.
Dominy, R.
Downing, S. J.
Duckham, F. W.
Dunn, A. F.
Dyke, E. G.
Ellis, W. B.
Elston, A. W.
Endicott, H. F. F.
Ewings, A. J.
Exell, A. S.
Finnimore, T. D.
Fodone, T. D.
Foxworthy, A. S.
Galt, E. J.
Gibson, T. F.
Gibson, E. W. K.
Gill, V. J.
Gill, H. W.
Ginger, L. S.
Glanville, R. C. S.
Glass, E.
Glass, J. K.
Gloyn, H. J. O.
Goodman, G. G.
Govier, F. L.
Grant, F. J.
Green, T.
Greenslade, S. J.

Gregory, H. C.
Guppy, F. W.
Hamilton, L. R.
Harris, R. E. V.
Harding, C. H.
Harris, W. H.
Harse, H. F.
Havill, S. C.
Haydon, K. W.
Hayes, J.
Hayward, B. R.
Higgs, S.
Hill, E. G.
Hill, E. N.
Hoare, R.
Hodge, W. D.
Hooper, H.
Hooper, H. E.
Hopkins, A. H.
Hoskin, C. R.
Howe, F.
Hudson, F. J.
Hulland, W. S.
Jackson, E. G.
Jarrett, F. C.
Jefferies, F. C.
Johns, A. S. B.
Johnson, J. A.
Jones, A. A.
Jones, H.
Keene, F. W.
Kendall, P. H.,
　　D.C.M.
Kennard, H. A.
Kilburn, H. B.
King, E. A. R.
Lamacraft, A.
Lanceley, D. W.
Long, R. B.
Luscombe, P. R.
Madge, K. R.
Mallaband, J. H.
Manley, F. J. H.
Manley, J. C.
Mardon, W. C.
Margrett, J. E.
Martin, A. M.
Martin, W. J.
Middleweek, E. L.
Millman, F. B.

Miller, A. W.
Milton, E. J.
Mitchell, A.
Moore, A. J.
Mogridge, J.
Moudy, D. L.
Mullett, S.
Murphy, P. J.
Northcott, W. H.
Page, S. J.
Parker, G. F.
Pearce, R. G.
Peardon, W. E.
Pearson, J. J.
Perry, J.
Perry, H. S.
Perryman, R. A. J.
Peters, F. J.
Pethybridge, W. G.
Pim, K. A.
Pooley, R. S.
Pratt, N. J.
Purnell, G. C.
Pyle, E. C.
Pyle, F. G.
Quaintance, S. J.
Radford, L. A.
Ridler, J.
Roberts, W. T.,
　　M.C., T.D.
Robson, R.
Rogers, A. E.
Row, L. A.
Russell, A. S.
Salmon, M. F.
Saunders, H. A. C.
Searle, F. G.
Serle, R. O.
Sherriff, E.
Sherwill, A. H.
Shobbrook, H.
Short, D.
Siddorn, R. J. C. K.
Sloman, A. R.
Smith, C. J.
Smith, F. N. C.
Smith, W. H. C.
Southward, W. H. C.
Sterrett, W. J.
Stevens, W. H.

131

Stone, J. E.
Stoneham, J.
Stoneham, W. S.
Sylvester, W. R. T.
Tarner, W. J.
Taylor, F. W. G.
Taylor, F. W.
Tett, J. C.
Thoday, F. A., T.D.
Thomas, D. I.
Thorn, F. C.
Tibby, F.
Tidball, F. D.

Tolman, L. C.
Tonkin, A. B.
Tonkin, F.
Tout, C. J.
Tucker, P.
Turner, W. H.
Twigg, J. B.
Vicary, A.
Voisey, C. A.
Vosper, T. C.
Waller, S.
Ware, T. J.
Ware, W. T. H.

Warwick, T. G.
Webber, W. A.
Wellington, F.
Williams, T. C.
Wilkinson-Bailey, W.
Wills, E. A.
Wilson, S.
Wilson, H. T.
Wise, E. G.
Woollacott, L.
Woodland, H. C.
Wyatt, T. W.

"B" COMPANY

Adams, A. J.
Adams, P. G.
Allen, F. L.
Allen, L.
Alwyn, F.
Andrew, H. H.
Ash, W. H.
Ashley, D. A.
Atkins, R. J.
Ayear, B.
Back, F. W.
Badcock, F. G.
Bagwell, W. G.
Baldwin, N. L.
Bayley, R. K.
Bealey, H. G. C.
Bending, W. J. R.
Berryman, S. R.
Blackmore, F. E.
Bleckley, C. A.
Bowden, A. E.
Bowles, S. J.
Boyland, W. H.
Bradford, S. T.
Bray, W.
Brimmell, M. W.
Broom, J. A.
Brown, S. E.
Brown, W. G.
Burrow, W. E.
Burwood, J.
Bussell, W.
Cairns, J. A.
Camble, F. T.
Camden, F. W.

Camfield, J. F.
Campbell, H. W.
Cann, A. J.
Canterbury, C. G.
Carmock, F.
Casley, R. S.
Casley, S.
Causley, S. G.
Challenger, R. A. H.
Challice, C. A.
Channing, G.
Chilcott, J. F.
Chislett, E. G.
Churchley, R. E.
Clark, S.
Clarke, C.
Clarke, L. W.
Clemett, L. A.
Climmer, L. G.
Clitherce, F.
Collard, F.
Collard, R.
Collett, G. F. G.
Colley, J. L. B.
Coombe, R. B.
Cornish, W.
Courtenay, L.
Cowley, H. W.
Creedy, A.
Cropp, L. C.
Cummings, A. M.
Dalley, A. F.
Davis, G.
Davis, W. J.
Dinham, P. A.

Edward, B.
Dumbleton, H. F.
Duncan, L. C.
Ebden, F. W.
Edwards, J. F.
Evans, E. G.
Fernham, R. J.
Flack, T. F.
Fulford, A. C.
Gardiner, A. E.
Garnsey, K. J.
Gage, C. P.
Gilbert, W. J.
Gillard, F. C.
Godfrey, J. C. H.
Goldsworthy, T. W.
Grant, F. W.
Gregory, H.
Hall, K. J.
Hancock, R. G.
Harding, E. O.
Harnell, C. H.
Harris, J. P.
Harrison, C. N.
Harrison, K. B.
Hayman, W.
Hember, J. H.
Hicks, D. S.
Hoare, M. C. B.
Hodge, J. H.
Hole, F. J. E.
Holland, W. H.
Hunns, C.
Hunt, K. W. N.
Hurford, H. W.

Husson, R. C.
Ireland, W. H.
Isaac, S. H. B.
Isaac, W. H.
Iversen, S.
Jerman, A. R.
Jones, A.
Jones, D. G.
Kemp, J. R.
King, J. C.
Knight, H. S.
Knott, S. J.
Laing, A. D.
Lang, W.
Larcombe, H. F.
Lemon, A. E.
Le Prevost, L. I.
Lethbridge, E. F.
Leythorn, H. J.
Lias, H. J.
Loosemore, C. H.
Mann, F. G.
Marley, R. W.
Marknell, L. S.
Masson, T.
McCarty, B.
McLelland, H.
Miller, E. V.
Miller, M. W.
Moore, L.
Morgan, L.
Morrish, A. W.
Morse, F. P.
Mulkerrens, S. F.
Murdoch, R. R.
Napper, H. J.
Neal, R. T.
Neale, G. L.
Norris, G.
Parker, A. L.

Parr, G. F. A.
Payne, W. F. H.,
    B.E.M.
Pearse, H.
Pongelly, A. J.
Pennington, E.
Perry, B. F.
Phillips, R. C.
Phillips, W.
Pincon, R.
Potter, J. E.
Pratt, S. J.
Price, A. C.
Pritchard, C. B.
Prout, F. C.
Pulling, R. H.
Rainbird, A.
Redfearn, D. S.
Read, A. T.
Row, R. E.
Richards, A.
Riley, W. H. E.
Robbans, J. A.
Roberts, C. H. G.
Ross, J. H.
Saunders, N. G.
Scunders, T. F.
Savidge, H. S.
Sayer, E. J.
Searle, A. N.
Shaxton, F. E.
Skinner, W. J.
Smith, L.
Sparey, A. J.
Stanton, E. R.
Stark, A.
Steele, J. R.
Steer, R. S. J.
Stonehouse, C. J.
Stoneham, E. A. R.

Stroud, R. J.
Swinford, W. G.
Sydenham, F. B.
Tapp, F. J.
Taylor, H. J.
Taylor, R. J.
Taylor, S. M.
Thompson, J. S.
Thorne, E.
Thorne, M.
Tonkin, R. C.
Toyne, A. C.
Trude, W.
Tyrell, H.
Uren, T. V .
Venn, W. D. G.
Walkey, D. G.
Way, E.
Wareham, D. M., M.C.
Webb, P.
Westcott, T. J.
White, S. G. S.
Whitfield, W. G.
Whitworth, A. V.
Wilkes, G. A.
Williams, G. A.
Williams, F. H.
Willis, F.
Wilson, B.
Woodbridge, H. F.
Woolway, W. R.
Worth, J. A.
Wride, C. P.
Wright, F. E.
Wright, W. A.
Wyld, F. G.
Yates, G. J.
Young, A. P., M.C.

"C" COMPANY

Adams, F. W.
Allen, F. J.
Alford, S. F.
Alcock, R.
Algar, F.
Andrews, A. L.
Ashford, L.
Back, R. J.

Baker, W. J.
Barrett, F. E.
Bates, L. K.
Bennett, H.
Bennellick, G.
Bennett, H. A. G.
Beer, W. E. T.
Bennett, S. O.

Best, F. J.
Bishop, E. C.
Blackmore, F.
Bond, L. W.
Bonner, E.
Boothby, R. C.
Bowden, F. L.
Braund, F. L.

Breading, L. A.
Brend, L. G.
Brewer, A. J.
Brewer, R. G.
Brewer, W. H.
Browne, J. H.
Browning, J.
Browning, R. D.
Browning, R. D.
Burden, W. C.
Burnett, N. J.
Byrne, J. A.
Byrnett, H. J. T.
Campion, W.
Cann, W. L.
Cann, W. T.
Cann, W. T. J.
Carew, D. R.
Carnell, C.
Carpenter, A. W.
Carr, F. W.
Casling, W. R.
Clapp, H. T.
Clatworthy, G. P.
Cleak, A. J.
Conibear, F. H.
Cook, A. T.
Collings, D. W.
Coombe, F.
Cooper, W.
Cowler, B. F.
Culler, J. E.
Curwood, F. H.
Dart, G. T.
Dart, W. G.
Davey, W. H.
Day, A.
Denning, R. S.
Dickins, S. S.
Dickins, A. J.
Dipstake, S. E.
Discombe, R. H.
Dockree, A. J.
Donnelly, T.
Drake, F. E. L.
Durant, F. G.
Edwards, A. G.
Elson, E. J.
Escott, F. H.
Escott, W.

Evans, J. S.
Eveleigh, A. G.
Eveleigh, E. E.
Ewings, W. T.
Farrell, L.
Ferris, A. F.
Follett, L. T.
Foster, F. W.
Frayne, C. S.
Fry, F. E.
Furdon, H.
Furzer, W. J.
Gardner, L. S.
Gay, A. G.
Geoghagen, S.
Grafton, D. J.
Gater, A. J.
Greenslade, T., D.C.M.
Greenslade, H. C.
Greenslade, J.
Gubbin, G. R.
Hall, A.
Hammett, F.
Hammond, H. F.
Hancock, J.
Harber, W.
Harris, F. J.
Hart, A. T.
Hartnell, E.
Hatton, A. C.
Haydon, H. C.
Haydon, T.
Hayman, J. R.
Hayward, P.
Hayler, G. W.
Hawkins, P. A.
Hellier, D. W.
Heyburn, L. E.
Higgins, F.
Hill, F. C.
Hillman, J.
Hillman, J. E.
Hitchcock, E. E.
Hitchcock, W.
Hoare, H.
Hodgeon, H.
Holder, G. W.
Hodgeon, J. P.
Holland, R. S.

Holland, A. S.
Hunt, P.
Hunt, P.
Hunt, W.
Hutchings, W. J.
Jago, P. E.
James, H. G.
Jarrett, W. W.
Jarvis, S. J.
Jerrett, R. H. T.
Jordan, O. E.
King, E. F.
King, G.
Kemp, E. A.
Kenyon, N.
Lake, L.
Leat, D. J.
Lee, R. S.
Lewis, J. P.
Liddon, L. J.
Loynes, E. C.
Luke, C. G.
Lyne, A. J.
McLaren, W.
Manley, A. H.
Maggs, W. C.
Mann, H. A.
Marsden, H. W.
Martin, T. S.
Mathews, E. A.
Mear, H.
Melhuish, R. J. A.
Menear, F.
Miller, A. H.
Mills, H. R. R.
Milton, R. A.
Moir, W. F.
Montgomery, D.
Morrish, F. G.
Morrish, R. W.
Mounstevens, F. J.
Murrin, W. W.
Newbury, C. C.
Newbury, R. C.
Newberry, R.
Newman, R. B.
Newcombe, G. J.
Newton, J. V.
Nicholls, T.
Norman, F. C.

Northcott, W.
Northcott, C. E.
Noton, G.
Oliver, J. P.
Pope, M. H.
Parr, F.
Parr, F.
Parson, F. C.
Pearce, A. H.
Pearce, W. H.
Pengilley, L. A.
Perkins, A. L.
Peters, P. R.
Pike, P. G.
Pike, W. R.
Pollard, F. W.
Potter, F.
Poulton, W.
Powell, T. C.
Powell, G. Y.
Prout, M. C.
Prowse, J. F.
Purnell, F. G.
Purrington, A. E.
Purrington, D. W.
Quinn, H. H.
Ranson, P. G.
Raphael, J.
Ridgeway, A. J.
Ridgeway, S. H.
Robins, L. W.
Rosser, A. C.
Rushmere, J.
Sage, F. J.
Samuels, J.
Sandle, W. C.

Sanford, H. E.
Sampson, H.
Scott, C. H.
Seabrook, K.
Seaward, F. C.
Setter, J. G. C.
Shear, R.
Sheppard, R. J.
Smerdon, S. J.
Shervington, E.
Short, S. L.
Simmons, J. H.
Slack, L. J.
Sloman, R. P. J.
Smith, L. C.
Snell, A. R.
Soper, L. R.
Soper, P.
Spicer, G. E.
Spray, R.
Squire, E. P.
Stabb, W.
Stephens, J.
Stevens, H. F.
Stokes, S. J. D.
Stokes, W. L.
Stone, E. J.
Streat, W. R. J.
Syers, W. C.
Tancock, R. W.
Tattersell, G.
Thomas, E. H.
Thomas, G. W.
Thompson, E. J.
Tobin, J. W.
Tooze, J. H.

Tozer, E.
Troke, P.
Troke, W.
Thompson, A. F.
Tucker, S. J.
Tuckett, C.
Vanstone, E.
Wadsworth, H.
Walkey, C. F.
Walroad, R. E.
Ward, G. A. R.
Warre, W. R.
Watkins, P. J.
Weeks, F. J.
Wellaway, F.
Wellaway, R. J.
Westlake, P. C.
White, C. W.
White, H.
White, R. F.
White, W.
Willey, R. M.
Williams, A. C.
Williams, P.
Willis, J. B.
Willmot, S. J.
Wills, F.
Wills, P. R.
Wilson, M. J.
Wiseman, W.
Woodley, A.
Woodward, F.
Worth, H.
Youldon, W.

"D" COMPANY

Adams, F. G. J.
Allen, W. H.
Badcock, E. G.
Bainborough, E. G.
Baldwin, A. T.
Berford, J.
Barnes, J.
Barnes, E.
Bellworthy, F. T. J.
Binns, G. C.
Bidgood, E. G.

Blanchford, R.
Bolt, J.
Bolt, J.
Bood, A. H.
Braddick, H. G.
Braunton, N. H.
Bower, L. S.
Brinicombe, F. A.
Bleackley, J.
Brown, E. S.
Brown, G. A.

Browning, C. J.
Bryant, R. J.
Cann, P. F.
Chalk, H. J.
Chugg, P. G.
Clare, E. T.
Cleave, R.
Cloughton, C.
Cole, C. S.
Cole, E. A.
Coles, F. S.

Coulman, W. T. L.
Connesley, T.
Corkhill, N.
Cox, C.
Crouch, A. E., M.M.
Curtis, E.
Dare, C. T.
Davis, D. H.
Davis, W. S.
Dexter, R.
Dumbleton, F.
Dyer, E. P.
Edwards, H. G.
Ferguson, R. G.
Fewings, A. W.
Fletcher, J.
Free, E. E.
Fry, A. G.
Gale, K. J.
Gale, R.
Gale, T. G.
Gallin, C.
Gibbs, R. A.
Gibbings, F. E.
Gifford, J. N.
Giles, W. N.
Glass, R. J.
Green, B. W.
Gribble, R. B.
Hammett, R. C.
Hammond, L. H.
Harding, F. G.
Harris, F. W. G.
Hawley, J.
Heal, G. F. R.
Hitchcock, W. H.
Hoare, F.
Hoddinott, R. B.
Hole, W. M.
Hockings, H. P.
Hooker, W. J.
Horwood, A. W.
Herford, T. H. A.
Hussey, B. H.
Hussey, J. G.
Ibbett, F. J.
Inglefield, S. E.
James, J. E.
Jeffery, F. C.

Johns, S.
Johns, W. G.
Johnson, B. R.
Jones, S. R.
Kemp, W.
Kenshole, J. J. H.
Laishley, M. F.
Lane, C. T.
Le Prevost, W. E.
Layman, L. J.
Liell, T.
Look, H. E.
Loney, K. W.
Lugg, E. G.
Mackrel, E.
Mallett, F. G.
Marles, G.
Masters, C.
Maunder, J.
Maunder, W.
McLary, W. M.
McRill, J.
Miller, H.
Mills, R. W. J.
Mitchell, L. E.
Morgridge, W. C.
Needs, E. C.
Nex, W. G.
Norman, H. W.
Northcott, W. R.
Oddy, A. E. D.
Ofield, W. W.
Pardey, J. H.
Pearce, G. A.
Pepper, E. E.
Portman, W.
Peters, H.
Peters, W.
Phillips, G.
Pidgeon, G. W.
Pincott, N. A.
Pike, W. H. G.
Podbury, W. O.
Powell, S. R.
Prowne, H. C.
Pugley, L. J.
Pym, D. A. J.
Radcliffe, D. W.
Radford, J. T.

Ritchie, F. W.
Roberts, E. W.
Robson, K. S.
Rogers, W. J.
Rowe, W. J.
Searle, L. J.
Seaward, W. H.
Sellick, W.
Shaw, W. H.
Short, L. J.
Sidlow, W.
Skelly, J. B.
Smith, F.
Smith, X. G.
Soper, L.
Stidston, T. H.
Stockham, L. S.
Streat, D. J.
Sweet, F. H.
Taylor, W. H.
Taylor, C.
Taylor, C. H.
Taylor, E. T.
Thayer, J.
Thorn, P. D.
Thyer, W. L.
Tilbrook, L. A.
Townsend, W. F.
Tredwin, L.
Tregale, G. W.
Tregale, K. J.
Tucker, C. W. J.
Tucker, F.
Vickery, J.
Voaden, J., M.M.
Walsh, G. G.
Ward, S. A.
Warran, S.
Wedlake, E. J.
Westlake, G. K.
Westcott Guido, V. W.
West, E. G.
Williams, T. V.
Winter, E. A.
Woolcott, B. G.
Woodward, D. E. H.
Woodward, S. C.

"E" (G.W.R.) COMPANY

Aspey, P. W.
Back, H.
Bearne, W. R.
Beer, L.
Beer, S. J.
Bear, S. W.
Bell, C. T. M.
Ball, O. C.
Bidgood, F.
Boobyer, A. C.
Bowden, P. A.
Bown, A. J.
Brooks, C. R.
Brown, D. J.
Brown, F. W.
Brown, E. L.
Buckley, A. J.
Bullay, A.
Butler, R. E.
Canham, D.
Cann, A. J.
Cape, S. A.
Cheney, A.
Churchward, T. G.
Clarke, E.
Clatworthy, E. W.
Connett, C. H.
Copp, G. W. T.
Cornelius, H. S.
Cornish, H. E. T.
Cornish, S. R.
Courtney, H. J.
Cox, G. F.
Crooker, H.
Crosse, A. H.
Crelley, S. R.
Curgenven, H. G.
Davey, T. E.
Davies, J. D.
Downing, R. H.
Drew, A. J.
Drew, A. A.
Drew, W.
Dunn, W. H.
Edworthy, F.
Elliott, F. W.
Evans, W. J.
Ewings, W. J.
Ewings, E. G.

Ewings, R. C.
Ewings, W. A.
Farmer, W.
Fear, H. E.
Guernsey, H. S.
Greenham, E. S.
Greenslade, F.
Greenslade, W. J.
Groves, F. D.
Guerin, E. W.
Hale, R. G.
Haly, S. H.
Hamilton, R.
Harman, W.
Harris, R. L.
Harris, W.
Hartnell, A.
Haydon, G. T.
Haydon, J. E.
Haydon, T. G.
Haydon, T. M.
Hellier, W. S.
Hill, M. W.
Hodder, W. J.
Hodges, G. R.
Hole, W.
Hollier, S. T.
Hook, W.
Hooper, D. J.
Hooper, H.
Hooper, J. D.
Howell, W. G.
Hunt, J.
Hunter, F. J.
Huxtable, C.
Johnston, H. J.
Jones, G. D.
Jordan, J. R.
Keys, W. H. P.
King, F. W.
King, P.
Lear, L. J.
Lewis, F. G.
Long, H. J.
McCassey, B. L.
Martin, J. L.
Marshall, W. A.
Matthews, F. N.
Mathews, H. A. H.

Maunder, J. A.
Mears, W. R.
Meredith, E.
Milton, J. S.
Montacute, M. G.
Morgan, F. C.
Mugford, S. S.
Neal, C. F.
Nickels, L. F.
Norman, C.
Oak, S. E.
Packham, F. J.
Page, G. J.
Panes, C. R.
Parkyan, A. H.
Perry, L. W.
Phillips, L. A.
Pike, J.
Pike, M. W.
Please, J. C.
Pope, E. H.
Poulton, F. T.
Powell, C. E. E.
Pullen, C. H. B.
Redcliffe, F.
Radford, H. L.
Reed, S. R.
Ricards, L. W.
Rice, L. R.
Ridgeway, W. H.
Robertson, W. H.
Rogers, W. A. J.
Salter, L. C.
Saxton, S. P.
Searle, E.
Shattock, H. E.
Shore, M. R.
Shute, W. E.
Simons, E. F.
Smart, H. S.
Smith, F. N.
Spratt, E.
Squire, A. F. J.
Summer, D. S.
Symonds, G. R.
Tape, J.
Taylor, L. G.
Totterdell, J. D.
Underhill, R. J.

Vallance, T. G.
Vercoe, H.
Vernon, T. H. A.
Vincent, R. T.
Warren, H. J.
Watts, F. E. W.

Westcott, W. J.
Western, C. W. J.
White, A. L.
Wills, W. A.
Wiltshire, F.
Wotton, R. H.

Wood, G. S.
Wyburn, T.
Wyke, W. J.
Yendall, A. W.

HEADQUARTERS COMPANY ADMINISTRATION

Allen, H. W.
Baker, J. H.
Bale, E. G.
Bartlett, C. J.
Broom, H. G.
Clulee, E. N.
Down, S. W.

Huxtable, A. F.
Leidlaw, J. A.
Lovell, W. L.
Mundy, A. B.
Needham, W. W.
Peach, C. A.
Page, V. R. C.

Powelsland, T. P.
Rind, J.
Russell, S. C.
Turner, B. P.
Wright, W. J.

HEADQUARTERS COMPANY — MACHINE GUN PLATOON

Andrews, T. E.
Battishill, F. A.
Bendle, F. J.
Boorne, A. H.
Cann, R. H.
Cudmore, F. H.
Currey, A. W. C.
Chudley, F. J.
Davey, W. J.
Dane, F. C. E.
Davey, A. C.
Ezard, E. H. R.
Gale, J. H.
Gratton, C. H. H.
Harris, C. S.

Hawkins, W. J.
Heard, B. H.
Hinchcliffe, H.
Harvey-Hurst.
Hurved, R. A. C.
Hutchins, R. A.
Jackson, J.
King, F.
Langdon, H. R.
Mardon, G. H.
Milton, F. H.
Panter, W. C.
Pearse, G. V.
Prouse, H.
Purchase, T. A.

Richards, G. T.
Rose, T. L.
Skinner, L. D.
Skinner, T. R.
Stocker, E. G.
Taylor, E. J. C.
Tavener, H. J.
Telling, R. C.
Till, R. J.
Tucker, G. H.
Walpole, K. R.
Whiteway, A. W.
Willey, W. D.
Wright, W. D.
Wright, F. M.

BATTALION TRANSPORT

Alford, W. B.
Arnold, A. E.
Blackbourne, J. A.
Cousins, W. H.
Cousins, L. J.
Courtney, E. G.
Chalk, T.
Edwards, H.
Edgar, E. E.
Eva, W. G.
Faulkner, A. G.

Fulford, T. R.
Goodman, C. V.
Hall, S. J.
Hamlyn, V. E.
Haymon, R. W.
Heale, F. G.
Hoskin, H. A.
Ingram, T. L.
Kiff, T. H.
Newcombe, W. H. J.
Powell, F. H.

Puttick, F. L.
Radford, A. S.
Rouse, E. G.
Rogers, E. J. R.
Southcott, L. G. W.
Willmott, P. H.
Wills, W. R.
Wheatley, E. P.
Wood, E. C.
Woodcock, S. W.

HEADQUARTERS COMPANY — PIONEERS

Bastin, H.
Bedford, C. E.
Bilsborough, J. H.
Bryant, H.
Browning, C. A. C.
Clifford, P. W.
Clarke, F. G.
Davies, C.
Davis, H.
Force, W. J.

Gifford, F. C.
Guppy, S. A.
Hole, E. E.
Hooper, H. E.
Howell, W. E. R.
Johnson, W. C.
Lazarus, P. F.
Johnson, A. J.
Long, E. D.
Lobb, R. A.

Maunder, R. W.
Murch, A. R.
Perry, M.
Perry, M.
Pitt, A. W.
Tomlin, F. C.
Tutton, H.
Twiggs, C. J.

HEADQUARTERS COMPANY — CLIFTON HILL RECORDS

Bentham, J. A.
Champion, C. W.
Cole, F.
Gardner, F. H.
Harris, F. J.

Heard, A.
Hooper, W. H.
James, W. D.
Pedlingham, S. E.
Setterfield, J. F.

Shute, F. J.
Syms, H. C.
Tout, W. J.

HEADQUARTERS COMPANY — SECTOR SIGNALS

Blythe, L.
Castling, R.
Clapp, S. J.
Cridland, R.
Davey, A. E. D.
De Lisle, L.
Flay, S.

Forsyth, S. J.
Harding, C. J.
Harding, W. P.
Hearn, H. S.
Hubert, H. B.
Luxon, G. M.
Powell, H. T.

Punsberry, R. G.
Riddett, S. A.
Steer, D. G.
Tout, W. W.
Whitton, G. W.
Wood, W. J.
Wood, B. F.

HEADQUARTERS COMPANY—SUB-ARTILLERY PLATOON

Bassett, S. H.
Binnie, W. D.
Blackmore, R. T.
Bovington, G. H.
Bonner, I. E.
Bradley, R. C.
Brown, F. J.
Chalmers, F. A.
Chandler, H. G.
Cockett, F. R.
Cowler, R.

Dennis, L.
Finn, G. H.
Glover, H. J.
Harris, R. T. G.
Heapd, H. E.
Hunter, J. R.
Jordan, S. N.
Manning, R. C.
Messenger, W.
Nash, S. C.
Salter, A. F.

Sharman, R. A.
Sharland, G.
Smith, R. E.
Symes, E. C. R.
Toy, F. G.
Tomkins, F. A.
Wells, E. W.
Youldon, S.
Wood, R. J.
Wilson, D.

SAPPER COMPANY

Alford, D.
Anniss, R. S.
Andrews, A.
Armstrong, J. A.
Atkins, P. J.
Atkins, W. C.
Barber, J. T. G.
Bainborough, W.

Bennett, J. D.
Bishop, G. E.
Boddy, K.
Browning, H. P.
Bray, W. R.
Cavill, H. J.
Charlesworth, G.
Clatworthy, A. J.

Clarke, W. F.
Cornish, W. J.
Cole, F. H. C.
Cole, P. J.
Cornish, A. H.
Cornish, R.
Cornish, A. G. M.
Davies, A. G.

Dare, D. T.	Johnson, R. G.	Prince, H.
Edwards, H. C.	Johnson, R. T.	Purrington, R. J.
Edwards, G. F.	James, J.	Radford, J.
Elstone, E.	James, L.	Reeves, G. P.
Ellis, W. H.	James, F. L.	Robbins, H. W.
Ewings, E. J.	Jarvis, L.	Robinson, A. A.
Ewings, F. R.	Kenneddy, J. T.	Rogers, F. R.
Ferris, G. C.	Kettell, W. E.	Rundle, E. J.
Frost, C. R.	Ketell, W. A. J.	Sane, J.
Frost, C. R. M.	Lippett, W. A.	Saunders, O.
Fry, C. W.	Luke, R. L.	Scott, M.
Foster, R. W.	Martin, W. J.	Scott, W. G.
Fursdon, S. J.	Maunder, B. V. H.	Shapley, A. W. C.
Gardiner, H. G.	Mills, L. S.	Sheppard, W. J.
Gidley, W.	Moore, R.	Simpson, F. R.
Gidley, E. G.	Moat, A. G.	Squire, A.
Gidley, A. W.	Moase, W. J.	Taylor, W. H. G.
Gingell, P.	Morris, W. C. G.	Taylor, F.
Giled, T. J.	Mudge, W. J.	Walkey, L.
Goss, H.	Mudge, J.	Watson, T. R.
Harvey, A. J.	Norman, H. J.	Watts, T. D.
Hayman, C. W. R.	Norman, W. G.	Wilins, R. E.
Harris, A. T.	Osborne, W. J.	Wilcox, F. S. P.
Heil, A. V.	Parr, H. F. J.	Wiseman, H. J.
Herd, W. G. C.	Parr, W.	Wood, G.
Hodges, A. J. M.	Pennington, E.	Wyatt, W.
Hodges, W. S. H.	Perry, A.	Wyatt, C. E.
Hoar, F. S.	Peters, F. J. H.	
Hucker, G. T.	Pope, L. E.	

WARRANT OFFICERS, SGTS. AND CPLS.
B.H.Q.

Howe, F. J. (R.S.M.), Warrant Officer (Class I).

Martin, J. (C.S.M.), Warrant Officer

Manley, W. (C.S.M.), Warrant Officer

Hewitt, W. H. (R.Q.M.S.)

Jennings, J. M. (Deputy R.Q.M.S.)

SGTS.

Ash, W. R.	Hart, E. L.	Porter, A.
Beer, V. S.	Hartvell, C. L. C. P.	Pritchard, B. T.
Gresswell, W. C. J.	Johns, F.	Rayner, S.

CPLS.

Down, C. A.	Jones, H. E.	Setter, H. E. C.

WARRANT OFFICERS, SGTS. AND CPLS.
"A" COY.

Jefferies, F. C. (C.S.M.), Warrant Officer

Cheeseworth, F. N. (C.Q.M.S.)

SGTS.

Baker, H.	Ellis, W. H.	Russell, A. F. S.
Cummings, W.	Jones, A. A.	Stoneham, W. S.
Coombe, J. C.	Lamacraft, A.	Serle, R. O.
Glass, T. K.	Manley, W. C.	Tett, J. C.
Green, T.	Marden, W. C.	Taylor, F. R.
Goodman, G. G.	Middleweek, E.	Tucker, P.
Higgs, S.	Pooley, S.	Twigg, J. B.
Elston, A. W.	Parker, G. F.	

CPLS.

Bolton, G. W.	Kendall, P. H.	Stoneham, J.
Davis, T. O.	(D.C.M.)	Tarner, W. J.
Govier, F. L.	Margretts, J. E.	Webber, A. W.
Galt, E. J.	Pratt, N. J.	Wellington, F.
Grant, F. J.	Peardon, W. E.	Ware, J. J.
Hopkins, H. H.	Searle, F. G. J.	
Keene, F. W.	Starrett, W. J.	

WARRANT OFFICERS, SGTS. AND CPLS.
"B" COY.

Camfield, J. F. (C.S.M.), Warrant Officer

Payne, W. F. H., B.E.M. (C.Q.M.S.)

SGTS.

Burrow, W. B.	Lias, H. J.	Sydenham, F. B.
Churchley, R. E.	Markwell, L. S.	Taylor, H. T.
Colley, J. L. B.	Morgan, L.	Tonkin, H. T.
Cornish, W.	Pengelly, A. J.	Westcott, J. J.
Dalley, E. F.	Perry, B. F.	Whitworth, A. V.
Dumbleton, H. F.	Prout, F. G.	Wilkes, G. A.
Harrison, K. E.	Saunders, T. F.	
Jones, A.	Shaxton, E. H.	

141

CPLS.

Ash, W. H.	Harding, E. D.	Reed, A. T.
Allen, F. L.	Harris, C. N.	Richards, A.
Andrews, H. H.	Lethbridge, E. F.	Robbens, J. A.
Cairns, J. A.	Masson, T.	Tapp, F. J.
Camden, F. W.	Morse, F. P.	Venn, W. P. G.
Casley, R. S.	Pinson, R.	Way, E.
Gardiner, A. E.	Pratt, S. J.	White, S. G. S.
Harrison, C. N.	Price, A. C.	Yates, G. J.

WARRANT OFFICERS, SGTS. AND CPLS.

"C" COY.

Westlake, P. C. (C.S.M.), Warrant Officer

Rosser, A. C. (C.Q.M.S.)

SGTS.

Greenslade, J.	Dipsdale, S. E.	Setter, J.
Newman, R. B.	Fry, F. E.	Smerdon, S. J.
Pollard, F. W.	Hart, A. T.	Squires, E. P.
Breading, L. A.	Hill, F. C.	Tobin, J.
Brewer, R. G.	Hitchcock, W.	Tooze, J.
Browning, R.	James, H. G.	Wadsworth, H.
Casling, W. R.	Kenyon, N.	
Culler, J. C.	Manley, A. H.	

CPLS.

Barrett, F.	Jarvis, S. J.	Tucker, S.
Brend, L. G.	King, E. F.	White, H.
Carpenter, A. W.	Oliver, J. P.	Willey, R.M.
Ferris, A. F.	Perkins, A. L.	Youldon, W.
Follett, L. T. H.	Pike, P. G.	
Gubbin, G. R.	Soper, L. R.	

WARRANT OFFICERS, SGTS. AND CPLS.

"D" COY.

Dare, O. D. (C.S.M.), Warrant Officer

Oddy, A. E. D. (C.Q.M.S.)

SGTS.

Baldwin, A. T.	Horwood, A. W.	Nothcott, W. R.
Bolt, J.	Lane, C. T.	Peters, W.
Cole, C. S.	Leyman	Voaden, J. (M.M.)
Dyer, E. P.	McRill, J.	Woodward, D. E. H.
Pree, E. E.	Maunder, W. R. M.	Woodward, S. C.

CPLS.

Adams, F. G. J.
Bainborough, J.
Barford, J.
Bellworthy, J. F. T.
Bilgood, E. G.

Brown, G. A.
Conneeley, J.
Fenings, A. W.
Johnson, B. R.
Maunder, J.

Sidlow, W.
Sweet, F. H.
Townsend, W. F.

WARRANT OFFICERS, SGTS. AND CPLS.
"E" COY.

Bell, C. T. M. (C.S.M.), Warrant Officer

Howell, W. G. (C.Q.M.S.)

SGTS.

Aspey, P. W.
Brown, E. W. L.
Bulley, A.

Clarke, E. L.
Harris, R. L.
Harris, W.

Haydon, J. E.
Hook, W.
Norman, C.

CPLS.

Farmer, W. A.
Jordan, J. R.
Mathews, F. N.

Mathews, A. H. A.
Reed, S. R.
Watts, F. E. W.

White, A. L.
Wyburn, T.

WARRANT OFFICERS, SGTS. AND CPLS.
H.Q. COY. — ADMINISTRATION

Lovell, W. L. (C.S.M.), Warrant Officer

Mundy, A. B. (C.Q.M.S.)

SGTS.

Bartlett, C. J.
Laidlaw, J. A. R.

Needham, W. W.
Powlesland, T. P.

Wright, W. J.

SGTS. AND CPLS. — SUB-ARTILLERY

SGTS.

Binnie, E. D.

Cockett, F. R.
Wood, R. J.

Wilson, D.

CPLS.

Salter, A. F.

SGTS. AND CPLS. — PIONEERS

SGTS.

Force, W. J.

Gifford, F. C.,
Acting C.S.M.

Maunder, R. W.

SGTS. AND CPLS.—SECTOR SIGNALS

SGTS.

Hubert, H. B.

CPLS.

Luxon, G. M.	Riddett, S. A.	Whitton, G. W.

WARRANT OFFICERS, SGTS. AND CPLS.
H.Q. COY.—MACHINE GUN

Purchase, T. A. (C.S.M.), Warrant Officer

Hutchins, R. A. (C.Q.M.S.)

SGTS.

Bondle, F. J.	Cann, R. H.	Telling, R. C.
Bourne, A. H.	Prouse, A.	Wilton, R. A.

CPLS.

Langdon, H. R.
Tucker, G. H.

SGTS. AND CPLS. — TRANSPORT

SGTS.

Faulkner, A. G.	Rogers, E. J. R.	Woodcock, S. W.

CPLS.

Alford, W. B.	Chalk, T.	Goodman, C. C.

WARRANT OFFICERS, SGTS. AND CPLS.
SAPPERS COY.

Prince, H. (C.S.M.), Warrant Officer

SGTS.

Elstone, E.	Ellis, W. H.	Scott, W. G.

CPLS.

Bray, W. R.	Foster, R. W.	Ketell, W. A. J.
Edwards, H. C.	Harris, A. T.	

SGTS. AND CPLS. — BTN. SIGNALS

SGTS.

Green, F. A.   Martin, H. J.   Turner, W. H.

CPLS.

Derges, H. G.   Padbury, I. R.   Palmer, J. C.

P.S.I.'s WHO HAVE SERVED WITH THE BATTALION

Budd, B. J.   Freestone, F.   Williams, T. J. F.
Callender, H. J.   Hill, A.
Cowell, J. N.   Mabin, A. W.

VOLUNTEERS WHO HAD LEFT THE BATTALION
BEFORE "STAND DOWN."

Austin, F.
Ash, H. F. B.
Arundell, G. F. H.
Ashton, J.
Arnold, W. G.
Ashtead, E. N.
Alford, W. B. J.
Alsford, T. J.
Allcorn, H.
Aggett, J.
Adams, A. R.
Adams, J. H.
Adams, T. H. B.
Acres, B. B.
Atkins, G.
Atkins, W. C.
Ashley, A. D.
Abrahams, I. J.
Abbot, H.
Ackroyd, J. W.
Adams, G. J.
Adams, W. J.
Addicott, W. J.
Addicott, T.
Adams, R. R.
Adams, M. S.
Adams, J.
Adams, E.
Adams, T. H. B.
Aggett, C. T. P.
Aggett, J.
Aggett, K. L.
Alexander, H.
Allan, A. B.
Allan, J. M.
Allen, F. W.
Allen, H. F.
Allen, T. B.
Alsop, A. J.
Alexander, C. N.
Alford, I. G.
Amery, H. J.
Ambler, G.
Amor, A.
Anderton, H.
Andreozzi, F. A.

Andrew, S. G.
Andrews, C.
Andrews, J. L.
Anker, F. S.
Andrews, T. E.
Andrews, W. G.
Angel, H. G.
Anning, F. H.
Anstice, F. W.
Anstey, A.
Apsey, G. R.
Arthur, E. R.
Armstrong, A.
Arburary, W. H. G.
Arnold, J.
Arnold, K. J. E.
Ashworth, G.
Ashton, A.
Ashlin, J. W.
Ash, F. C.
Atkins, J.
Audley, G. W.
Axford, K. H.
Ayshford, A. T.
Atkins, P. J.
Armstrong, A. D.
Alford, O. F.
Andrews, T. E.
Aggett, A. J.
Aspden, J. L.
Armstrong, H. J.
Armstrong, C. J.
Arthurs, W. F.
Anstey, R. A.
Anning, E. W.
Abraham, W. S. C.
Aggett, H. R.
Allen, A. W. G.
Allwood, R. J.
Back, F. S.
Bamsey, W. A. W.
Barner, R. W.
Barry, H. A.
Bartlett, S. R.
Bearne, A. E.
Bennett, G.

Bennett, T. C.
Bowman, T.
Brooks, E.
Brown, G. A.
Butler, B. R.
Bury, N. C.
Butcher, A. H.
Bunce, J. F.
Bye, G.
Becket, R. H.
Baker, G.
Ball, W. B.
Barkell, D. G.
Baker, A. A.
Banbury, R. W.
Baker, A. E.
Baylie, A. A.
Brown, W. R.
Brewer, F.
Brewer, K. W.
Brook, W. F.
Brimble, O.
Brown, J. A.
Bye, E. J.
Bush, H. T.
Bowden, P. J.
Burrowns, C. W.
Butcher, J.
Burnell, A. E.
Burrows, C. W.
Boult, S. J.
Bell, A. B.
Bainborough, A.
Blackwell, R. W.
Best, W. J.
Baker, C. S.
Bryant, J.
Byne, A. C.
Bennelick, L.
Boult, T. G.
Bowden, F. C.
Boult, J. W.
Bolt, N.
Bourke, W. G.
Bouchard, W. S.
Borradale, R. O.

Booth, A. S.	Barnes, W. H.	Bowden, P. A.
Bowden, R. J.	Bowditch, G. W.	Brown, F. J.
Bovgourd, W. M.	Beer, V. E.	Brown, G. A.
Bowers, W. D.	Beech, F. W.	Brock, W. J.
Browning, C. J.	Bedford, J. F.	Brown, R. C.
Browning, F.	Beckett, E.	Bricknell, C. A.
Ball, E.	Beck, E.	Braddon, R. C. P.
Boundy, L. D.	Broom, H. J.	Bewer, H. W.
Bee, J.	Barrett, L. G.	Bryant, G. H.
Ball, F. W.	Bennet, W. E.	Brewer, W. H.
Best, H.	Blair, W. A.	Brooks, A. G. M.
Boult, W. G.	Baines, A. R.	Brindley, J. R.
Bond, E. E.	Badcock, J.	Bending, F. W. C.
Brown, P. L.	Brockley, O.	Battin, A. H.
Brookes, K. G.	Brewer, G. J.	Bastin, R.
Boult, R. H.	Blackmore, F. C.	Bennett, S. W.
Bowring, G. L.	Blackmore, F.	Bennett, W. E.
Borrett, S. C.	Berryman, F. J.	Bennett, R. F.
Bowden, J. H.	Baker, S. J.	Bennellick, F.
Bowerman, W.	Baker, J.	Balkwill, J.
Bowden, D. R.	Baker, L. W.	Baxter, H. J.
Bowden, W. G.	Baker, W. P.	Bassett, D. C.
Bolt, R. H.	Brewer, W. H.	Brown, F. W.
Bond, R. F.	Barlow, T.	Browning, A. J.
Bowden, A.	Boyes, F. E. F.	Brown, R. N.
Bennelick, F.	Bownes, K. A.	Browne, E. F.
Bendle, A. W.	Bryant, W. J.	Bell, V. F.
Bellamy, W.	Body, F. R. H.	Bedford, P.
Boardman, W. H.	Boon, C.	Burt, N. H.
Blaker, W.	Bolt, C. S.	Butcher, J. G. C.
Blakeley, B. W.	Bond, F. J.	Butler, D.
Blake, R. S.	Bell, R. H.	Bowerman, R.
Blades, R. F.	Beer, E. C.	Bowden, E. M.
Blackwell, R. W.	Berry, A. J.	Bowden, W. H.
Bowles, A. A. D.	Berry, F. T.	Bowden, G.
Brindley, J. R.	Berry, H.	Blackmore, R. T.
Bartlett, G. W. C.	Berry, T.	Bradford, W. W. T.
Bartlett, G.	Benning, A. E.	Brown, H.
Bartlett, D. G.	Bending, H. S.	Bromell, J. G.
Bartlett, J. R.	Beesley, E. D.	Brown, N.
Bartlett, P. J.	Bevan, F.	Brewer, R.
Back, J. S.	Bennelick, R. G.	Brown, H. W.
Back, J. R.	Beer, W. W.	Bradbury, F. G.
Bonner, T. F. H.	Bradbury, J. C.	Brown, S. G.
Bashford, K.	Brimacombe, L. R.	Brealey, F. J.
Bullard, B. R.	Bauer, H. J.	Browning, L. V.
Banting, J.	Back, I. G.	Bradbury, N.
Baker, K.	Barber, M. W.	Brook, W. F.
Butcher, H. J.	Baker, F.	Bache, H. S.
Barnett, R.	Brown, A. F.	Bayley, H. G.

Banks, F. W.
Bath, F. L.
Baskerville, C. L.
Banfield, D. B. J.
Barber, J. T. G.
Baldwin, W. H.
Balchin, W. G.
Boult, R. J.
Boobyer, P.
Bennet, R.
Brunning, N. C.
Blackmore, J. B.
Brewer, W. H.
Bishop, E. C.
Beaven, H. O.
Brown, W.
Beal, A. J.
Bebell, T. W.
Broadhead, R. W.
Bristow, R. E. J.
Bright, J.
Bright, E. L.
Bright, A. E. H.
Brigden, J. L.
Brierley, R. V.
Brewer, L. G. F.
Brealey, K. A.
Breading, D.
Bray, J. S.
Billing, S.
Bayley, H. G.
Bennellick, P.
Bellamy, A. E.
Bond, A. R. J.
Bond, R.
Bolt, R. H.
Bolt, A. L.
Bolt, E. J.
Bartlett, F. J.
Bartlett, K. F.
Bartlett, G. F.
Bartlett, L. W. A.
Bartlett, N. H.
Bartlett, W. F.
Bartlett, W. F.
Bartlett, J.
Barnes, J. E. C.
Blackman, W. C.
Bennett, J. M.
Bird, W. A.
Bishop, H. H.

Bishop, J. P.
Bishop, W. H.
Bishop, E. R.
Bird, H. B.
Bird, H. S.
Birch, P. C.
Birch, H. C.
Bilverstone, S. H.
Bidgood, R.
Beadon, J. A.
Blackmore, R.
Blackmore, E. A. W.
Blunt, E. R.
Bloomfield, R. J.
Bloomer, H.
Blong, P.
Blanchford, H.
Blaksley, J. O.
Bowden, S. R.
Blunt, A. V.
Blackmore, R. J.
Bickel, R. F. J.
Blackmore, R.
Brignall, J. E.
Boston, F. E.
Blakwill, D. J.
Brown, W. C.
Baker, J. P.
Bate-Jones, R. G.
Barrett, A.
Barker, N. J.
Bainborough, C. W.
Bailey, H.
Back, P. E.
Butler, H. T.
Brimacombe, L. R.
Bauer, H. J.
Back, I. G.
Barber, M. W.
Bye, W. E.
Bell, W. R.
Bennett, R.
Beddy, P. L.
Bedford, W. S.
Berry, S. J.
Beach, G.
Bickle, F. J.
Biddulph, C.
Burrows,
   D. E. St. John
Burrows, H. W.

Burns, K. P.
Burkitt, C. E.
Burke, P.
Burgoyne, F. E.
Burgess, F. G.
Burford, J. H.
Bunn, A. W.
Buller, M. H.
Bull, R. W.
Budd, G.
Budd, W. H.
Brown, J. H.
Brookfield, W.
Baker, F. G. P.
Baker, H. P.
Baker, T.
Baker, W. A.
Barrington, G.
Bernett, E.
Barker, J. R.
Beeston, A.
Bazley, W. H.
Bayley, R. C.
Brant, W. H.
Brant, F.
Brailey, M.
Bradley, W.
Bradford, F. G.
Bradford, G. J.
Bradford, S. F. G.
Bradbeer, C. F.
Brabon, J.
Bryant, H. H.
Bruton, G. L.
Browning, M. T.
Brazil, A. H.
Beaumont, R.
Black, E. G.
Back, B. W.
Beele, A. D.
Bonning, J. H. I.
Batten, B.
Banfield, D.
Bond, R.
Bennett, A. J.
Bunker, E. B.
Bradford, L. J.
Ball, W. B.
Brannam, A. J.
Brewer, A. G.
Bennett, B. A.

Challacombe, C. H.
Chaffe, L.
Comins, F.
Coles, H. G. P.
Cox, F. A.
Collins, W. S. H.
Collard, G. H. J.
Colton, M. J.
Cornish, J. H.
Copp, B. H.
Coombe, B. L.
Cotterill, I. E.
Coles, R. F.
Clapp, R. J.
Clark, W. H.
Clark, R. G.
Clarke, H.
Clark, G.
Clarke, F.
Cockerhead, W. J.
Cole, W. T.
Cornish, G. W.
Cole, T. J. G.
Coombe, E. A.
Courtney, F.
Coles, C. E.
Colbeck, E.
Cox, C.
Cornish, J. E.
Cornish, P. G.
Cope, G. A. R.
Cox, B. R. W.
Coater, N. B.
Cole, F.
Coles, C. E.
Coleman, E. F.
Commins, F. C.
Cox, P. C.
Conway, G.
Crossman, F. E.
Crocker, C. F.
Craner, S.
Climmer, W. T.
Crossinggum, A. B.
Croyden, A. J.
Creed, W. R.
Cole, T.
Cole, C. J.
Coldfridge, W. H.
Collicott, W. J.

Curtis, W. H.
Curtis, J. C.
Cumming, W. J.
Curgenven, H. G.
Cullen, J.
Cullingworth, P. C.
Cutland, F. W.
Curtis, R. C.
Curtis, L. S.
Curtis, W. D.
Curson, R. E.
Cumes, W. H.
Crook, G. J.
Crook, A. W.
Croft, R. J.
Crees, W.
Craze, S. P.
Crawshaw, W.
Craig, F. D.
Crabb, S. F.
Crouch, A. R. H.
Cross, H. R.
Crossley, M. C.
Crisp, W. G.
Creek, W. A.
Crabbe, G. F.
Crowe, H.
Copp, R. C.
Cooke, F. J.
Cooke, W. S.
Cooke, W. N.
Conibear, R.
Coneybear, W.
Commins, A. C.
Combstock, F. W.
Colyer, A. T. C.
Colmer, J. C. V.
Collins, J. S.
Collings, D. W. G.
Collins, T. S. D.
Collins, W.
Collett, A.
Collard, D. F. H.
Collard, C.
Coles, S. C.
Coles, N.
Coles, B. J.
Cole, W. A.
Coombes, C.
Cooke, H. D. H.

Courtney, H. J.
Courtney, F.
Courtney, F. E.
Coram, F. E.
Coombes, C.
Cobley, R. A. W.
Cochlin, J. W.
Cockcroft, A. H.
Collard, R.
Collett, G. F. G.
Curtis, L. M. M.
Cockram, F.
Condliffe, J.
Cumming, R. F.
Carter, A.
Camble, G. W. P.
Carpenter, P. L. J.
Coles, C. W. K.
Climo, H. H.
Clark, T. D.
Climmer, F. G.
Chick, E. Q.
Chanter, C. W.
Cherry, J. R.
Chambers, W. J.
Clapp, R. F.
Coates, M. L.
Copp, J. H.
Curtis, A.
Cox, R. H.
Cummings, G. S.
Cudmore, R. E.
Cummings, J. C.
Curran, S. C.
Challenger, G. B.
Chapman, D. B.
Collard, K.
Coverdale, H. J.
Capon, H. J.
Creber, F. A.
Cowler, R.
Court, S. P.
Copp, R. W.
Chalk, T. R.
Copp, P. F. J.
Conder, C.
Collinge, T. S.
Cornish, H.
Cridkand, R. M.
Carpenter, M.

149

Collinson, F.
Cole, W. V. J.
Curtis, W. F.
Carpenter, K. F.
Carpenter, A.
Connett, G.
Croft, W. S.
Clatworthy, J. W.
Carter, R. W.
Chubb, C. A.
Cleave, W.
Commins, H.
Challice, A. L. J.
Cossey, A. A.
Chadwick, W.
Cann, L. O.
Cann, J.
Cann, G. C.
Carah, J. W.
Cawsey, W. H.
Camp, L. G.
Cameron, D. B.
Carpenter, V. L.
Carpenter, W. D.
Camble, F. T.
Cawthorn, D. J.
Cawston, E. R.
Cawsey, W. H.
Catchpole, E.
Castling, R.
Carthew, P. C.
Carter, V. M.
Carter, E. C.
Carter, A. J. G.
Carr, R. W.
Carpenter, T. W.
Cann, D. G.
Campbell, A. W.
Cummings, A. J.
Cameron, G. F.
Chambers, W. G.
Caryl, P. A. C.
Carpenter, V. L.
Carter, J. R.
Cann, D. G.
Carpenter, H. C.
Capel, H. G.
Cann, G.
Carpenter, T.
Callard, W. G.

Callaway, R. C.
Carter, J. R. L.
Churchill, C. F.
Chandler, V. C.
Churchward, E. I.
Cheriton, L. V.
Cheesman, P. W.
Challice, W. J. S.
Chamberlain, W.
Clarke, A. F.
Clarke, W. H.
Climo, H. R. H.
Cleveland, G.
Clements, W. J. P.
Clements, A. E.
Clements, S. H.
Clayton, E. B.
Clarke, F. T.
Clapp, S. W.
Clarke, G. M.
Clark, W.
Clampitt, W. H.
Clapp, S.
Challice, C. A.
Chudley, W.
Chesterfield, C.
Chambers, A. H.
Chamberlain, T.
Childs, C. G.
Churchward, G. L.
Challacombe, D.
Chapplow, W. L.
Chapple, D. J.
Chapple, D. J.
Chapman, C.
Chilcott, C.
Chowings, S. F.
Chick, F.
Cheriton, W. H.
Cheadle, W.
Chudley, W. J.
Chudley, W. A.
Chapman, H. F.
Chapman, A. E.
Channon, H. E.
Champion, A. E.
Chammings, R. S.
Chamberlain, E. M.
Chambers, S. E.
Chambers, F. G.

Camble, A. P.
Carpenter, W. A. C.
Channing, R.
Chapman, C. C.
Cocks, W. R.
Coleman, T. G.
Cosway, L. H.
Cotton, W. J.
Cox, W. C.
Denford, R. J.
Denford, T. J.
Durden, R. P.
Davis, J. J.
Dansham, L. G.
Derrington, A. P.
Dan, C. R.
Doble, I. C.
Dodge, I. J.
Doble, G. B.
Downing, J. T.
Discombe, G. S.
Denham, G. C.
Densham, J. W.
Dell, T. H.
Derry, R. C.
Darke, H.
Davis, R.
Dare, J. E.
Davies, W. H.
Dare, I. W.
Davey, H. W.
Davey, J. J.
Dare, R. C.
Davey, H. T.
Dyson, R. W.
Dyer, A. C. E.
Dyson, W. R.
Davey, F. H. W.
Dermed, F. T.
Denison, S.
Densham, R. W.
Derrick A.
Davey, R. G.
Dimond, G. R. C.
Duguid, E. S.
Dorothy, R. A.
Dunster, F. R.
Davey, K. J.
Davey, A. J.
Doroth, F. R.

Dicker, A.
Dart, C. A.
Davey, H.
Down, W. H.
Downing, W. N.
Davey, A. E.
Deviell, W.
Dakyns, G. F. G.
Dyer, D. S.
Dyson, W. E.
Dunn, D. G.
Drayton, K. W.
Drew, P. W. G.
Dare, A. E.
Dart, W. S.
Darke, C. A.
Duddridge, F.
Darke, A. T.
Dale, J.
Davey, W. G.
Davey, C. W.
Davey, A. E. D.
Davey, F. J.
Darvill, W. E.
Dart, W. S.
Dart, S.
Dart, C. H.
Dart, B. J. C.
Darlington, R. R.
Darles, A. E.
Darke, A. J.
Darke, A. T.
Darke, F.
Dare, C. A.
Dansey, C. H.
Daltrey, E. C.
Dack, R. J. T.
Davey, S. E.
Davey, H.
Day, L.
Davey, T. R.
Downing, A. W.
Downing, A. N.
Dorrington, D. R.
Dorothy, R. A.
Diment, F.
Dickson, F. W.
Dinele, A. G.
Dinner, A. J.
Dixon, D. P.

Discombe, W. E.
Davey, A. J. G.
De Mowbray, M. S.
Derrick, C. R.
Deane, G. W.
Deans, J. C. G.
Dent, N.
Dayman, W.
Davey, A. W. R.
Dawe, J. J.
Davison, D. P.
Davis, M. O. A.
Davies, D. L.
Davies, D. W.
Davies, G. V.
Dawe, F. J.
Dymond, C. W.
Dymond, P. G.
Dyer, T.
Dyer, R.
Durant, F. G.
Duffy, W. J.
Duigan, J.
Dummett, T. H.
Dunn, A. C.
Dunn, L. T.
Dunn, D. A.
Dunne, D. P. J.
Drake, D. L. T.
Drake, P.
Drake, H. F.
Drake, D.
Drury, H. M. R.
Drummond, D. C.
Drodge, J. L.
Drew, F. R.
Drew, L.
Draper, T. E.
Drake, C. H.
Downham, R. S.
Down, P. D.
Down, R. A.
Dobson, W. A.
Dock, J.
Dodge, C. H.
Dodge, I. J.
Dodd, C.
Dodd, F. J.
Dobson, J. N.
Doble, R. F. B.

Dorothy, A. T.
Dowson, H.
Downs, F.
Evans, J. F. A.
Eayres, G. F. A.
Errington, W. A.
Evans, A. G.
Evely, J. P.
Eveleigh, P. A.
Eveleigh, F. C.
Eveleigh, R. E. C.
Elson, A.
Ellis, F. H. A.
Elliot, F. C.
Elliot, F. L.
Edwards, D. A.
Elliott, R.
Evans, W. H.
Evans, R. G.
Evans, H. E.
Edwars, A. E.
Evans, W. R.
Edmonds, W. A.
Edwars, E. H.
Ellacott, E.
Ellis, M. W.
Elston, S. A.
Elsegood, H. A.
Ellion, J.
Elliot, J. S.
Ellis, A. F.
Elston, F. S.
Elliot, S.
Eggleton, L. F.
Egerton, J.
Edwars, L. W.
Edwards, T. G.
Edyvean, D.
Edgington, R. C.
Edwards, A. M.
Edmonds, H. V.
Edwards, N. C.
Edwards, W. R.
Edwards, W. J.
Edwards, S. J.
Ebdon, F. S.
Ebdon, F. J.
Eastland, N.
Eager, K. R. W.
Eakers, R.

East, F. H.
Eaton, F. C.
Easterbrook, C. M.
Ewings, A. R.
Evans, D. W.
Evans, N. M.
Evans, K. W.
Evered, R. C. S.
Evered, H. G. H.
Evans, E. V. J.
Evans, W. A.
Evans, D. C.
Evemy, L. A.
Everett, A. W.
Eustace, R. W.
Escott, L. T.
Escott, C.
Escott, J. B.
Erredge, R. E. A.
Endicott, L. G.
England, L. S.
Emery, T. J.
Emery, E. D.
Emery, R. P.
Ellis, H.
Ellis, R. E.
Ellis, R. T.
Ellis, J. W.
Elliott, F. R.
Elliott, R. D.
Elliott, C. G.
Eddy, S. G.
Edmonds, J.
Elliott, J. E.
Ferguson, H. J.,
    M.B.E.
Furner, T. R.
Ferguson, L. R.
Fletcher, W. H.
Fry, P. T.
Frost, S.
Fox, W. H.
Ford, G. F.
Ford, C. W.
Ford, C. N.
Fuchs, L.
Fry, F. H.
Freeman, N. E.
Frost, K.
Frost, J. T.

Frost, H.
Friend, W. C.
Friend, L.
French, T.
Freestone, W. F. L.
Franklin, C. H.
Franklin, W.
Ford, B. L.
Ford, C. C. W.
Foster, W. H.
Foster, E. C.
Forrest, C.
Forrest, C.
Forrest, H.
Flood, C. H.
Flanders, M. H.
Fitt, C. S.
Fisher, F. L.
Finn, H. J.
Field, J. E. C.
Findlay, N. R.
Fish, G. R.
Fenning, A. D. W.
Fenn, H. G.
Fewings, A. W.
Falla, R. J.
Farley, A. E.
Farmer, R.
Farnham, P.
Farthing, A. E. J.
Faulkner, L. C.
Faville, E.
Fay, L. M.
Flintoft, W.
Farley, A. E.
Farmer, J. H.
Fitzjohn, W. J.
Fitzpatrick, S. A.
Flower, J. G.
Fletcher, W. H.
Foster, G. C.
Ford, F. V.
Frost, C. F. M.
Fay, L. O.
French, S. J.
Francis, H.
Fussell, H. J.
Forman, H. I.
Furber, J. M.
Fesler, R. R.

Ford, S. J.
Fairchild, H.
Forrest, P.
Finch, L. C.
Fenwick, J. T. H.
Ford, W. S.
Fewins, L. G.
Gray, F. S.
Gilhooly, F.
Gregory, H. V.
Gee, P.
Gander, E.
Grant, D. D.
Godding, H. W.
Gubb, H. W. A. E.
Guiver, C. Y.
Guthrie, E. J.
Guy, E. J.
Guy, F. A. W.
Guy, E. J.
Grabham, J.
Greenham, E. S. A.
Green, L. A.
Green, E. G.
Green, R.
Grimes, R. G.
Griffiths, T. S.
Greeney, E. J.
Grover, P.
Grose, W. P. J.
Grundrod, A.
Grifith, E. R.
Griffin, H.
Gribble, J. W.
Gregory, D.
Gregory, R. J. W.
Gregory, C. J.
Geegory, L. E.
Greenslade, F. J.
Greenslade, R. H.
Greenaway, G. W.
Greenaway, W. R.
Green, W. H. F.
Green, W. E.
Grant, W. G.
Gratwicke, E. H.
Graham, A.
Grace, A. S.
Graham, J. T.
Graham, F.

Godfrey, A. S. J.
Goldsmith, B.
Goby, W. D.
Goby, L.
Gore, J. J. L.
Gould, H. C.
Gough, G. H.
Goss, J. W.
Goodliffe, D.
Good, C.
Goldworthy, R. H.
Goldsworth, B.
Godwin, A.
Godfrey, P. H.
Gorter, H. G. B.
Goad, W. H.
Guvier, H. G. S.
Gliddon, A.
Gliddon, W. P.
Gratwicke, C. R.
Glenn, W. A. P.
Glasborow, H. F.
Glass, G.
Glass, R.
Glanville, L.
Glanvill, C. N. G.
Giles, W. T.
Gilbert, F. H.
Gifford, J.
Gibson, S. C.
Gibbs, W. H.
Gibbs, G. H.
Gibbs, R. F. C.
Gibbs, F. G.
Gibbons, R. E.
Gillins, V.
Ginger, L. S.
Gillard, T. J.
Gillard, F. J.
Ghent, A. R.
Gage, C. A.
Gale, C. P.
Gale, P.
Gallin, C.
Gale, R. H.
Gapper, J. K.
Gasson, W.
Granham, D. R.
Gardner, J.
Gardiner, P. L.

Gard, P. W.
Gatti, S. J.
Gater, A. J.
Gayton, K. G.
Gaskell, W. H.
Galt, J.
Gater, A. J.
Gray, G. W. E.
Greenslade, F. J.
Green, S.
Grant, S.
Griffiths, H.
Green, W. H.
Gunn, W. E.
Guppy, S. P.
Greeaway, R. G.
Greenslade, T.
Gotham, E. J.
Goldworthy, F. E.
Gittins, W. G.
Gilbert, C. S.
Gill, W.
Gillard, P. C.
Gillard, J. B.
Gill, R. G.
Gillard, S. E.
Gill, W. R.
Gaplin, J. S.
Gard, P. W.
Gard, G. A.
Gale, W.
Gil, G. E.
Gendle, F. W.
Giga, C. E.
Gordin, B. A.
Girsham, G. H.
Greenaway, R. T.
Green, F.
Green, T. P.
Groves, V. C.
Godbeer, R. R.
Glanville, F. C. G.
Gladstone, K. S. M.
Gorfin, F. J.
Gratwicke, E. H.
Goss, C. R.
Gibson, H. A.
Garnham, B.
Gribble, J. W.
Gregory, W. G.

Gardener, E. F.
Gardner, P.
Gitsham, E. G.
Golesworthy, M. F. R.
Gosney, J. E.
Gunn, C. G.
Ham, R. G.
Hart, E. J.
Hay, M. B.
Hepple, H. G.
Hobbs, S.
Horne, E. W.,
   D.S.O.
Hutchings, R.
Harman, D. W.
Harling, A.
Harding, S. J.
Harding, R. H.
Hansford, H. G.
Hannaford, S.
Hannaford, J. B.
Hannaford, F. W.
Hancock, C.
Hancock, J. C.
Hardman, R.
Holland, H. R.
Hodder, A. J.
Hollingdale, J. R.
Hodge, F.
Hogden, C. H.
Hogg, A. M.
Holland, W. J.
Hole, W. G.
Hole, F. G.
Holdsworth, F.
Hodges, L. J.
Hocking, P. B.
Hocking, C. D.
Hobbs, L. H.
Hoare, F. G.
Hoar, F.
Hoar, R. W.
Horner, A. E. W.
Horne, S. N.
Hopkins, J. A. G.
Hope, M. G.
Hooper, W. A.
Hooper, R. S. A.
Hooper, H. E.
Hooper, J. S.

Hooper, W. G. C.
Hooper, R. N.
Honey, K. F.
Holway, P. J. J.
Holton, M. J.
Holman, S. G.
Holman, H. W.
Holmana, T. H. A.
Holloway, M. I.
Holland, L.
Hoyte, J.
Howland, A. A.
Howe, H. R.
Howard, W. T.
Howard, R. A.
Howard, J. P. E.
Howard, R. G.
Houghton, R.
Hosegrove, T. W. E.
Horton, W. G.
Horsham, H. J.
Halls, W. J. G.
Hucker, C. D.
Hutchings, R.
Hunter, W. F.
Hutchings, D. G.
Hughes, H. W.
Hubbard, F. T. P.
Hull, V. N.
Hurley, P. L.
Hutchings, W. R.
Hunt, F. A.
Hunt, A. J.
Hurved, H. H. C.
Hucker, G. T.
Hutchins, E. J.
Huxham, K. C.
Hurchings, L. F.
Hutchings, L. A.
Hutchings, J. W. P.
Hutchings, G. V.
Hutchings, W. J.
Hudson, F.
Hutchings, F. J.
Hussey, R. G.
Hussey, R. G.
Hurved, H. H.
Huntingford, P. W.
Hunt, G. G.
Hunns, C. H.

Humphries, J. R.
Humphrey, M. J.
Hugo, L. G.
Hugo, C.
Hughes, H. C.
Hayward, G. W.
Haigh, F.
Helder, E.
Harrison, H.
Hopains, A. D.
Hooper, B. E.
Heal, W. R.
Hoseroye, D.
Horrox, W. L.
Homeyard, E. W.
Howe, H. T.
Hodge, F.
Hodgon, R.
Hooper, D.
Hocking, D. J.
Hodgson, G. B.
Holmes, W. C.
Hooper, R. T.
Hoad, C.
Howe, S.
Hoyte, C. W.
Hucker, A.
Hughes, E. J.
Hutchings, W. P.
Hunwicks, G.
Hughes, W. J.
Hudson, L. W. R.
Hughes, A. J.
Hunt, P.
Hilton, J. G.
Hensby, G. S.
Heath, L. J.
Heard, F. W. J.
Hember, D. G.
Haycock, B. W.
Harris, H. R.
Hammong, M. A.
Hall, C.
Hammett, S. J.
Harris, L. J.
Havell, P. A.
Hardy, R. S.
Hackworthy, D. A.
Hannaford, G.
Hannaford, F. W.

Haydon, W. G.
Hawker, R. G.
Hammett, E. V.
Harris, L.
Halfpenny, D. R.
Habberfield, V. A.
Harding, L. T. H.
Harris, A. F.
Hurford, A. J.
Hamilton, D.
Hatch, T. S.
Harvey, P. L.
Hoare, L.
Holman, K.
Holman, S. G.
House, F.
Holman, M. S.
Howard, T. R. J.
House, J. D.
Hooper, K. C.
Holman, H. W.
Holmes, G. L.
Hopton, F. C.
Hodkinson, W. T.
Hodge, L. W. E.
Hooper, J. D. G.
Hooper, R. T.
Holmes, W. R.
Harries, S.
Haydon, W. J.
Hawkes, A. S.
Harris, W.
Hayward, L. J.
Hayward, J.
Hammond, H. F.
Hawke, P. O.
Hazelwood, L. H.
Hammond, E. V. J.
Hamlyn, V. E.
Hainworth, F. V.
Harding, I. V.
Harvey, M. F. C.
Harvey, H. H.
Harvey, W. H.
Harvey, R.
Hart, H. F. J.
Harris, P.
Harris, I. S.
Harris, H.
Harris, F. E.

Harris, S. W. G.
Harris, D. M.
Harris, E. A. J.
Harris, E. J.
Harris, B.
Harris, S.
Harries, A. E.
Harper, R. S. B.
Harris, R. E. V.
Hackworthy, L. J.
Harrison, C. N.
Hawkins, A. J.
Havill, S. C.
Hatherley, J.
Hatherley, J.
Haskell, C. T.
Hawkins, S. J.
Hayward, J. V.
Hayward, F. C.
Haynes, G. V.
Hayman, G. A. C.
Hayman, A. T.
Hayler, W.
Hayes, F.
Hayes, E. J.
Haydon, W.
Hiscock, L. G.
Hibbs, E. F.
Hickmott, R. G.
Heard, W. J.
Hearle, G. M.
Heale, J.
Hexter, M.
Heyburn, C. R.
Heywood, L. A. J.
Heyburn, L. E.
Hensby, G. S.
Henley, E.
Henderson, G. E.
Helmore, G. A.
Hellier, A. G.
Hector, R.
Hecker, S.
Heal, S. D.
Heywood, A. S.
Hind, C. E. K.
Hills, C.
Hill, G. G.
Hillman, W.
Hitchcock, J. L.

Higgs, A.
Hicks, A. W.
Hiscock, J. E.
Hill, D. W. C.
Hill, W.
Hill, D. I.
Hill, J.
Hill, F. J.
Hill, C. E.
Hill, G. T. R.
Hill, T. L. R.
Hicks, W.
Hibberd, P. H.
Hitchcock, A. V.
Hiscock, C.
Hilton, P.
Hill, W. C. S.
Hicks, E. D.
Haywood, R.
Howard, W. H.
Howard, L. J.
Howard, L.
Harris, W. G.
Headland, H. C.
Hubber, W. G.
Harris, D. M.
Holmes, W. G.
Haydon, G.
Hooper, E.
Huish, J. B.
Hutchins, L.
Howard, W. F.
Hamon, S. C.
Huish, C. F.
Hitchman, A. G.
Hodge, G. W.
Harris, D.
Hayman, F. G. W.
Hughes, F. D.
Harris, F. W.
Hartnell, L. B.
Heap, G. V. M.
Hunt, A. J.
Hughes, P.
Howard, W. T.
Hayman, C.
Hooper, B. E.
Haywood, H. G.
Huddy, A.
Hopkinson, W. T.

Hart, L. E.
Harvey, E. W.
Helyar, C. E.
Harris, W. J.
Hill, H.
Honslow, F. H.
Hobjecn, G.
Hoer, W.
Holdin, J. W.
Hamilton, E. J.
Hartwill, C. H.
Hoer, P. E.
Hammond, F. A.
Hames, H. R.
Halsted, R.
Hall, A.
Hall, H.
Hall, F.
Haliburton-Bourke, E. C.
Halfyard, F.
Haley, H. C.
Hackworthy, D. A.
Harcourt, P. A.
Harrison, R.
Hancock, T.
Hay, C.
Harmer, B. H.
Izzard, W. H.
Ireland, W. H.
Ireland, C. S.
Ireland, S. J.
Ireland, W.
Ireland, A. W.
Ireland, W. H.
Impey, W.
Isaac, E. J.
Isaac, A. G.
Isaacs, E. T. J.
Isaac, R. M.
Irving, L.
Irish, W. N.
Inken, S. A.
Inken, F. G.
Ingram, G. H.
Iles, W. B.
Iles, D.
Iremonger, E.
Isaac, W. H.
Isaac, H.

Ingham, W.
Ives, J.
Irving, J.
Johns, W. T.
James, S.
Jones, T. C.
Jose, E. J.
Joy, W. H.
Joslin, C. F.
Jones, F. W.
Jones, A. E.
Joslin, E. W.
Jordan, R. W.
Jones, J. P.
Jones, F. C.
Jones, H. W.
Jones, H. K.
Jones, S. K.
Jones, S. L.
Jones, T. W.
Jones, W. R. T.
Johnstone, G. J.
Johnstone, G. G.
Johnstone, J.
Johnstone, T. W.
Johnson, R. T.
Johnson, F. G.
Johnsone, E. R. H.
Johns, S. V.
Johns, F. W.
Jelley, J.
Jezzard, G. T.
Jewell, A. J.
Jenne, T. G.
Jenkins, A. M.
Jeffrey, W. H.
Jeffery, D.
Jefferson, R. G.
Jarvis, H.
Jarvis, D.
Jarman, W. E.
James, F. L.
James, R. D. F.
James, D. R.
James, W. G.
James, H. C.
Jackson, J.
Jackson, J.
Jackson, W. F.
Jacobs, A. J.

Jackson, H.
Jarrett, W. R. G.
James, B.
James, F. T. H.
James, J. W.
Jackman, W. J.
Jury, D. L.
Judson, R. H.
Jones, R. W.
Johnston, A. H.
Jones, O. T.
Johnston, C. A.
Joy, E. R.
Jordan, A. E. O.
Jones, E.
Jones, L. R.
Jennings, T. G.
Jewell, I. E. F.
James, J.
Jacques, R. D.
Jackson, A. F. A.
Jones, A. C.
Jeffery, G.
Jones, R. D.
Jarman, F.
Jones, D. C.
Jones, D. C.
James, W. E.
Johns, F.
Juniper, L. C.
Jones, H. B.
Jordan, W. S.
Jewell, D. A.
James, F. G.
Jones, H. A.
Johnson, W.
Kingham, V.
Keene, F. W.
Kevern, W. H.
Kevern, A. T.
Kay, R. G.
Knight, M. W.
Knight, H. E. B.
Kingdon, E. J.
Kiff, C.
Kingdon, S. R.
Kong, G. B.
Kerry, A. E.
Knibbs, P. J.
Kingham, E.

Kerswell, R. W.
Knapman, R. T.
Keast, M. B.
Knights, L. J.
Kennard, A. L.
Kerslade, A. J.
Kingsland, B.
Kofoed, A. M. C.
Knapp, E.
Knee, G.
Knight, E.
Knight, E. F.
Knights, C. J.
Kingsom, W.
Kingsbury, A.
Kingsland, F. H.
Kingdon, E. J.
King, M. H. G.
King, K. W.
King, C. W.
King, W. H.
King, G. A. J.
King, G. A.
Kearey, R. L.
Kelsal, J. A.
Kerslake, W. J. H.
Kemp, R.
Kemp, S. G.
Kevern, C.
Kerswill, L. G.
Kerslake, J. M.
Kenwood, E. J.
Kenward, K. S.
Kennedy, W. J.
Kendall, H. M.
Kempsford, E. C.
Kemp, L. V.
Kemp, J. A.
Kelson, W. H.
Kelly, L. R.
Kelly, C. L.
Kelland, F. T.
Keene, J.
Lugg, E.
Lazarus, P. F.
Loveless, R. J.
Lympaney, C. H.
Leverett, F.
Levy, W.
Lewis, F. C.

Lewis, J.
Lewis, J. K.
Lewis, L. F. A.
Lewendon, W. T.
Lea, E. F. B.
Lindsay, W.
Lightfoot, C. J.
Lightowler, A. L.
Lindon, N. L.
Lindsay, D. C.
Lippett, R. C.
Liscombe, F. T.
Litchfield, J. H.
Little, J. A. J.
Lockwood, A.
Lock, A.
Loader, T. F.
Lock, K. C.
Lock, W. J.
Lock, S.
Lodge, J. C.
Lomas, J.
Loney, B.
Long, H. B.
Long, F. J.
Longstaff, F. C.
Loosemore, C. H.
Loughman, W. C.
Lone, I. R.
Lovering, G. J.
Lowe, J. W.
Lower, T. H.
Lowton, P.
Lucas, W. H.
Lucas, R. W.
Luke, E. F.
Luvatte, C. E.
Luxton, A. W.
Luxton, A. E.
Lyne, R. T.
Lye, C.
Lyne, A. J.
Lyne, J. H.
Lyne, F.
Lyne, W. M.
Langford, F. H.
Lendon, K. W.
Lendon, H. R.
Lee, R. S.
Lee, F. S.

Lee, F. J.
Lee, J. H.
Lear, P. R.
Leach, A. J.
Lendon, K. W.
Leggatt, E. W.
Leigh, F. S.
Lewis, W. H.
Lee, P. G.
Laythorne, C. H.
Lawson, G. W.
Lavington, W. C. R.
Laundon, J. E.
Larken, A. E.
Langdon, K. W.
Langdon, H.
Langabeer, W. H.
Lane, R. J.
Lane, E. R.
Landrey, C. J.
Lampen, R. J.
Lambert, J.
Lake, H. C.
Lamacraft, S.
Lake, P. H.
Lugg, E.
Lake, A. J.
Labey, T. C.
Lawson, D. W. E.
Laing, E. G.
Legg, B. F.
Leatherland, R. L.
Lee, G. L.
Lee, T. H.
Lee, A. G.
Leyman, R.
Lee, H. J.
Leggett, T. W.
Larcombe, R. J.
Lake, C. E.
Langdon, N. G.
Laskey, R. J.
Lamble, F. R.
Laskey, J. H.
Lashbrook, G. F.
Lambrechts, N. C.
Langworthy, W. J.
Lamacraft, F. F. A.
Lark, K. R.
Lavis, J. W.

Laskey, E. L.
Larbalestier, G. E.
Lasket, M.
Lang, A. J.
Latham, C. A.
Lay, C.
Leaman, D.
Long, R. C. L.
Lake, F. L.
Luxton, A. E.
Lock, N. H.
Laskey, A. A. H.
Legg, D. L.
Langworthy, F. N.
Loosemore, A. M.
Luscombe, W. H.
Luxton, S. B.
Luscombe, S.
Luke, R. T.
Launder, P.
Lake, R. H.
Langabeer, L. F.
Laskey, W. G.
Luxton, J.
Lockyear, V. N.
Lovell, T. J.
Lowe, G.
Lockyear, L.
Lloyd, R.
Lee, R. G.
Luff, R. N.
Lodge, J.
Lawrence, G. L.
Lane, R. G.
Lyne, N. C.
Lord, C. W. J.
Langdon, W. G.
Latham, A. J.
Lawrence, J.
Lawrence, J. J.
Leat, J. W.
Leney, T. G.
Lock, R. H.
Lodge, T. B.
Lovell, W. F.
Marks, R.
Marks, G. H.
Maunder, W. R.
May, T. G.
Meilton, H. F.

Melhuish, C. J.
Mellish, E. F. W.
Milford, E. F.
Miller, S. E.
Mitchell, J. M.
Muxlow, J.
Muxlow, J. C. J.
Miller, M. W.
Masters, C.
Mellish, L. D.
Manning, J. H.
Milican, W. G.
Milford, V. C.
Miles, P. G.
Midson, T.
Mitchell, J.
Mitchell, P. E.
Mitchell, J. A.
Mills, J. S.
Mildon, T. G.
Miller, W.
Mingo, C. A.
Mills, G. T.
Mitcham, C. T.
Mills, H. W.
Mead, C. J.
Meadors, J.
Milton, L. R.
Mitchell, G. G. M.
Marley, S. G.
Moss, L. M.
Murray, T. A.
Mountstevens, G. H.
Moulton, S. J.
Mortimore, J. H.
Mortimore, H. J.
Morse, K.
McConnell, J. R.
McGann, J. S.
McKimm, T. G.
McPherson, A.
McGill, R. J.
Marsden, H. G.
Millman, A. C.
Mills, E. W.
Miller, F. J.
Miller, R. C.
Milton, F. H.
Milligan, S. A.
Milton, S. G.

Mills, G. H.
Milican, T. R.
Medway, D. A.
McLean, M.
McAndrews, F. C.
Mares, A. E.
Manley, R. J. H.
Mardon, W. C.
Maunder, F. E.
Martin, B.
Miller, J. F.
McKie, J.
McCarthy, P. F.
McGrafth, S. A.
Mallett, F. G.
Major, S. G.
Manning, R.
Maddock, D.
Martin, H. W. H.
Mallett, S. B.
Martin, W. G.
MacKenzie, A.
Maynard, W.
Marshall, W.
May, W. A.
McMahon, P. R.
Milligan, S. A.
Morrish, R. W.
Milfin, W. J.
Millman, W. D.
McHardy, J.
Mann, H. V.
Marshall, S. D.
Marks, G.
Mansfield, J. R.
Marchant, H. E. W.
Marris, T. C.
Marshall, J. E.
Marsden, G. W.
Mayne, W.
Mayne, D. J.
May, W. R.
Marks, P. W.
Manley, A.
Manley, G.
Marks, R.
Maunder, H. C.
Mather, J. C.
Moore, B. W.
Moore, H. J.

Moore, C. C.
Moore, R. C.
Morgan, G. O.
Morgan, R. J
Morgan, W. H.
Morrish, P.
Moore, G.
Montgomery, H. A.
Molloy, A. T.
Morton, W. L.
Montandon, C.
Morrish, J.
Moss, F. F. S.
Moseley, J. W.
Mortimer, L.
Moore, L. W.
Monk, S. E.
Morris, M. J.
Moore, L.
Morgan, K. A.
Michelmore, H. T.
Mitchell, J. H.
Metcalfe, H.
Melville, H. F.
McLaren, W.
McCarthy, W.
Martin, J. B. L.
Martin, H. E.
Martin, R. C.
Murphy, M.
Murley, R. O.
Murdoch, E. R.
Monkley, F. G.
Moore, G. T.
Morgan, S. J. C.
Mortimore, J.
Morros, F. J.
Montandon, E. J.
Mole, A. G.
Moule, W. H. J.
Milton, L. R.
McGill, S. H.
May, A. T.
Moxe, C. J.
Maunder, H. T.
Mallon, E.
Morgan, H. S.
Morrish, R. W.
Mason, J. D.
Mimms, A. T.

Mitchell, H.
Mitchell, N. F.
Mitchell, C. R.
Mitchell, E. W.
Mitchell, W.
Meilton, S.
Medway, F.
Mears, F. E.
Meager, R. J.
Meyers, G. W. C.
Mears, E.
Marriner, R.
Mardon, J. L.
Morrish, A. S.
Marchant, K. J.
Mander, A. L.
Mann, D.
Mannley, S. W. A.
Murphy, W. H.
Mumford, A. G.
Mullarkey, O. S.
Mugford, L. J.
Muckle, W. P.
Munray, J.
Munson, W. G.
Morey, W. H.
Monkley, L. J.
Macpherson, M.
Moist, R.
Moore, P. R.
Major, H. A.
Maidment, B.
Mahony, J.
Madge, C. D.
Madge, E. W. J.
Madge, K. A.
Madge, J. W.
Maddicks, E. P. H.
Martin, T. S.
Martin, L. D.
Martin, J. B.
Martin, H. W. H.
Maunder, J. A.
Maunder, R. J.
Matthews, S. W.
Matthews, E. A.
Matters, T. J.
Mason, J. I.
Masters, F. H.
Martin, W. H.

Martyr, E. G.
Mardon, F. G.
Madden, N. T.
Matta, L. M.
Maynard, R.
Matters, T. C.
May, R. H.
Mann, A.
Mardon, G. E.
Mathews, E. C.
Musk, A. L.
Major, F. G.
Mardon, A. E.
Mawhinney, R. J.
McLary, T. I.
Mapledoram, H. C.
Mason, N. E.
Moore, G. A.
Marsh, C. H.
Miller, C.
Mann, H.
Marley, W. E.
Martin, D.
May, F. W.
McLoughlin, F.
Moist, E.
Morgan, R. G.
Martin, F.
Moore, L. W.
Mann, G. B.
MacDonald, H.
Mayes, A. E.
McGahey, J. F.
Newcombe, E.
Nash, T. J.
Nash, P. A.
Napper, G. A. E.
Neate, H. W. G.
Newbery, C. C.
Needham, R. G.
Newton, A.
Newbarry, R. J.
Nethercott, R. A.
Neale, H. E.
Neale, R. F.
New-Berry, W. G. W.
Newcombe, W. T. N.
Needs, W. J.
Newberry, H. V.
Newcombe, D.

Newton, T. G.
Newton, A. H.
Nicoll, G. W.
Nicholls, A. C.
Nicholls, H. E.
Nicolls, I. A.
Nott, R. W.
Nott, R. J.
Norton, F. C.
Notly, W. K.
Nourse, W. J. A.
Norman, E.
Norris, A. W.
Northcott, W. H.
Northcott, H. R.
Northcott, W. R.
Norton, R. W. J.
Norton, J. C.
Nuttall, S. W.
Napper, F. W.
Naden, P.
Neville, F. T.
Newman, R. P.
Nichols, A. S.
Nickols, H. G.
Nichols, A. E.
Northcott, M. W. F.
Nickols, D. W.
Newlands, R. T.
Newcombe, A. J.
Nunn, G .H. R.
Nuck, C. E.
Newcombe, T. R.
Newton, S.
Norman, C. A.
Norton, W. J. C.
Newton, T. L.
Nagle, E. G. B.
Newman, J. W.
Norman, H. J.
Norrish, J. R. C.
Norton, C. W.
Ostler, E. C. H.
Owen, A. B.
Owen, R. H. W.
Owens, R. F.
Owen, B. W.
Ousley, E. J.
Ousley, L. W.
Osborne, A. J.

Orchard, J. G. **R.**
Orchard, R. O.
Opie, E. J.
Oliver, E. V.
Oliver, R. W. F.
Olver, J. H.
Oke, R. G.
Oke, A. J.
Oakley, R. F.
Oatway, F.
Ofield, B.
Oke, W. L.
Orchard, R. J.
Orchard, W. H.
Osgood, F. F.
Ousley, C. E. **J.**
Owen, E. G.
Owens, H. S.
Orton, J. H.
Oates, M.
O'Sullivan, D. C.
Oak, C. A.
Palmer. A. A.
Pratt, S. J.
Palmer, C. F.
Payne, A. E.
Pennington, E.
Pike, E. R.
Phillips, H. E.
Pye, E. H.
Pym, R.
Pym, K.
Pule, L. A.
Pyle, D. J. J.
Pym, T. W.
Pugsley, A. E.
Pullin, D. H.
Pullen, F. G.
Prowse, A. G.
Prince, S. G.
Prigg, A. E.
Priddy, H.
Price. L. R.
Price, F. W.
Price, J. S.
Preston, T. L.
Preston, W. H. **A.**
Preston, F.
Pratt, K. L. L.
Preece, W. J.

Pratt, F. W.
Prangnell, C. T. **R.**
Prance, S. R.
Preece, J. H.
Pratt, C. A.
Postgate, R. S.
Poore, R.
Pollard, G. F.
Potter, W. J.
Powesland, S. G.
Powley, A. S.
Powell, P. H. G.
Potter, W. T.
Potter, R. J.
Potter, R. A.
Pope, S. H.
Pope, J. W.
Popham, R. R.
Plumer, A. B.
Plumpton, P. O.
Plumer, C. F.
Pitt, W.
Pitt, L. G.
Piper, W. E. H.
Pinson, R.
Pinn, H.
Pincott, N. A.
Pincott, G. E.
Pincott, G. E.
Piller, A. G.
Pill, J. T.
Pike, W. H. G.
Pike, P. G.
Pike, J.
Pike, C. H.
Pike, F. G.
Pidgeon, W. V.
Pickering, J.
Pittard, L. M.
Phillips, J. O .
Phillips, P. D.
Phillips, L.
Phillips, D.
Phillips, P. H.
Phillips, R. F.
Phelps, W. T.
Pethybridge, L. G.
Petherbridge, F. W. J.
Petherick, D. M.
Perry, P. J.

Perry, G.
Perrott, K. R. M.
Perkins, W. O.
Perkins, M. G. F.
Perkins, M. T.
Pepprell, H. G.
Penwarden, F. L.
Peel, F. J.
Pearson, H. W.
Pearless, R. C.
Pearce, R. W.
Pearce, A. E.
Pearce, A. E.
Penwell, S. C.
Pearson, D. R.
Peasegood, A.
Penney, D. A.
Penhaligon, M. E.
Perry, K. R.
Pearson, J. J.
Perryman, S. G.
Penny, C.
Perkin, M. G. F. **A.**
Perry, R.
Patch, B.
Passmore, R.
Passmore, A. J.
Pascoe, A.
Paddon, W. K.
Pascoe, E. A. C.
Partridge, W. J. H.
Partridge, R.
Partridge, L. G. R.
Parsons, C.
Partridge, G.
Parsons, F. T.
Parsons, A. T.
Parsons, C. F.
Parsons, R. J.
Parsons, C. H.
Parrott, H. A. G.
Patt, E. A.
Parr, A. W. H.
Parkinson, C. E.
Parkhouse, H.
Parkhouse, E.
Parker, O.
Parker, J. R.
Pariter, S. T.
Parish, P. E.

Palmer, T.
Palfrey, L. G.
Paterson, R.
Pavey, S. M. J.
Pateyjohns, P.
Payne, C. H.
Payne, D. M.
Paltridge, A. E.
Parrott, C. E.
Parkhouse, S. H.
Parker, F.
Parkes, F. H.
Pateman, C. A.
Parker, G. A.
Paul, W. S.
Parsons, D. J.
Parsons, W. E.
Palfrey, A. E.
Parsons, C. H.
Parker, J. R.
Price, G. W.
Purvis, W. J.
Pym, J. W.
Pritchard, B. H. B.
Patchchett, H. D.
Parsons, D. A.
Penney, G. E. R.
Pengilliy, C. J.
Penhaligon, J.
Perry, G.
Pearse, S. E. B.
Pengilley, R.
Phillips, A.
Phillips, J. W.
Physick, D. H.
Pitts, R. G.
Pine, P. G.
Pitts, J.
Platts, J. H. W.
Pooley, E.
Pope, H.
Palmer, B.
Passmore, G. H.
Paineter, F. C.
Plasom, F. S. G.
Poole, C. H.
Philip, W. E.
Pulman, E. C.
Parkhouse, R. W.
Pike, W. G.

Peters, E. J.
Pritchard, H. H.
Passmore, J.
Preston, H. J. A.
Pitts, J. B.
Purvis, F.
Parr, R. W.
Paddon, G.
Parr, L. J.
Proctor, W. L.
Palmer, D. J. L.
Pyle, N. F.
Palfreyman, G. E.
Palmer, A. W. S.
Parker, J. L.
Perry, A. W.
Pope, G. A.
Prince, A. J.
Quantick, H.
Quaintance, S. J.
Quartly, J. H.
Quick, H. J.
Quantick, H.
Robert, G. G.
Rundle, F. A.
Renouf, F. J.
Rundle, C. R.
Rose, H. J.
Rundle, G. B.
Ryan, V. G.
Rutherford, G.
Russell, L.
Russell, N. J.
Rush, F. H.
Rundle, E. G.
Rudling, F. T.
Ruse, F. H.
Rundle, F. G.
Russell, P. E.
Rundle, F. H. W.
Rowsby, S. W.
Rowland, W. F.
Rowland, F. G.
Rowe, W. J.
Rowden, C.
Routley, G. S.
Roseyeare, L.
Rose, D.
Rookes, C. S.
Robinson, E.

Robinson, L. J.
Robinson, C. J. B.
Robinson, A. I.
Robins, G. E.
Robins, G. W.
Roberts, W.
Roberts, R. H.
Roberts, D. J.
Roberts, N. W.
Robbins, W. H.
Robbins, L. A.
Roach, A.
Rowe, E. F.
Roden, L. M.
Rowsell, W. C.
Robinson, W. C.
Rockey, F. J.
Rowe, A. S.
Rowden, R. J.
Roberts, F. C.
Roberts, H.
Richards, D. W. B.
Richards, J. H.
Richards, S. F.
Rice, L. J.
Rice, D. V.
Rice, A. E.
Rice, G.
Richards, L. G.
Richards, G.
Richards, H. C.
Richards, A.
Richards, L. W.
Richard, W. H.
Rice, W.
Rigg, A. W.
Richards, V.
Riggs. E. E.
Reynolds, T. H.
Reynolds, D. W.
Reynolds, D. J. H.
Reilly, T.
Reeves, G. P. H.
Reeves. C. A. C.
Reeve, H. L.
Reed, H. E.
Reed, A. H.
Redclift. W. J.
Retter, E. R.
Reed, L.

Reed, D. G.
Reed, W. H.
Rawlings, F.
Ratcliffe, D. G. A.
Rait, A. C.
Radmore, C. H.
Raddan, F. E.
Radford, E. A. B.
Raphael, K. J. F.
Randall, E. N.
Randall, S. C.
Raddon, R. F.
Randall. C.
Rance, A. C.
Raw, L. P.
Rait, A. C.
Rankman, W. H.
Rushmore, G.
Roper, J. W.
Richards, L. W.
Rowland, R. S. A.
Roxburgh, P. R. N.
Rowden, R. C.
Rowe, W.
Roberts, K. G.
Roberts, W. J.
Rowland, R. E.
Rowland, W.
Rowsell, W.
Ridge, F.
Ridout, A. C.
Richards, W.
Rippon, W. C.
Ridd, H. C.
Ridout, E. F.
Richards, A. E.
Richards, W. J. S.
Richardson, R. A.
Ridewood, C. C.
Rich, H. C.
Richards, F.
Reid, G. I.
Ritter, K. G. E.
Reed, A. J.
Rowland, R. S. A.
Richards, W. G.
Roberts, W. F.
Robbins, H.
Robinson, A. I.
Row, R.

Roche, G. M.
Roach, T. D.
Read, R. W.
Rowe, H. C.
Russell, E.
Rudd, R. L.
Roberts, R.
Rowe, A. S.
Roberts, F.
Roberts, T.
Rice, F. D.
Ridd, F. C.
Rouse, C. J.
Raddan, L. A. E.
Rees, H. G.
Ridgeway, F. J.
Rooke, F. C.
Rundle, W. H.
Salter, B.
Salter, R. T.
Samuelson, C. H. F.
Smale, N. R.
Squibb, W. F.
Squire, E. S.
Salter, A. G.
Sowden, J. R.
Spurway, D. M.
Speller, C. K.
Sparey, A. J.
Sprague, A. E.
Sparkes, P. L.
Spencer, L. G.
Silcock, T. F.
Simmance, H. W.
Simmons, J. H.
Simmons, C. A.
Sims, G. N.
Simons, A. H. B.
Simpsons, C. J.
Skinner, W. W.
Skinner, L. C.
Skillington, H.
Stephens, W. J.
Stevens, H. F.
Stidton, R. J.
Stile, T. J.
Stocker, H. J.
Stokks, W.
Stone, A. F.
Stoneham, J.

Stoneham, G. D.
Stoneham, M.
Stookes, T.
Stookes, E.
Storry, R.
Streat, W.
Strong, E.
Stowell, S. H.
Summers, C. H.
Swain, T. M.
Steer, C.
Stephens, H. J. T.
Stephens, H. H.
Stephenson, R. H.
Symmons, A. E.
Smith, F. P.
Smith, R. B.
Smith, F. R.
Smith, C. W.
Smith, H. W.
Smith, A. A.
Smith, C. B.
Smith, G. G.
Smith, P. A.
Smith, J. H.
Smith, W. H.
Smith, W. H.
Smith, J. A.
Smale, H. G.
Snows, W. H.
Snows, I. H.
Snows, G. J.
Snell, A. L.
Snell, J. J.
Snows, W. H.
Snowdon, P.
Solomon, T. J. V.
Soper, L.
Southcott, C.
Southwell, W. H. F.
Sandle, R. T. A.
Simpson-Gray, M. T.
Squire, R. A.
Shephard, S.
Stokes, E.
Sagar, J. N.
Sanvitale, W.
Sage, H. O.
Smith, P.
Simon, C. D.

Sacre, F. E.
Stevenson, A. P.
Snow, T. A. G.
Stevens, F. P.
Spargo, T. T.
Stone, J. D.
Starr, E. F.
Stone, E. E.
Stoneham, F. R.
Streer, W. H.
Stoneham, F.
Stabb, B. F. A.
Strachan, A.
Stabb, T. A.
Stacey, C. H.
Stamp, J. M.
Stanbury, H.
Stediford, H. J.
Steed, R. J.
Steer, S. H.
Swift, G. R.
Symmons, A. E.
Symons, N. H.
Simons, T. R. J.
Sylvester, F. H.
Spicer, W. J.
Spicer, W. J. A.
Spiller, C. H.
Spiller, L. H.
Shute, C. C.
Shapland, C. J. C.
Shepherd, R. J.
Shephard, E.
Shapcott, F.
Shepherd, S. R.
Shapland, C. J. C.
Sharland, G. A.
Sharpe, H. A.
Shayler, P. H.
Shaw, J.
Shaw, W. H.
Shears, C .A. B.
Shenton, P. E.
Shepheard, W. V. I.
Shilson, E. M.
Shabbrook, L. V.
Smalldon, R. C.
Smart, C. V.
Smith, T.
Smith, P. W.

Smart, L. J.
Smale, H.
Smale, W. E.
Smith, L. G.
Stacey, G. D.
Stevens, A. E.
Strawbridge, A. J.
Stentiford, W. H.
Strawbridge, S. G.
Stevens, W. H.
Stocker, N. E. L.
Stark, J. L.
Stephens, J. H.
Stephens, J. P.
Spivey, H. P.
Spratt, I. S.
Sobey, W. J.
Southard, E. J. T.
Southall, J. R.
Snell, I. H.
Snell, L. G.
Snow, I.
Snow, R. R.
Skoines, E. G.
Skelton, C. M.
Skidmore, W. E.
Skinner, A. H.
Skinner, J. L.
Slader, W. T.
Smith, W. H.
Shooter, D. N.
Shooter, H. H.
Shooter, A. H.
Shorland, F. H. G.
Short, S. A.
Shute, W. G.
Searle, L. J.
Sellick, A. J.
Sellick, R.
Sene, J. E.
Sercombe, W. J.
Setter, K. E.
Seward, W. H.
Smoldon, L. J.
Smith, S. J. L.
Smith, H.
Smith, A. E.
Shute, F. J.
Salter, L. F.
Salter, S.

Sabine, D. S.
Salter, H. J.
Sanders, L.
Sanders, J.
Salter, S. G.
Sampson, A. C.
Salter, L. C.
Selley, S.
Selley, R. P.
Savage, W. H.
Salter, G. W.
Sandle, A.
Sargeant, G. P.
Sargent, H. S.
Saunders, C. W.
Savage, E. R. J.
Sayers, T.
Sayers, B. W.
Salter, L. H.
Scribbins, H.
Slade, W. W. H.
Sussex, S. P.
Stott, L.
Stephens, G. G.
Stevens, W. H.
Stocker, R. C. D.
Staddon, V. T.
Steer, A. J.
Sharman, W. R.
Shapley, C. G.
Shear, M. R.
Sandy, G. A.
Salter, F. R.
Saul, F.
Scaddan, J. R.
Sculpher, F.
Sculpher, G. H.
Scale, G.
Scott, R. G.
Scott, C. H.
Scrowston, G. R.
Scriven, S. J.
Scriven, T.
Searle, E.
Sercombe, R. W.
Seward, L. J.
Seabright, F. C.
Seale, G. H.
Searle, C. H. L.
Shepherd, C. G.

Shepherd, W. A.
Short, H. J.
Snow, W. T.
Scrivens, A. E.
Seward, H. G.
Sercombe, S.
Seaward, C.
Salter, J. H.
Smith, L. W.
Sprague, R. M.
Sharp, C.
Saunders, L. A.
Shank, J. J.
Sparks, H.
Smythe, W. R.
Stone, E. J.
Soper, R. J.
Snow, H. H.
Sharland, W. C.
Southard, L. G.
Scott, E. G.
Setter, C. M.
Sinclair, J. E.
Stookes, C.
Spoors, R. E.
Snell, C. E.
Staddon, E. R.
Suter, L. R.
Smith, A. D.
Searle, R. J.
Searle, E. V.
Stickland, R.
Starr, A. H.
Spoors, R. E.
Shorland, J. C.
Stevens, D. R.
Stone, E. J.
Snell, A. R.
Sanders, E.
Sluman, H.
Spicer, R. F.
Shore, A. F.
Smyth, R. J.
Shears, C. S.
Sheppard, H. G.
Simpson, J.
Sellick, P. J. W.
Seach, D.
Shephard, H. A.
Taylor, D.

Toy, D. R.
Toogood, J. E.
Till, E. A.
Tozer, P.
Toms, S.
Tipple, R. O.
Tixard, R. H.
Torode, F. J.
Thomas, H. J.
Thomas, A. R. H.
Thorn, F. J.
Thorpe, M. G.
Thorogood, H. C.
Thomson, G. A.
Thompson, H. G.
Thorn, A. E.
Thorne, C.
Thorne, E.
Tickell, R. A. G.
Tilbury, R.
Titchener, P. A. A.
Tiso, W. R.
Tiltman, E.
Thorne, R. G.
Thorpe, A.
Thomas, W. J.
Thomas, W. S.
Thorne, R. D.
Thomas, A.
Thomas, D.
Thomas, E. H.
Thomas, F. J.
Thomas, K. J.
Thomas, E.
Thew, P. A. G.
Telford, W. E. H.
Tucker, G.
Tape, J.
Talbot, F. C.
Tansley, W. E. G.
Talbot, E. J.
Tancock, J.
Tancock, S. J.
Tagg, A. A.
Taylor, E. A. G.
Taylor, R. M. D.
Taylor, L. T.
Tavener, R. S.
Taylor, F. J.
Taylor, D. J.

Taylor, C. J.
Taylor, R. J.
Taylor, A. S.
Taylor, F.
Taylor, E. E.
Tavener, A. E. F.
Tavener, R. L.
Tatham, J. A.
Tapp, W. H.
Tapp, W. H.
Tolcher, A. S.
Tolman, J. H.
Toleman, S. L.
Tomlin, F. C.
Tenge, W. G.
Tonkin, W. K.
Toms, A. G.
Tonkin, J. W. T.
Tonkin, C. V.
Towill, W. J.
Tootell, J. A. R.
Twitchin, W. G.
Twiggs, W. H.
Tucker, D. W.
Tuckett, W.
Tucker, A. S.
Tucker, G. R.
Turner, D. H.
Turner, C. R.
Turl, L. J. L.
Tuckett, R. L.
Tuckett, F.
Tuckett, C.
Tuckett, C. P.
Tuckett, W. J.
Tucker, E. G.
Tucker, C. W.
Turnbull, W. C. C.
Tucker, S. R. G.
Tucker, F. J.
Tripe, S. H.
Tregale, R. H.
Trott, P. L.
Tremlett, V. G.
Trevithick, W. C.
Trace, A. J.
Tricker, W. J.
Trout, R. A.
Trenberth, R. N.
Tremlett, H. G. W.

164

Trelaven, W.
Treharne, J.
Toogood, E. **R. R.**
Townsend, A. W.
Taleman, J.
Toasland, G. **B.**
Tomlin, R.
Tomkins, F. A.
Toward, F. P.
Tootell, L. W.
Tooze, R.
Townsend, L. G.
Tozer, L. G.
Toze, F. W.
Toyne, W. B.
Toye, T. H.
Townsend, R. C.
Tatchell, F. D.
Tapper, K. E. T.
Tamlin, E. A.
Taylor, W. R. O.
Tapp, G. H.
Taylor, W. H.
Tansley, W. E.
Thorne, W. J.
Thorpe, D. J.
Tibble, S. C.
Tozer, L. G.
Turl, E. G.
Tricker, R. F. R.
Till, F. N.
Tarner, F. W. L.
Turner, A. G.
Trebble, J.
Turner, F.
Tolley, S.
Tucker, C. R.
Trengove, C. E.
Twitchin, J.
Tucker, R. F.
Tubbs, R. R. F.
Tucker, F.
Tuckett, F.
Tapp, E. T.
Templeman, F.
Tucker, W. H.
Thomsett, A. H.
Upright, K. R.
Uzzell, E.
Urch, J. W.

Upsher, H.
Vooght, G. H.
Vosper, F. W.
Vickery, E. W. J.
Vinnicombe, F. C.
Vincent, F. W.
Venner, H. A.
Vincent, G. F.
Virtue, L.
Vinnicombe, W. G.
Vincent, C. W. E.
Vincent, C. E.
Vowden, W. H.
Voisey, R. H. J.
Vyse, A. H.
Vosper, F. J.
Vittles, T.
Vittles, R.
Vickery, A. J.
Vickery, R. A.
Vaughan, W. F.
Valentine, E. E.
Vardy, P. B.
Valentine, W. H.
Vanstone, A. J.
Vercoe, H.
Veitch, A.
Veryard, C.
Venning, C. H. V.
Vicary, H. A.
Vickery, R. A.
Vickery, R. B.
Vickery, S. L.
Vickery, R.
Vickery, G. A.
Vickery, N. E.
Vickery, L. W.
Vicary, A.
Vickery, T. E.
Vanstone, E. J. A.
Vale, G. T.
Vanstone, R. J.
Vicary, W. R.
Verhagen, D. H.
Vicary, A. E.
Willey, M. D.
Willwy, M. C.
Wagner, C.
Webb, R. H.
Weston, M. J.

Westcott, E. B.
Whidden, H. R.
Wills, W. A.
Westcott, W. G. **H. S.**
Walters, B. T.
Ware, S.
Wotton, H.
Wotton, E. W. L.
Woolway, F. R.
Worth, F.
Woodward, L.
Woodward, H. F.
Woods, H. F. G.
Woods, H. C.
Woodrow, J. W.
Woodridge, E. J.
Woodman, J. B.
Woodley, P. N.
Woodland, W. F.
Woodhall, D.
Woodcock, D. S.
Woodbury, W.
Woodbridge, W. **R.**
Woodbridge, C. **E.**
Wood, W.
Wood, H. E.
Wood, H.
Wood, K. W.
Wollacott, C. J.
Wood, C.
Woodward, F.
Woodgates, S. J.
Wooldridge, H. J.
Woodland, L. J.
Woolway, F. W.
Wood, D. R.
Woodland, R. J.
Woollen, E. J.
Wotten, H.
Woodbridge, R. F.
Wood, H. L.
Woodland, C.
Woodland, F. G.
Woodland, L. W.
Wood, R. C.
Winfield, E. J.
Wills, D. A.
Wilmot, S. J.
Willmington, E.
Williamson, H.

Williams, K.	Williams, M.	Wood, D. C.
Williams, P. H.	Williams, L. R.	Webber, E. J.
Williams, J. J.	Williams, F. H.	Williams, L. S.
Williams, A. R. R.	Windsor, C.	Williams, G. V.
Williams, J.	Willey, E. J.	Wills, W. R.
Williams, H. A.	Williams, B.	Willcocks, S.
Williams, D. E.	Williams, J.	Western, A. R.
Williams, A. H. J.	Willey, D. H.	Wannell, H. J.
Williams, J. R.	Willcox, A. E.	Westcott, W. G. A.
Wilson, S. C.	Williams, R. H.	Wellman, G. T.
Wills, L. V.	Wilson, G. H.	Westaway, F. J.
Wilson, F. T.	Willey, A. G.	Were, P. J.
Wilson, E. F.	Wickens, R. M.	West, S .
Wilson, W. B.	Wills, L.	Webber, S. G.
Wilson, D.	Williams, P.	Welch, E. F.
Wilson, W. H.	Widgery, J. J.	Western, A.
Walters, F.	Williams, B. G.	Wells, I. V.
Wilson, J.	Williams, A. C. H.	Welland, T. L.
Wreford, J.	Williams, E. C. K.	Welch, D. C. E. H.
Wreford, L. E.	Webber, N.	Wedgwood, B.
Wright, A. D.	Westlake, S. G.	Weeks, S.
Wright, C. G.	Western, C. W.	Webber, T. R.
Wright, J. D.	Westcott, P. G.	Webber, A. J.
Wright, F. J.	Westaway, S. C.	Webber, F.
Wright, J. D.	Westall, C. E.	Webber, R. C.
Wykes, L. G.	Wells, A. H.	Webber, R. J.
Wyatt, W. T.	Witton, T.	Webber, W. R.
Wyeth, J. H.	Westcott, F. R.	Webb, S. H. T.
West, E. A.	Williams, C. W.	Webb, W. J.
Wood, F.	Willett, L. H.	Welling, W. J.
Ware, R. C.	Webber, W. E.	West, R. H. J.
Weymouth, R. H. F.	Wright, E. A.	Welch, C. E. J.
Wright, E. T.	Williams, W. A. D.	West, W. E.
Wills, R. W.	Westcott, G. E.	Westcott, A. E.
Westle, F.	Wells, C. E.	Weeks, G.
Watts, P. S.	Willmot, A. H.	Webber, R. W. G.
Wing, J. E.	Westcott, W. P.	Webber, F.
Ware, A. J.	Welch, A.	Westcott, W. E.
Wills, W. C. S.	Woodhall, D. B.	Western, A. R.
Wright, D. A. E.	Watts, W. H.	Wills, W. J.
Wilkinson, J. M.	Whidden, H. R.	Wilson, J. G.
Willcocks, F. L.	Ward, H. J.	Williams, W. G.
Wilkins, A. G.	Wragg, L. S.	Wills, W. G.
Wildgoose, J. H.	Westell, J. W.	Wills, E. A.
Widgery, R. N.	Walmsley, J. C.	Willis, H. F.
Wickens, W. D.	Wedgwood, W.	Willey, R. M.
Wise, E. G.	Wilson, R.	Whitworth, E. C.
Wilcocks, W. C.	Wilson, J.	Whitty, C. E.
Willey, J. E.	Williams, L. R.	Whitton, L. T.
Wilson, R.	Willmott, F. G.	Whittle, A. H. J.

Whittle, R. O.
Whittington, R. G.
Whittam, A. H.
Whiting, W. R.
Whitfield, G. A.
Whiteley, D.
White, C. H.
White, F. J.
Whitbread, L. H.
Whidden, A. K.
Whelan, C.
Wheaton, W. B.
Wheatley, J. E. C.
Wharton, S.
White, P. G.
White, F. A.
Whiter, J. W.
Whitley, N. J.
Whitton, P.
Whitfield, A. N.
Whitthorn, R. A.
Wheaton, F. C.
Whitthorne, A. L.
Whelan, C.
White, W. H. J.
White, R.
Wharton, A.
Wharton, S.
Wallen, A.
Ware, E. T.
West, S. T.
Western, J. W.,
O.B.E., T.D.

Wheaton, W. B.
White, J. D.
Williams, D. T.
Wills, A. R.
Windrum, W. G.
Wonnacott, R.
Woodland, C. J.
Woolcott, R.
Wright, A. E.
Wheaton, R.
Wadman, L. W.
Warren, P. J.
Walrond, C. G.
Walker, J. J.
Walter, F. J.
Warren, R. J.
Wyper, D.
Wallis, E. R.
Walmsley, C. J.
Walbeoff, L. A.
Walsh, A. J.
Waushope, E. J.
Watts, P. E.
Watkins, O. H.
Warwick, A. J.
Warren, H. J.
Warne, R. G.
Warren, J. K.
Ward, P. E.
Ward, R. D.
Ward, E. R.
Ward, T.
Ward, L. F.

Walters, G.
Walters, S. J.
Wallis, A. F.
Wallen, A. W. H.
Walker, C. J.
Walduck, D. E.
Wain, J.
Warwick, K. H.
Watson, E.
Walker, E.
Warren, R.
Warne, B. R.
Wallen, A. D. G.
Youngson, A. G.
York, G. W.
Young, B.
Young, W. A. P.
Young, A. G.
Young, K. E.
Yeo, G.
Yeo, R. D.
Yeo, H. H.
Yeo, R. K. G.
Yendall, C.
Yelland, A. H.
Yendall, K. F.
Yandell, H. G. C.
Young, B.
Yeo, H. I.
Youldon, F. S.
Yelland, A. E.
Zabban, L. H.

Lightning Source UK Ltd.
Milton Keynes UK
UKHW020434290819
348709UK00005BA/150/P

9 781783 311613